T0386131

THE ROMANTIC IMPERATIVE

FREDERICK C. BEISER

The Romantic Imperative

The Concept of Early
German Romanticism

HARVARD UNIVERSITY PRESS

Cambridge, Massachusetts, and London, England   2003

First Harvard University Press paperback edition, 2006

Library of Congress Cataloging-in-Publication Data

Beiser, Frederick C., 1949–
  The romantic imperative : the concept of early German romanticism /
Frederick C. Beiser.
    p.   cm.
Includes bibliographical references and index.
ISBN 0-674-01180-5 (cloth: alk. paper)
ISBN 0-674-01980-6 (pbk.)
1. Romanticism—Germany. 2. Philosophy, German—18th century.
3. German literature—History and criticism. I. Title.
  PT363.P5B45 2003
    830.9′12—dc21   2003056574

For Julie Ann Beiser

CONTENTS

PREFACE

These essays are attempts to define and explain aspects of early German romanticism, the period known as *Frühromantik*, which flourished from 1797 to 1802. They are essentially introductory, an attempt to guide the anglophone reader through unfamiliar territory. More specifically, my aim is to introduce the *philosophy* behind early German romanticism—its epistemology, metaphysics, ethics, and politics—and to show its relevance for the period's literature, criticism, and aesthetics. While the literature, criticism, and aesthetics of *Frühromantik* have always attracted interest and attention, the same cannot be said for its metaphysics, epistemology, and ethics; yet the former can be understood only through the latter.

Since my aim is introductory, the first four essays attempt to identify the characteristic goals and ideals of *Frühromantik*. Attempts to determine the "essence" of the movement—what the Germans called *Wesensbestimmung*-or *Begriffsbestimmung der Romantik*—were once very common, especially in the German tradition of scholarship. Because of a growing historical nominalism, such studies are considered very unfashionable today. My aim in these essays, however, is not to determine the "concept" or "essence" of *Frühromantik*, still less of *Romantik* in general, as if these terms denote some kind of archetype or eternal intellectual pattern beneath or behind the phenomena. My only task has been to find *some* common goals and traits among a specific group of thinkers at a specific time and place. Even the most skeptical nominalist cannot banish such empirical generalizations. We need to have some survey of the forest, no matter how unique its individual trees.

The main critical thrust of these essays is directed against postmodernist interpretations of *Frühromantik*, especially the works of Paul de Man, Manfred Frank, Isaiah Berlin, Ernst Behler, Phillipe Lacoue-Labarthe, and Jean-Luc Nancy. While I have learned much from these scholars, I believe their interpretation of *Frühromantik* is one-sided and anachronistic. It understands that period essentially as an anticipation of postmodernism and imposes contemporary concerns upon it. For all its affinities with postmodernism, *Frühromantik* remains a unique historical phenomena, still very much part of the eighteenth century. Several of the essays (Chapters 2–5) therefore attempt to right the balance of postmodernist interpretations and to reinstate the rationalist dimension of *Frühromantik*.

A crucial issue in understanding *Frühromantik* is its complicated ambivalent relation to the German Enlightenment, or *Aufklärung*. Although this appears to be a purely historiographical issue, it is crucial in determining the very identity of *Frühromantik*. It is indeed the underlying issue behind postmodernist interpretations, which, sometimes unwittingly, revive the old interpretation of *Frühromantik* as a reaction against the *Aufklärung*. For these reasons, several essays are devoted to this issue (Chapters 3–5).

Some essays, especially the first and second, were written in reaction against the still predominant literary approach to *Frühromantik*, which sees it as an essentially literary, critical, and aesthetic movement. For much too long this approach has let a literary tail wag a cultural and philosophical dog. Yet romantic literature was only one part of a broader intellectual and cultural movement, and it is intelligible only in the light of romantic philosophy, especially its epistemology, metaphysics, ethics, and politics. If the romantics gave pride of place to the aesthetic, giving it superiority to philosophy as a guide to truth, that was only for all too epistemological and metaphysical reasons. Powerful voices have protested against the narrowness of the literary approach—among them Rudolf Haym, Walter Benjamin, Oskar Walzel, and Paul Kluckhohn—but their protests have rarely affected dominant practice. No one should think that the days of literary scholasticism are over. The literary approach has been reasserted very recently by one of the foremost scholars of *Frühromantik*, Ernst Behler. Scholars continue to attempt to get to the essence of *Romantik* by analyzing the use and origins of a mere phrase (namely, *romantische Poesie*) (see Chapter 1). Worst of all, the practice of postmodernist scholars has been to make vast generalizations about *Frühromantik* from features of its literary style (see Chapter 2).

My own approach to *Frühromantik* stresses the primacy of its moral and political values, and their dominant role in its aesthetics and religion. Some of the following essays (Chapters 2, 3, and 6) have therefore been written against the still common view that *Frühromantik* was essentially apolitical. In stressing the political dimension of romantic aesthetics, I do not mean to claim that the romantics engaged overtly in political activity, still less that their politics came from retreating into a moral and aesthetic sphere that stood sovereign over the political realm. Neither of these views captures the uniqueness of the political situation of the romantics in the 1790s, when political views were more overt but organized political action from below was still prohibited. The primacy of the ethical and political in *Frühromantik* means that the romantics subordinated the aesthetic and religious to ethical and political ends. They defined the highest good not as aesthetic contemplation but as human self-realization, the development of humanity. No less than Plato and Aristotle, they insisted that this ideal is realizable only within society and the state. These ethical and political values played a decisive role in the romantic agenda: they are the ultimate purpose behind its aesthetics, its philosophy of history, and *Naturphilosophie*.

My method is basically hermeneutical and historical, an approach defended and practiced by the romantics themselves. This means that I attempt to interpret the romantics from within, according to their own goals and historical context. As far as possible, I have tried to bracket alien vocabulary and to reconstruct the romantics in their historical individuality. This is not because I see the romantics as a historical phenomenon of no contemporary relevance—the very opposite is the case—but because there are many ways of seeing their relevance to our contemporary interests, and as many ways as there are such interests. I do not think that it is the task of the philosophical historian to prejudge relevance by imposing one contemporary perspective on the past. The relevance of the romantics should not be read into their texts; rather, it should be inferred from them, *after* the work of historical reconstruction. My fundamental task here has been historical reconstruction.

My approach to *Frühromantik* has been chiefly inspired by Rudolf Haym's brilliant book *Die romantische Schule* (Berlin: Gaertner, 1870). I see my own work as a continuation of Haym's original project. It was Haym who first stressed the need for a detailed investigation into the origins of *Frühromantik*, who first insisted on bracketing political and cultural prejudices, and who first made it a subject of historical study. The earlier efforts of Heine, Hettner, and Gervinus were amateurish by comparison, and marred by the political prejudices Haym wanted to overcome. Haym fully appreciated the fundamental importance of philosophy for *Frühromantik*, and he had a holistic approach that did full justice to its multidisciplinary nature. While he never ceased to be critical of the romantics, his criticisms came after a sympathetic reconstruction of the material. To be sure, much in Haym is now out of date; some of his interpretations are simplistic; and he never fully practiced the impartiality he demanded. Still, his concern for impartiality, historical depth, sympathetic reconstruction, and holism are as valid now as they were in 1870. In fundamental respects Haym set the standard that contemporary work has yet to match.

Some of my work on *Frühromantik* has appeared on previous occasions, more specifically, in the article "Romanticism" for the *Routledge Encyclopedia of Philosophy* (vol. 8, 348–352); in chapters 9–11 of my book *Enlightenment, Revolution, and Romanticism* (Cambridge: Harvard University Press, 1992), which discuss romantic political theory; in the introduction to *The Early Political Writings of the German Romantics* (Cambridge: Cambridge University Press, 1996), and finally in four chapters (Part III, 1–4) of *German Idealism* (Cambridge: Harvard University Press, 2002), which treat romantic metaphysics and epistemology. Although some of the essays here are based on my earlier work, they refine and improve it; the other essays cover new ground.

The ten essays were written on various occasions in the past ten years. Most of them appear for the first time in this book; a few have been published before, but almost all of these have been heavily revised for this volume. The first chapter was written for a lecture given in February 2000 at South Stockholm College, Stockholm, Sweden, for the inauguration of its comparative literature program. An early version of the second chapter was written for a lecture at the Fishbein Center for the History of Science at the University of Chicago. A revised version appeared in German as "Die deutsche Frühromantik," in *Philosophie, Kunst, Wissenschaft. Gedenkschrift Heinrich Kutzner* (Würzburg: Königshausen and Neumann, 2001), pp. 38–52. This essay has been heavily revised since, and the version that appears here is virtually new. The third chapter, now heavily revised, was a contribution to James Schmidt's *What Is Enlightenment?* (Berkeley: University of California Press, 1996), pp. 317–329. The fourth chapter was written for a Schleiermacher conference at Drew University in April 1999, and it has not appeared before. The fifth essay is new to this volume; it was accepted for publication in the *Journal of the History of Ideas* but never appeared. The sixth was originally published in *Philosophers on Education*, edited by Amélie Rorty (London: Routledge, 1998), pp. 284–289, and it has been revised for this edition. The seventh essay appears here for the first time, though earlier versions of sections 5–8 appear in the Schlegel chapter of my *German Idealism;* this chapter is an attempt to rethink Schlegel's philosophical development from my earlier *Enlightenment, Revolution, and Romanticism*, pp. 245–263. The eighth essay was originally written for a volume titled *Philosophical Romanticism*, edited by Nikolas Kompridis, which is forthcoming from Routledge in 2004. Earlier versions of Chapter 9 were given as lectures in several places: at Sheffield University in May 1999, the University of Arizona in September 1999, the University of Stockholm in February 2000, the Dibner Institute for Science and Technology in November 2000, and the NEH conference on Early German Romanticism in July 2001. The essay will be published as part of the Dibner series on the History and Philosophy of Science, *Dibner Institute Studies in the History of Science and Technology*. Chapter 10 was written for a lecture series on the philosophy of religion held at Boston University in October 2001, and it has not appeared before.

Because the essays were written separately, there is some overlap and therefore repetition. Since I expect that many readers will want to read the essays independently, I have not removed all the repetitious passages. For those readers who wish to read the essays in sequence I can only beg their patience and indulgence.

My study of *Frühromantik* goes back to student days at Oxford, when I first fell under the spell of Schelling and Novalis, not really knowing that they were part of a broader intellectual movement called *Frühromantik*. For a philosopher in those days to study *Frühromantik* at Oxford was a strange and solitary affair. Oxford was then, and remains now, a bastion of scholasticism; and *Frühromantik*, if it is anything, is the negation of scholasticism. In one memorable meeting I was encouraged in my efforts by Isaiah Berlin; I only wish that I had more opportunity to benefit from his company.

Over the years my studies of *Frühromantik* have profited from the work of many individuals, only a few of whom I can mention here. I have learned much from Karl Ameriks, Michel Chaouli, Manfred Frank, Paul Franks, Micheal Friedman, Charles Lewis, Michael Morgan, Bill Rasch, Robert Richards, and Simon Shaffer. I am also grateful to the many participants at the Dibner Institute meetings in November 2000, and at the NEH Summer Institute at Fort Collins Colorado in the summer of 2001; their good spirits and sharp wits encouraged me to clarify many of my views about *Frühromantik*. Last but not least, I am especially grateful to Michel Chaouli, Ian Balfour, and an anonymous reviewer for comments on the final manuscript. I only hope I have done justice to their many suggestions and criticisms.

Der romantische Imperativ fordert die Mischung aller Dichtarten. All Natur und Wissenschaft soll Kunst werden—Kunst soll Natur werden und Wissenschaft.

Imperativ: die Poesie soll sittlich und die Sittlichkeit soll poetisch sein.

—From Friedrich Schlegel's Notebooks, 1797–1798

THE ROMANTIC IMPERATIVE

Introduction:
Romanticism Now and Then

After more than a century of neglect in the English-speaking world, there are signs of a growing interest in the philosophy of early German romanticism.[1] Since 1990 several books in English have appeared on aspects of *Frühromantik*;[2] French and German works on the topic have been translated;[3] translations of romantic writings have appeared;[4] and, last but not least, in 2001 an NEH Summer Institute was devoted to philosophical aspects of *Frühromantik*.[5] Slowly but surely, the consensus is building that early German romanticism was not only a literary but also a philosophical movement.

The reasons for the neglect of early romantic philosophy have been various. There have been potent *political* reasons. Since World War II, romanticism has been discredited by both liberals and Marxists alike as the ideology of fascism, and not least because many Nazis embraced it as party ideology. There have also been *academic* reasons. Because romanticism is usually understood as a literary and critical movement, it has been made the special preserve of literary critics and historians. Not least, there have been *philosophical* reasons. The growth of analytic philosophy in the anglophone world has led to a skepticism and intolerance toward alternative ways of doing philosophy. Finally, there have been *scholarly* reasons. Some of the most important manuscript materials regarding the philosophy of the German romantics have been published only since World War II. The fragments of Novalis, Hölderlin, and Friedrich Schlegel have been published in critical editions only in the 1960s. While some of this material had been available before, it was not in reliable or critical editions.

Whatever the reasons for the neglect of early German romantic philosophy, the renewal of interest in it is long overdue. This revival stems partially from a growing—if sometimes begrudging—recognition of the historical im-

1

portance of *Frühromantik*. Its historical significance rests on several factors. First, the early romantics broke with major aspects of the Cartesian legacy: its mechanical conception of nature, its dualism between mind and body, its foundationalist belief in certain first principles, and its belief in a self-illuminating subjectivity. Second, the young romantics also questioned some of the fundamental assumptions behind Enlightenment rationalism: the possibility of an ahistorical reason, of classical standards of criticism, and of self-evident first principles. Third, the early romantics were also innovators in virtually every field of philosophy. In metaphysics, they developed an organic concept of nature to compete with the mechanical paradigm of the Enlightenment. In ethics, they stressed the importance of love and individuality in reaction against the formalism of Kant's and Fichte's ethics. And, in aesthetics, they undermined the standards and values of classicism, developing instead new methods of criticism that respected the context and individuality of the text. Finally, in politics, the romantics questioned the individualism behind modern contract theory, reviving the classical communitarian tradition of Plato and Aristotle. It was indeed the romantics who first identified and addressed some of the fundamental problems of modern civil society: anomie, atomism, and alienation.

Quite apart from its historical importance, many of the aims and problems of romantic philosophy are still vital today. Like many contemporary philosophers, the young romantics sought an epistemology that valued criticism yet escaped skepticism, one that recognized the failures of foundationalism yet did not surrender to relativism. Their goals in the philosophy of mind have also lost none of their relevance: the romantics sought a naturalism that was not a reductivist materialism, a middle path between the extremes of dualism and mechanism. The chief problem of their political philosophy remains a central issue today: How is it possible to reconcile the demands of community and those of individual liberty? Finally, their aims in aesthetics are still a desideratum—how to avoid the extremes of a dictatorial classicism and an anarchic subjectivism? If these goals and problems sound familiar, that is in no small measure because we are the heirs of the romantic legacy.

All these are sufficient reasons for a close study of early German romantic philosophy. But they have not been the sole reason for the romantic renaissance. Perhaps its chief source lies in the increasing awareness of the affinity of *Frühromantik* with postmodernism. To many, the early romantics were postmodernists *avant la lettre*. Like the postmodernists, they were skeptical of the possibility of foundationalism, of universal standards of criticism, of complete systems, and of self-illuminating subjects. Centuries before Foucault, they were apostles of sexual freedom, critics of sexual stereotypes, and defenders of personal liberty. They were also pioneers in the development of hermeneutics and founders of historicist literary criticism. Many scholars are beginning to recognize that antifoundationalism, historicism, and hermeneutics had their origins not in the twentieth century—in thinkers like Heidegger, Wittgenstein, Gadamer, or Dewey—but at the close of the eighteenth century in the reaction against the *Aufklärung* among the early romantic generation.

Nevertheless, despite the contemporary relevance of *Frühromantik*, we must be careful to avoid anachronism. We must strive to understand its historical individuality. For, if the early romantics are our contemporaries in some respects, they are not so in others. They were indeed still the children of the eighteenth century, *Kinder der Aufklärung*. In crucial respects they were very far from postmodernism. First, they differed in their Platonism, their belief in a single universal reason, in the archetypes, ideas, or forms that manifest themselves in nature and history. The claim that the young romantics insisted that truth and value is a matter for the individual to decide fails to come to terms with the profound influence of Platonism on Hölderlin, Schelling, Schleiermacher, Friedrich Schlegel, and Novalis.[6] For all the importance that the romantics gave to individuality, they never ceased to hold that there are fundamental moral or natural laws that apply to everyone alike.[7] Second, the romantics were also far from postmodernism in their striving and longing for unity and wholeness, their demand that we overcome the fundamental divisions of modern life. While the romantics recognized difference, and indeed celebrated it, they also believed that we should strive to reintegrate it within the wider wholes of state, society, and nature. At least arguably, postmodernism begins with the claim that these divisions are a *fait accompli* and that there is no point striving to overcome them. Third, the romantics remained religious, and indeed even mystical. While their religion had a pantheistic rather than theistic or deistic foundation, they never lost some of the crucial aspects of the religious attitude toward the world. It was indeed the self-conscious goal of Friedrich Schlegel, Novalis, Schelling, and Schleiermacher to revive this attitude, which is apparent in their call for a new religious mythology and bible for the modern world. But is there any place for the absolute in postmodernism?

Despite these disparities between *Frühromantik* and postmodernism, the predominate trend in recent interpretations of the philosophy of *Früh-*

romantik has been postmodernist. I have chiefly in mind the work of Paul de Man, Azade Seyhan, Alice Kuzniar, Phillipe Lacoue-Labarthe, Jean-Luc Nancy, Manfred Frank,[8] and Isaiah Berlin, who was something of a postmodernist *avant la lettre*.[9] With some qualifications, it is even necessary to add to this list Ernst Behler, the doyen of *Frühromantik* scholarship.[10] While these scholars often disagree with one another and are not always so explicit, they come together in two respects: in understanding *Frühromantik* as antirationalist, and in stressing its affinities with postmodern concerns. There is an important element of truth in these interpretations because, in *some* crucial respects, the early romantics did react against the legacy of the Enlightenment. It must be said, however, that the postmodernists have pushed their case too far, so that it has become one-sided and anachronistic. For in other important respects, the early romantics continued with, and indeed radicalized, the legacy of the Enlightenment. They never lost their beliefs in the need for and value of self-restraint, criticism, and systematicity. They continued to believe in the desirability of *Bildung*, the possibility of progress, the perfectability of the human race, and even the creation of the Kingdom of God on earth. While they were not so naive to believe that we would actually *achieve* these ideals, they did hold we could, through constant striving, *approach* them.

The need to find a middle path between the extremes of rationalist and irrationalist interpretations is clear from Friedrich Schlegel's famous dictum that philosophy both must have and cannot have a system.[11] Romantic irony begins with the attempt to straddle that dilemma, with the constant striving for a system combined with the self-critical awareness that it is unattainable. Postmodernists stress why the romantics think we cannot have a system; but they understate the romantic demand forever to strive for one.[12] It was indeed just this demand that drove Friedrich Schlegel, Schleiermacher, Schelling, and Novalis to construct systems of their own.[13] To be sure, their efforts were only sketches or drafts *(Entwurfe)*, written in the realization that there could be no perfect exposition of *the* system; but they still show unmistakably that the romantics were not committed in principle to writing fragments forever.[14]

Prima facie it is difficult to understand how the romantics' skepticism about certain foundations, complete systems, and infallible standards of criticism went hand-in-hand with their Platonism and rationalism. But this difficulty only shows our own limited historical horizons. It comes from the legacy of early modern rationalism, more specifically the philosophies of

Descartes, Leibniz, Malebranche, and Spinoza, whose rationalism expressed itself in systems and first principles. In the Platonic tradition, however, skepticism sometimes went hand-in-hand with rationalism. While many Platonists believed that the world is in principle intelligible, they did not think that our own finite human intellects could grasp the eternal forms, except through a glass darkly. Like Socrates, they held both that there is a realm of pure being and that the wise man knows he knows nothing. It is a mistake to conflate their skepticism about our capacity to grasp this order with an affirmation of the irrationality of the world itself. The romantics were decidedly *not* the missionaries of Dionysus in the sense of Schopenhauer and Nietzsche, who affirmed the irrationality of reality.[15] When Friedrich Schlegel expressed his doubts about the complete comprehensibility of the world he was affirming not its intrinsic irrationality but simply its incomprehensibility *for us,* for our *finite human* reason.[16] Schlegel has been the central figure for postmodernist interpretations of *Frühromantik;* yet he confessed that Plato had been the chief inspiration behind his philosophy, and held that the true philosophy is idealism, which he defined in Platonic terms.[17]

Of course, the individuality of *Frühromantik,* its fundamental differences from postmodernism, should also not prohibit us from seeing some of its fundamental affinities. But the chief goal of the philosophical historian should first and foremost be to reconstruct the individuality of *Frühromantik,* to understand it from within according to its own context and characteristic ideals. To be sure, this goal too is only another infinite ideal that we can approach but never attain; but, for all the reasons stated above, I think the struggle toward it is eminently worthwhile. The ten essays here are efforts in that direction.

CHAPTER 1

The Meaning of "Romantic Poetry"

1. Aims and Scruples

"Romanticism," Arthur Lovejoy wrote in 1923, is "the scandal of literary history and criticism." Lovejoy argued that it would be better just to abandon such a woolly concept, because scholars kept giving completely conflicting accounts of its meaning. What one scholar saw as the very spirit or essence of romanticism another saw as its exact antithesis. This problem arose not simply from having opposing interpretations of the same texts, Lovejoy noted, but also from the lack of agreement about which texts should be counted as romantic in the first place. To remedy such anarchy, he recommended talking about "romanticisms" in the plural rather than "romanticism" in the singular.[1]

Since Lovejoy wrote these provocative lines, there have been some notable attempts to answer him. Some scholars have attempted to find common features behind the apparently contradictory aspects of romanticism,[2] while others have discerned universal patterns behind the use of the term "romantic" in various European countries.[3] Although much of this work has been informative and illuminating, it is questionable whether it takes us very far. The problem is that these common features and universal patterns are too general and anemic to help us understand *one* of the romanticisms, that is, the specific goals, ideals, and beliefs of thinkers working in a particular intellectual context. Even worse, such generalizations are very fragile, since they can be easily refuted by citing a few contrary instances. For these reasons, it is still prudent to follow Lovejoy's advice.

So, in the spirit of Lovejoy, I want to lay aside any claims to speak about romanticism in general and to focus instead on *one* of the romanticisms. I would like to examine one brief period of intellectual life in Germany in the

6

late eighteenth and early nineteenth centuries, the period known in German as *Frühromantik* and in English as early German romanticism. Scholars generally agree about the approximate dates of *Frühromantik:* it began in the summer of 1797 and declined in the summer of 1801.[4] There is also little disagreement about who were the central figures of this movement. They were W. H. Wackenroder (1773–1801), F. W. J. Schelling (1775–1845), F. D. Schleiermacher (1767–1834), Friedrich Schlegel (1772–1829) and his brother August Wilhelm Schlegel (1767–1845), Ludwig Tieck (1773–1853), and Friedrich von Hardenberg (1772–1801), better known by his pen name "Novalis."

I would like to ask today one very basic question about *Frühromantik*. Namely, what did the young romantics mean by "romantic poetry" *(romantische Poesie)?* To be sure, this is no easy question, and it would take several volumes to answer it fully. Friedrich Schlegel himself warned his brother that he could not provide him with an adequate account of what he meant by romantic poetry since it would be 125 sheets long.[5] I do not pretend here to provide anything like a full explanation of the meaning of this very difficult and elusive phrase. I am going to set aside all questions about its etymology and suspend any discussion of its philosophical foundations. All I want to do now is to raise one very basic question about the meaning of this phrase. Namely, to what does it apply? Or, in short, what were the young romantics talking about when they spoke of romantic poetry?

I choose to examine the concept of *romantische Poesie* because it still provides the best point of entry into the magical and mysterious world of early German romanticism. There can be no doubt that this concept was pivotal for the young romantics themselves. It expressed or presupposed many of their basic interests and ideals, and they sometimes used it to distinguish their ideas from those of the past. Nevertheless, despite its importance for them, it is necessary to note that the young romantics did *not* define themselves in terms of this concept. They never referred to themselves as *die Romantiker* or as *die romantische Schule*. The term was first applied to a later group of romantics only in 1805, and then it was used only satirically; it acquired a neutral connotation, more akin to the contemporary meaning, only in the 1820s.[6] Still, provided that we recognize that the romantics did not define themselves with this term, the anachronism in calling them romantics is not vicious; indeed, the concept of *romantische Poesie* was so crucial for the young romantics that we are justified in naming them after it.

Of course, the importance of the concept of romantic poetry for the young romantics has been recognized long ago. It has been the subject of intensive investigation by many eminent scholars, among them Rudolf Haym, Arthur Lovejoy, Hans Eichner, and Ernst Behler. It might well be asked, therefore, what point there can be in reexamining it. My main reason for doing so is that I want to reexamine the traditional, and still very prevalent, conception of early German romanticism. According to that conception, *Frühromantik* was an essentially literary and critical movement, whose main goal was to develop a new form of literature and criticism in reaction against neoclassical literature and criticism.[7] This interpretation has taken as its centerpiece and foundation the concept of *romantische Poesie,* which it assumes designates nothing more than a new kind of literature and criticism.

Let me lay down my cards right now and confess that I think that the traditional interpretation has been a disaster. The main problem behind it is that it has justified an academic division of labor that has had two very damaging consequences for the study of *Frühromantik.* First, most philosophers ignore the subject because they think that the central concerns of early romanticism fall within the realm of literature. Second, the subject has been almost the exclusive preserve of literary scholars, who do not focus sufficient attention on the fundamental metaphysical, epistemological, ethical, and political ideas that are the real foundation of early romanticism. As a result, philosophers have narrow intellectual horizons, while literary scholars have a very amateurish understanding of their subject.

Still, though I think that the standard literary conception has had these sad consequences, I do not wish to rest my case on it. I wish to criticize the standard interpretation on its own grounds by reexamining the very texts that are supposed to support it. My chief complaint is that this interpretation cannot do justice to the main concept it intends to explain: romantic poetry. Against the traditional interpretation, I wish to put forward two theses about the meaning of this concept. First, it refers to not only literature, but also all the arts and sciences; there is indeed no reason to limit its meaning to literary works, since it also applies to sculpture, music, and painting. Second, it designates not only the arts and sciences but also human beings, nature, and the state. The aim of the early romantic aesthetic was indeed to romanticize the world itself, so that human beings, society, and the state could become works of art as well.

According to my interpretation, then, *romantische Poesie* designates not a form of literature or criticism but the romantics' general aesthetic ideal. This ideal was truly revolutionary: it demanded that we transform not only literature and criticism but all the arts and sciences; and it insisted that we break down the barriers between art and life, so that the world itself becomes "romanticized."[8]

2. The Standard Interpretation

So much by way of anticipation. Before I begin to criticize the standard interpretation, let me, for the sake of fairness, explain it in a little more detail. This will help us see its limitations.

The standard interpretation maintains that the central aim of the young romantics was to create a new *romantic* literature and criticism, which they developed in reaction against the *neoclassical* literature and criticism of the seventeenth and eighteenth centuries. This neoclassical literature could take two forms: it could refer to the neoclassical tradition of the earlier eighteenth century in France and Germany; or it could designate the neoclassicism of Goethe, Schiller, and Voß later in the eighteenth century, which was formulated in reaction against the romantics. Usually, the contrast between *Romantik* and *Klassik* applies to the literary values of the romantics versus those of later Goethe and Schiller.

Whatever the contrast with neoclassicism, the fundamental premise behind the standard interpretation is that the phrase *romantische Poesie* designates some form of literature. The only question that remains is *which* form, or precisely *how* we should characterize it.

It is important to see the precise assumptions behind this premise. It is *not* assumed, contrary to the associations of the term *Poesie*, that this phrase designates only poetry, that is, literature in verse form. Everyone recognizes that the romantics also used the phrase *romantische Poesie* to refer to works in prose. It is also *not* assumed that the phrase refers to some specific genre or style of poetry or prose, such as the lyric, epic, or idyll; for everyone also agrees that *romantische Poesie* refers to some mixture or synthesis of styles, a work that can combine many genres into one. What is assumed, however, is that the term *Poesie*—the genus of which *romantische Poesie* is only a species—designates some *literary use of language,* however eclectic in style, and whether in prose or verse.

There is some evidence to support such an interpretation, though most of it comes from Schlegel's early writings, especially those he wrote between 1795 and 1797, the rough dates of his early neoclassicist phase. Schlegel then used the term *Poesie* mainly to refer to poetry, especially the various forms of *verse,* such as lyric, epic, and satire. But he did not use the term exclusively in this narrow sense, because he also applied it to works written in prose. He found it odd, for example, that Herder did not think of the novels of early modern literature as *Poesie;* although these works were in prose, they were still for Schlegel "poetry in prose."[9] Schlegel's explicit definition of *Poesie* does seem to confirm the assumption that this term designates some literary use of language, any aesthetic production in words. According to his definition, "poetry is any use of language whose main or secondary goal is the beautiful."[10] Schlegel is also careful to distinguish poetry from the other arts. In one of his early fragments he makes poetry one of the three forms of art along with music and sculpture.[11] What distinguishes these three forms are their different media. While the medium of music is *movement* and while the medium of sculpture is *body,* the medium of poetry is *language.* So, in sum, for the young Schlegel, poetry is only one of the arts; it is that art whose medium is language; and its goal is to create beauty. That seems to confirm the crucial assumption behind the standard interpretation that *romantische Poesie* refers to some specific form of literature.

The crucial question remains, however, whether Schlegel continued to use the term *Poesie* in this sense when, in early 1797, he abandoned his neoclassicism and developed his concept of *romantische Poesie.* The tacit assumption behind the standard interpretation is that Schlegel *retained* his early concept of *Poesie* when he wrote his manifesto of *romantische Poesie* in *Athenäumsfragment* no. 116, the *locus classicus* for the early romantic definition. It is admitted that Schlegel later expanded the meaning of the concept of *Poesie,* so that by 1800 he applied it virtually to all forms of art, and indeed to nature itself. But it is still assumed that as late as 1798 he used the concept essentially in his earlier sense. It is indeed virtually taken for granted that *Poesie* refers to some literary production, whether in verse or in prose. The only question that has divided scholars has been *what kind* of literary production *romantische Poesie* is supposed to be.

The persistence of this assumption becomes apparent from a famous controversy about the precise meaning of *romantische Poesie* in *Athenäumsfragment* no. 116. The occasion for the controversy was Rudolf Haym's blunt claim, in his magisterial *Die romantische Schule,* that Schlegel's romantic poetry essentially referred to the modern novel, of which Goethe's *Wilhelm Meister* was the paradigm.[12] According to Haym, *romantische Poesie* was nothing less than *Romanpoesie,* where *Roman,* true to its German etymology, referred to the novel *(der Roman).* To prove his point, Haym noted the remarkable affinity between Schlegel's account of romantic poetry in *Athenäumsfragment* no. 116 and the characteristics he attributed to Goethe's *Wilhelm Meister* in his laudatory review of that work.

Although Haym's explanation is seductively simple, it was vehemently attacked by Arthur Lovejoy in a celebrated 1916 article on the grounds that it could not account for some very basic facts.[13] Against Haym, Lovejoy countered that Schlegel's romantic poetry had no essential connection with the modern novel, because Schlegel's paradigm of the romantic writer was Shakespeare, who was, of course, a dramatist. He then pointed out that Schlegel used the term "romantic" to designate "the romances of chivalry" and "medieval and early modern literature," whose main paradigms were Dante, Cervantes, and Shakespeare. Surely, these authors were not novelists in the modern sense of that term.

In 1956 Hans Eichner attempted to settle the dispute between Lovejoy and Haym by developing a theory that incorporated and corrected the main points of both.[14] Eichner could claim more authority than his predecessors because he had access to sources unavailable to them, namely, Schlegel's recently discovered literary notebooks. Basing his interpretation on this new material, Eichner argued that, in one respect, Haym was correct after all: romantic poetry was indeed that of the novel. Haym went astray, however, in equating the novel with Goethe's *Wilhelm Meister* or the modern prose novels of Fielding and Richardson. The *Roman* was not only a modern prose narrative, but, as Lovejoy insisted, it was the medieval and early modern romance. *Pace* Haym, such a romance could assume many forms; it could be drama as well as verse.

This dispute has been especially instructive—it would have to be invented if it did not already exist—and it deserves to be called classical in its own way. However, it is not my purpose here to assess the various positions held in the dispute. I have recounted its bare bones only to make one simple point: namely, that Haym, Lovejoy, and Eichner all assumed that *romantische Poesie* designates some form of literature. The only sticking point between them concerned the *precise form* of this literature. They never questioned their underlying assumption that the term *Poesie* in the phrase *romantische Poesie* signifies some literary use of language. It is just that assumption, however, that I now wish to question.

3. Down the Romantic Road

If we closely examine the development of Schlegel's concept of *romantische Poesie*, especially its evolution in his literary and philosophical notebooks from the summer of 1796 until late 1797, it soon becomes clear that this concept *cannot* refer merely to some form of literature. Although literature remains one of the *primary* forms of *romantische Poesie,* it is still very far from its *exclusive* form. Rather, Schlegel now extends and generalizes the concept, so that it becomes his ideal for *all* creative activity, no matter what the medium, whether written in language or not.

Let us briefly consider the main steps by which Schlegel generalized his concept of *romantische Poesie,* the chief stages involved in his stretching the original literary concept into its broader aesthetic meaning. There are four such steps, four stages of progressive generalization, which are more logically than chronologically distinguishable. All these steps were taken in Schlegel's literary and philosophical notebooks, in fragments written from 1796 to late 1797, at least several months before the composition of the *Athenäumsfragmente* in the spring of 1798.

The first step came from generalizing one of the salient features of early modern literature. For Schlegel, one of the defining characteristics of early modern literature in contrast to classical literature is that it is eclectic, encompassing a wide variety of styles or genres. While a work of classical literature would limit itself to one genre—so that, for example, a poem was either an idyll, a satire, or an epic—a work of early modern literature could encompass all these genres within itself. In his early neoclassical days, Schlegel regarded this feature of early modern literature as one of its worst attributes, because it seemed to be purely chaotic, having no basis other than a desire to please the reader.[15] Around 1796, however, Schlegel began to have doubts about his own neoclassicism. His faith in the superiority of classical art crumbled, so that he reconsidered the feasibility of reviving it in the modern age, which had very different needs and values from those of classical antiquity. Schlegel then learned to appreciate some of the distinctive qualities of modern literature, which seemed to be more appropriate for its age. The great vice of modern literature—its eclecticism—now became its great virtue. Its mixture of styles was now proof of that restless striving for wholeness, that eternal longing for unity, that was characteristic of modernity. It was the task of the modern age, Schlegel believed, to recreate the wholeness and unity of the ancient world, but now on a more sophisticated and self-conscious level that provided for the freedom and equality of everyone.[16] What had once been given by nature to the ancient Greeks—unity with oneself, with others, and with nature—now had to be recovered through free activity by modern man. Modern literature, in its creative use of many styles, expressed this striving to regain wholeness and totality.

This feature of early modern literature soon became for Schlegel *the* defining characteristic of *romantische Poesie*.[17] Once Schlegel had taken this step, however, he had already made his first crucial move in abstracting the concept of *romantisiche Poesie* from its strictly literary meaning. For if the mixture of styles is central to *romantische Poesie*, then the concept cannot refer to any specific style or genre of literature, whether in verse or prose. Any specific style would be comprised *within romantische Poesie*, so that it could not be a specific style itself. Nor was there any single form or way of combining all these styles, since Schlegel insisted that they could and should be combined in all kinds of ways, depending on the creativity and imagination of the writer.

Admittedly, the first step of generalization—defining *romantische Poesie* in terms of its eclecticism—still leaves it a form of literature. It is a very eclectic form of literature, to be sure, but it is still literature all the same, given that its medium remains language. Schlegel's second step, however, takes him beyond the threshold of language entirely. If *romantische Poesie* is essentially eclectic, comprising all manners of style and discourse, then it becomes pointless for the philologist to characterize and classify it strictly according to its stylistic features. There will be too many styles, and too many ways of combining them, for any purely linguistic classification to be useful. The only way to describe romantic poetry will then be in terms of its general aesthetic and moral qualities.

Sure enough, in his notebooks, Schlegel now begins to characterize and classify romantic works in just these terms. He defines them in terms of their *moral* qualities, such as whether they are ethical or political, or in terms of their *aesthetic* qualities, such as whether they are imaginative, imitative, and sentimental. The distinction between forms of romantic literature is now one of degree rather than kind, depending on which one of these qualities preponderates.[18] While Schlegel characterizes romantic works in terms of many different qualities in his notebooks, he seems to settle on three general qualities as definitive: *fantasy, mimesis,* and *sentimentality*.[19] A romantic work should be fantastic in that the author's imagination recognizes no law above himself and freely combines materials; it should be imitative in that it should contain a portrait of its whole age or reproduce the fullness of life; and it should be sentimental, not in the sense of expressing feelings, but in the sense of revealing the spirit of love. Clearly, these qualities are so general that they could apply to any genre of literature. But the crucial point to see now is that there is no reason to limit them to literature alone.

This is indeed Schlegel's third step. Once he began to characterize *romantische Poesie* in terms of its aesthetic rather than linguistic qualities, he was ready to apply this concept to virtually all the arts. For there is no reason why literature alone should be imaginative, sentimental, and imitative; it is obvious that these same general qualities could characterize sculpture, music, or painting. Sure enough, the early literary notebooks show that Schlegel had also taken just this step. There he began to apply the concept of the romantic to the other arts, especially to music, sculpture, and painting; he even went so far as to apply it to clothing and dance. Consider, for example, what he says in this revealing fragment: "Opera must be romantic, since music and painting are already so; and the modern art of dancing is perhaps a mixture of romantic fantasy and classical sculpture. One must surpass the ancients in this respect. Even modern clothing inclines toward the romantic."[20]

Prima facie it might seem as if Schlegel's description of the other arts as romantic was more by extension than meaning, more a courteous gesture than a settled conviction. For in his early writings he had written about *Poesie,* taken in the narrow sense of verse, as the highest of all the arts.[21] This is indeed just what we would expect for someone whose youthful ideal was to be the Winckelmann of classical poetry. Yet it is interesting to note that, by 1797, Schlegel had abandoned this conviction too. Anticipating Schopenhauer and Nietzsche, he now held that music is "the highest of the arts," and indeed "the art for the modern age."[22] It is important to recognize—for reasons soon to be explained—that the other arts were given a central role in the general aesthetic program of the *Athenäum.* It is indeed noteworthy that the longest article in the three volumes of that journal is devoted to the visual arts.[23]

Schlegel's fourth step is to extend the concept of *romantische Poesie* to the sciences. This step followed, in part, from the second. If the romantic is determined by its general aesthetic qualities, there is also no reason to limit it to the arts alone. The same concept could apply to the sciences as well, provided that they had an aesthetic exposition. It did not matter that the sciences had to use more discursive language; for they could combine this style with others, and so they would be just another kind of romantic art. This was indeed the ideal of all *Naturphilosophie:* a poetic exposition of science. Schlegel's fourth step also derives from his growing recognition that the arts and sciences have much more in common than he had earlier often assumed.[24] Partly because of the critique of foundationalist philosophy in Jena, he had ceased to think that philosophy, philology, ethics, and aesthetics could be rigorously scientific, where all propositions are derived from a single fundamental first principle and then placed in an incorrigible system. But the less the classical ideal of science seemed attainable, the more the traditional disciplines appeared to be more like the arts.

Whatever the precise epistemological status of the sciences, it seemed very artificial and arbitrary to exclude them from the romantic program, especially when they showed the same striving for wholeness, the same longing for unity, as that found in literature. If this striving and longing were to come closer to its ideal, then a truly romantic work would indeed have to be a *synthesis* of science and art. Hence in his notebooks Schlegel declares that science becomes perfect to the extent that it is art, and that art becomes perfect to the extent that it is science.[25] Schlegel had already seen such syntheses of science and art in the mythology of the past, and indeed in the Bible, which now became a model for romantic poetry.[26] The task for modern man was to recover the unity of art and science in ancient mythology; in other words, it was to create a new mythology, to write a new Bible.

If we add all these steps together, it should be clear that the concept of *romantische Poesie* does not apply only to literature, let alone merely a specific form of it; rather it also refers to any creative work whatsoever, whether literary, artistic, or scientific. Schlegel draws just this general conclusion in his notebooks: "All works of the mind should romanticize, approximating as much as possible to the romantic."[27] Playing on the close affinity in German between *der Roman* and *das romantische*, he insists that all works should now become *Romane*.[28]

4. The Concept of *Poesie*

All the developments reflected in Schlegel's notebooks in 1797 finally became fully explicit and self-conscious in the *Athenäum*, especially in his 1800 *Gespräch über die Poesie*. Here Schlegel is perfectly explicit in drawing the conclusion that *das romantische* cannot be described in terms of some genre or form of literature. Instead, he insists that it has to be explained in terms of its general aesthetic qualities; the romantic, as he puts it, is not "a kind" *(Gattung)* but "an element" *(ein Element)* of literature.[29]

More significantly, Schlegel intentionally explodes the narrow literary meaning of *Poesie* by explicitly identifying the poetic with the *creative power* in human beings, and indeed with the *productive principle* in nature itself.[30] To be sure, poetry in its literary form was the *highest* manifestation of this power, its most subtle and sophisticated product; yet it was still only *one* of its manifestations. To assume that literature is the only form of poetry is simply to mistake the part for the whole. Schlegel is now explicit that the poetic principle is active in all the arts, in the creation of sculptures, buildings, dramas, symphonies, and paintings, as well as in novels and poems. Indeed, any product of human creativity—at least insofar as it was beautiful—is poetic.

That Schlegel was deliberately and self-consciously departing from ordinary usage in using the term *Poesie* in this broad sense there cannot be any doubt. In one of the dialogues in the *Gespräch über Poesie* the character Amelia is very skeptical about giving the term such a wide meaning.[31] She comments rather acidly: "If it goes on like this, before too long one thing after another will be transformed into poetry." She then asks: "Is everything then poetry?" The character Lothario replies to Amelia's question by extending poetry to all the arts and sciences: "Every art and discipline that functions through language," he says, "when exercised as an art for its own sake . . . appears as poetry." But then the final word is had by the character Ludovico, who pushes the limits even beyond language: "And every art or discipline which does not manifest its nature through language possesses an invisible spirit, and that is poetry." If we take Ludovico seriously, *Poesie* does not even have to refer to linguistic creations, let alone literary ones.

If Schlegel's use of *Poesie* now seems eccentric and whimsical, it is important to recall that he was only going back to the classical sense of the term. The original sense of the poetic *(poiētikós)* was that which pertains to making or creating something.[32] It is this meaning that appears in Plato and Aristotle, who gave it a central role in their classification of the sciences. According to Diogenes Laertius, Plato had divided the sciences into three kinds: the theoretical (geometry, astronomy), the practical (politics and flute-playing), and the poetic (architecture and ship-building).[33] While the theoretical is contemplative and the practical executes some task, the poetic is creative or productive. Its task is to create things, whether it is a beautiful sculpture or a ship.

It is noteworthy that Schlegel was not alone in his broad use of the word. A similar, if not entirely identical, sense also appears in the writings of August Wilhelm Schlegel, Schelling, and Novalis. August Wilhelm declares that "poetry, taken in the widest sense, is the power to create the beautiful and to present it visually or audibly."[34] Schelling too often uses the term in the classical sense, where it means "the immediate production or creation of something real . . . invention in and for itself."[35] But he also gives the term a more technical metaphysical sense: it is that act of creativity by which the genius reveals the divine within himself by making the universal and ideal something particular and real. For Novalis too, *Poesie* has a very general meaning, so that it signifies "the free, active, and productive use of our organs."[36] Poetry sometimes designates an organic being that grows according to its own inner laws;[37] but it could also refer to "the great art of the construction of transcendental health," where a person developed the power to perceive everything as a beautiful whole.[38]

Some defenders of the standard interpretation have contended that the broad meaning Friedrich Schlegel gave to *Poesie* in the *Gespräch über Poesie* was not already in place when he wrote the *Athenäumsfragmente*.[39] But I think it is clear from the account I have already given of Schlegel's earlier intellectual development that this is incorrect. The testimony of the notebooks is clear and overwhelming: that, as early as 1797, Schlegel had already extended the concept of *romantische Poesie* to all the arts and sciences, and that he began to talk about the *Poesie* within nature itself.[40] What he stated in the *Athenäumsfragmente* was simply the final conclusion of a long development that had taken place nearly a year earlier. This becomes clear, I think, if we take another look at Schlegel's famous *Athenäumsfragment* no. 116. Now that we know something about the origin and context of this fragment, we can reread it in a new light.

It is an obvious point staring the reader in the face—indeed so obvious that it is easy to overlook it—that when Schlegel writes about *romantische Poesie* in *Athenäumsfragment* no. 116 he is *not* referring only to literary works, or indeed to the products of any activity. Rather, he is talking about creative *activity*, the *process* by which something is produced. This is indeed part of the point behind his famous comment that the most essential feature of any romantic work is "its becoming," the fact that it is never complete but that it destroys itself only to create itself forever anew. Furthermore, it is also plain that Schlegel is referring to creative activity *in general*, and not only to one *specific kind* of activity, such as writing poems or novels. This must be the case because the characteristics he ascribes to this activity are so general that they could apply to all forms of creative activity. Consider some of the chief characteristics he attributes to romantic poetry: that even in creating something it never loses the power of self-criticism; that it loses itself entirely in its object yet also has the power to stand back from it and its own activity; that it sees the necessity of constraint but recognizes none except those it imposes on itself; that it never comes to an end because its very essence consists in its "becoming." And so on. Clearly, such attributes also apply to the creative activity of a sculptor, painter, musician, or scientist, and there is no reason to limit them to the poet, writer, or dramatist. But this is not only the *implication* of, but also the *intention* behind, Schlegel's account of *romantische Poesie* in this fragment. For, in his earlier *Kritische Fragmente*,[41] Schlegel had already emphasized all these attributes as essential to irony, which he recommended as the proper attitude for *any* thinker trying to know the truth and to attain perfection.

This reading of *Athenäumsfragment* no. 116 is obvious, and it would be accepted by those scholars who advance the standard interpretation. Why, then, in the face of such evidence, do they continue to put forward their interpretation as if it were an established truth? The explanation does not lie entirely with the gravitational pull of the academic division of labor, though I suspect that this has been very seductive. Ultimately, the source of the problem lies with Schlegel himself, who was also confused about this very issue. It is important to see that his concept of *romantische Poesie* is ambiguous.[42] It could refer to his own philosophical ideal and be a normative concept, in which case it applied to all the arts and sciences; but it could also be a historical concept, in which case it referred to early modern forms of literature in contrast to classical forms. While Schlegel first used the term in a historical sense to designate some of the stylistic aspects of early modern literature, he later generalizes these into a normative concept for all the arts and sciences. Yet traces of the original historical concept remained even when he began to use it in the broader and normative sense. Schlegel himself would continue to use the concept to refer to early modern literature, and to distinguish it from neoclassicism, even after he had made it into his general ideal of all human creativity. He would not get out of the confusion until much later when he began to ascribe romantic qualities to the works of classical antiquity. I would like to excuse the advocates of the standard interpretation, then, on the grounds that they are the victims of Schlegel's own confusion.

5. Romanticizing the World

Now that we have seen the very broad meaning that the young romantics gave to *romantische Poesie*, it should be clear that their aesthetic revolution was much more ambitious and radical than anything ever dreamed of in the philosophy of the standard interpretation. The young romantics did not simply desire a new romantic literature and criticism to replace a neoclassical literature and criticism. Rather, they wanted to romanticize all the arts and sciences, so that there would also be a romantic painting, a romantic sculpture, and a romantic music, and so that there would be a romantic science as well as a romantic art. Furthermore, all these arts and sciences were then to be synthesized in a single work of art, which would be nothing less than the mythology of the modern age.

If this seems absurdly ambitious or preposterous, then I must warn you that it is really only the beginning. The aesthetic revolution of the young romantics was much more radical still, going far beyond any plans for the reform of the arts and sciences. For its ultimate aim was to romanticize the world itself, so that the individual, society, and the state would become works of art. To romanticize the world meant to make our lives into a novel or poem, so that they would regain the meaning, mystery, and magic they had lost in the fragmented modern world. We are all artists deep within ourselves, the young romantics fervently believed, and the goal of the romantic program is to awaken that talent slumbering within ourselves so that each of us makes his life into a beautiful whole. Hence it was a central goal of the young romantics to break down those barriers between art and life that had confined art to books, concert halls, and museums, and that had made the world a very ugly place.

This radical program to romanticize the world itself appears perfectly explicitly in some of Schlegel's early writings. Even in his early neoclassical essays the germs of the program are already apparent, for there Schlegel endorses Winckelmann's view that art and life were one in the ancient world.[43] In his early notebooks Schlegel is very explicit in calling for a return to that unity of life and art in the ancient world. There are some remarkable fragments, written in 1797, where Schlegel declares what he calls *"der romantische Imperativ,"* an obvious play on Kant's own categorical imperative. This romantic imperative demands that all of nature and science should become art, and that art should become nature and science.[44] Furthermore, it demands that poetry should be social as well as society poetic, and that poetry should be moral as morality should be poetic.[45] There should be nothing less than a contract between poetry and life, as Schlegel later puts it, so that poetry becomes lively and life becomes poetry.[46] All these demands follow from what Schlegel calls elsewhere the *"Genialischer Imperativ"*: the demand that we overcome the divisions of modern life and restore unity to *Bildung.*[47]

This radical program also appears perfectly explicitly in Schlegel's later *Kritische-* and *Athenäumsfragmente*. In *Kritische Fragment* no. 78 Schlegel states the romantic theme that the life of each individual should be a novel: "Each individual, who is cultivated and who cultivates himself, contains a novel in his inner self. But that he expresses and writes it down is not necessary."[48] The ambition to break down the barriers between art and life is made perfectly explicit in *Athenäumsfragment* no. 116: the goal of romantic poetry, Schlegel says in a passage echoing the earlier notebooks, is "to make not only poetry social and lively but also society and life poetic." Romantic poetry encompasses everything poetic, he further explains, so that it includes not only "the grand system of art" but even "the sigh, the kiss, that the creative child breathes in artless song."[49] But the most revealing statement of all appears in *Athenäumsfragment* no. 168, where Schlegel poses the question: "What philosophy is left for the poet?" His answer could not be more explicit: "That creative philosophy that originates in freedom and the belief in freedom, and that shows how the human spirit impresses its law on all things and how the world is its work of art."[50]

Like Schlegel, Novalis also had a radical aesthetic ideal. It was indeed Novalis who first declared the radical romantic manifesto in the striking sentence: "The world must be romanticized." To romanticize the world is to give it back its meaning, magic, and mystery, which had been lost through the growth of modern culture. Novalis was perfectly explicit in defining what he meant by romanticizing something: "When I give the commonplace a higher meaning, the customary a mysterious appearance, the known the dignity of the unknown, the finite the illusion of the infinite, I romanticize it."[51] To romanticize our lives in this manner, Novalis explained, means to make them into a novel. Our lives will then become an aesthetic whole, where everything has its place and takes on a special meaning. This is how he put the point in another fragment: "All the chance events of our lives are materials from which we can make what we like. Whoever is rich in spirit makes much of his life. Every acquaintance, every incident would be for the thoroughly spiritual person . . . the beginning of an endless novel."[52]

Novalis gave his aesthetic ideal a political significance as well as a moral one. It was not only the individual but also the state itself that had to become a work of art. Hence Novalis dubs his political ideal "the poetic state." The governing metaphor of this ideal is that life is a stage.[53] The ruler is director, the citizens are actors, and their roles are laws and customs.

6. Motives for the Radical Program

We are now finally in a position to formulate the very general meaning that the young romantics gave to their concept of *romantische Poesie*. Rather than signifying simply some new form of literature, this concept stood for the romantics' grand aesthetic ideal: the transformation of all the arts and sciences, and indeed all aspects of life, according to the demands of art. *Romantische Poesie* sometimes refers to the *activity* of aesthetic production, to all human *creativity* insofar as its object is the beautiful. As such, it refers to the activity of *romanticizing* the world, making something have the magic, meaning, and mystery of a novel or poem. But the term could also designate the *goal* or *end* of that activity: the world insofar as it has been made into a novel.

Such a grand ideal will make the romantics seem absurdly idealistic—indeed, dare I say, excessively "romantic." Yet it is important to note that they saw *romantische Poesie* only as an ideal, a goal we can approach but never completely attain. All that remained to our lot here on earth, they fully recognized, was the eternal *striving* and *longing* to achieve this goal.

The question still remains: Why did the romantics use the concept of *romantische Poesie* in such a broad sense? Why did they extend *Poesie* from its narrow literary meaning so that it would apply to all human creativity? Here I can only touch upon the philosophical and moral basis for this move. Suffice it to say for now that there were at least two reasons, both of them compelling.

First, to apply the term *Poesie* not only to literary creativity but to all artistic creativity, and indeed to the creativity of nature itself, stressed a point very important to Schlegel, Schelling, and Novalis around 1797: namely, the continuity between nature and art. They wanted to emphasize that *all* forms of human creativity are simply appearances, manifestations, and developments of the creativity of nature itself. For the young romantics, there was only a difference in degree, not one in kind, between the creativity of the artist and that productive power of the *natura naturans,* that universal power or energy behind all things, what Herder called *"die Urkraft aller Kräfte."* The creativity of the artist was simply the highest organization, manifestation, and development of the same fundamental organic power active throughout all of nature. Such a doctrine was important to them, though, not only because it placed art within its general metaphysical context, but also because it guaranteed the *truth* of aesthetic production. For if what the artist creates is also what nature creates through him, then his activity reveals, manifests, or expresses nature itself; it is indeed the *self-revelation* of nature. Art thus becomes, as Schelling famously argued, the organon and criterion of truth itself.[54]

Second, to apply the term *Poesie* not only to works of literature but to all forms of aesthetic production was necessary to achieve the romantics' fundamental goal: *Bildung,* the education of humanity, the development of all human powers into a whole. There can be no doubt that the young romantics saw all their efforts in literature and criticism as directed to this grand ideal. They swear their allegiance to *Bildung* in the preface to the *Athenäum,* their common journal.[55] Schlegel declares that *Bildung* alone is the highest good; and Novalis makes it his mission on earth to promote it.[56] *Bildung* means the complete development of all human powers, especially one's powers as a human being, but also those unique to oneself. Now given such a goal, it is obvious that it would be unduly narrow to limit the romantic program to literature alone. All the arts had to be enlisted in such an important cause, for all of them contributed in their own way to the many-sided development of a human being. Hence to apply the term *Poesie* to all the arts—to painting, sculpture, drama, and music as well as literature—made good sense since that drafted them all in the grand cause of aesthetic education.

Both of these points confirm the general reading of *romantische Poesie.* They show that the romantics were, for general philosophical and moral reasons, committed to extending the concept of *romantische Poesie* beyond its original literary domain. They also demonstrate the profound extent to which the early romantics' conception of *Poesie* must be understood within its general philosophical and historical context. To insist that we can talk about *romantische Poesie* hermetically, as if it were a technical concept of a completely self-contained discipline, undermines its essential purpose.[57] For the fundamental spirit behind the concept of *romantische Poesie* is holistic: to recreate the unity of all the arts and sciences, and to reestablish the unity of art and life. The chief problem with the standard interpretation is that it treats such a holistic concept in a partial, divisive manner. That, I believe, must stand as the final indictment against it.

Early German Romanticism:
A Characteristic

1. The Task of Characteristic

To interpret a literary work, Friedrich Schlegel once said, it is necessary to understand its *individuality,* what is unique to or distinctive about its style and way of seeing things. We can criticize a work, he held, only if we lay aside general norms and consider the author's own goals and circumstances. This method of interpretation, which attempts to define what is characteristic of a work by understanding the writer's aims and context, Schlegel called "characteristic" *(Charakteristik).*

What I would like to do now is to apply Schlegel's method to early German romanticism itself. I want to determine the goals, problems, and context of the romantic movement during its early formative years from the summer of 1796 to the summer of 1801, the period known as *Frühromantik.* My aim is to characterize the guiding ideals and issues behind some of the leading thinkers of the early romantic generation, specifically those of Friedrich Schlegel, August Wilhelm Schlegel, Novalis, the young Hegel, Schleiermacher, Schelling, and Hölderlin. I want to know what these young romantics were trying to achieve, and how their goals differ from earlier and later movements of thought, such as the Enlightenment *(Aufklärung)* and *Sturm und Drang.*

Of course, the characteristic of *Frühromantik* is old business, and some very eminent scholars—such as Rudolf Haym, Paul Kluckhohn, Fritz Strich, H. A. Korff, Benno von Wiese, and Ernst Behler, to name but a few—have already tried their hands at it.[1] It is with some trepidation, therefore, that I take up this task anew. My reason for doing so is my dissatisfaction with the traditional approach toward *Frühromantik,* which is still prevalent and indeed dominant today.[2] This approach regards *Frühromantik* as fundamentally a literary and critical movement, whose main purpose was to create a new romantic literature and criticism in opposition to neoclassical literature and criticism. The purpose of scholarship on *Frühromantik* is then to determine how romantic literature and criticism differ from neoclassical literature and criticism.

I have two chief complaints against this approach. First, it is far too narrow, failing to encompass *Frühromantik* in all its depth and breadth. Almost all scholars would agree that *Frühromantik* was not only a literary and critical movement, but also a cultural and philosophical one, and indeed one so broad that it encompassed virtually every field of culture and philosophy. Although this point was made long ago by Haym, literary scholars have paid it only lip-service.[3] Second, this approach also gives undue importance to the literary and critical dimension of *Frühromantik*. Admitting that this dimension is only one part of a whole, some literary scholars still regard it as the central or dominant part. They are led to this conclusion because they think that *Frühromantik* was essentially an aesthetic movement, whose main purpose was to revitalize German art. But there are serious problems with this reasoning. While it is indeed accurate to regard *Frühromantik* as an aesthetic movement, it would be wrong to limit the aesthetic exclusively to the literary and critical; here again that dimension was only one part of a broader aesthetic whole. Furthermore, it is a mistake to treat the aesthetic—even taken in a very broad sense—as if it were a self-sufficient domain, having autonomous or indeed sovereign status. Rather, romantic aesthetics derives its meaning and purpose from its philosophical context and its underlying ethical and political values.

Once we reject the traditional understanding of *Frühromantik,* the question of its characteristic remains wide open. What follows is an attempt to fill this gap. My characteristic of *Frühromantik* comprises three basic theses. My first thesis is that the central ideals of the romantics were primarily ethical and political rather than critical and literary. The ethical and political have primacy over the literary and critical in the sense that the romantic devotion to aesthetics was ultimately guided by their ethical and political ideals. These ideals were the ends for the sake of which they undertook their literary and critical work. If this is the case, then we must abandon, once and for all, one of the most common myths about romanticism: that it was essentially apolitical, an attempt to flee from social and political reality into the world of the literary imagination.[4] Rather than escaping moral and political issues for the sake of literature and criticism, the romantics subordinated their literature and criticism to their ethical and political ideals.

My second thesis is a more specific account of the romantics' ethical and political ideals. The romantics fundamental ethical ideal was *Bildung*, self-realization, the development of all human and individual powers into a whole. Their basic political ideal was community, the pursuit of the good life in the state. What both these ideals have in common is their aspiration toward unity: the attempt to unify all powers of the individual, and to reconcile him with others and nature. The goal of romantic striving was therefore essentially *holistic:* to create through reason that unity with oneself, others, and nature that had been given in antiquity.

My third thesis is that the romantic ideals of unity were an attempt to reaffirm wholeness in the face of the divisive tendencies of modern civil society. While these ideals were in crucial respects a reaction against modernity, they were in others an attempt to preserve some of its fundamental values: freedom, reason, and progress. It is therefore incorrect to characterize *Frühromantik* as either a complete endorsement or rejection of modernity. Rather, the romantic response was much more complex and ambivalent, typical of German reformism in the late 1790s.

2. The Highest Good

Prima facie it might seem to be impossible to determine the fundamental goals of the early romantics. It seems as if there are many ways to describe their goals, and as if they accept such a plurality of values that there is no way of reducing them down to one description. Though understandable, such skepticism is too hasty. It overlooks one very reliable way of determining the romantics' most basic values and ideals. This is to determine their answer to a fundamental question of ethics—namely, what is the highest good, the *summum bonum?*

This question is ancient, going back at least to Aristotle. In his *Nicomachean Ethics* Aristotle gave a precise and influential account of the concept of the highest good. He laid down two conditions of the highest good: first, it is *final*, because all other goods are only means to it; and, second, it is *complete*, because it cannot be improved by adding any other good to it.[5] Few philosophers quarreled with Aristotle's definition; they would dispute for centuries, however, about its precise interpretation. The specific meaning of the highest good was indeed the main subject of ethical discussion and controversy in antiquity and the Middle Ages.

In late-eighteenth-century Germany as well, Aristotle's question was still very much alive. The question had often been formulated in more theological terms—"What is the vocation of man" *(die Bestimmung des Menschen)?*—but the main issue was the same, since the vocation of man, the task assigned to him by Providence, was the end of life, the highest good. All aspiring philosophers had to take a position on this issue, and the young romantics were no exception. It was indeed no accident that Schlegel gave it a central place in his lectures on transcendental philosophy, and that the young Schleiermacher devotes two essays to it.[6] In his later years Schleiermacher would indeed argue that the revitalization of ethics as a philosophical discipline depended on returning to this ancient question.[7]

The early romantics' position on the highest good is perfectly clear and straightforward. "The highest good, and the source of everything useful," Friedrich Schlegel wrote in his *Ideen*, "is *Bildung*."[8] In his *Blütenstaub* Novalis put forward a similar view: "We are on a mission: we have been called upon for the education *(Bildung)* of the earth."[9] Along the same lines, Hölderlin told his brother that the goal most dear to himself was *"Bildung, Besserung des Menschengeschlects."*[10] In their common journal, the *Athenäum*, the romantics saw one overriding goal behind all their contributions: *Bildung*. They swore the following oath:

> Der Bildung Strahlen all' in Eins zu fassen,
> > Vom Kranken ganz zu scheiden das Gesunde,
> > Bestreben wir uns treu im freien Bunde. . . .[11]

The German term *Bildung* is notoriously untranslatable. Depending on the context, it can mean education, culture, and development. It means literally "formation," implying the development of something potential, inchoate, and implicit into something actual, organized, and explicit. Sometimes the various connotations of the term join together to signify the educational process or product of acculturation, or the ethical process or product of self-realization.

If we view the romantic ideal of *Bildung* from a general philosophical perspective, it would be most accurate to describe it as an ethics of self-realization. The classical account of such an ethics is Aristotle's *Nicomachean Ethics*, where the highest good is defined in terms of human excellence, the development of characteristic human virtues. In fundamental respects, the romantics go back to the Aristotelian tradition. In the classical world the principal alternatives to Aristotle's ethics of self-realization were hedonism and stoicism. While the hedonists defined the highest good in terms of pleasure alone, the stoics saw the supreme end of life as the execution of duty or cultivation of virtue alone. It is noteworthy that the romantics rejected—for very Aristotelian reasons—the two eighteenth-century counterparts of hedonism and stoicism: the empiricist ethics of Bentham and Helvetius, and the rationalist ethics of Kant and Fichte. The romantics criticized Kant's and Fichte's ethics of duty for exaggerating the importance of duty, for giving no place to feeling, pleasure, and desire within the highest good; and they faulted Bentham and Helvetius for pushing feeling, pleasure, and desire too far, for failing to see that devotion to pleasure alone would neglect the development of our characteristic human powers.

The most crucial and conspicuous feature of the romantic ideal of *Bildung* is that it is holistic. There were two aspects to this holism. First, it stressed the development of *all* our characteristic human powers, rejecting any one-sidedness that would develop one aspect of our humanity at the expense of others. Second, it emphasized that all these powers should be formed into an integrated, harmonious, and balanced whole. True to such holism, the romantics insisted that we should educate not only reason but also sensibility, not only the intellect but also feeling and sensation. They argued that sensibility—the power to sense, feel, and desire—is no less human than reason itself.[12] How we sense and feel as human beings differs markedly from any other animal.

The romantic ideal of *Bildung* was not only holistic but also individualistic. In other words, *Bildung* should consist in the development of not only our characteristic human powers, which we all share as human beings, but also our distinctive individual powers, which are unique to each of us. The romantics stressed that each individual had to realize his human powers in his own unique and individual fashion. No two persons were ever alike; each had characteristics that distinguished him from everyone else; complete self-realization demanded actualizing these distinctive characteristics no less than our universal ones. This ethic of individuality is especially marked in Friedrich Schlegel's and Schleiermacher's idea of "divine egoism," according to which the individual is sovereign over all the values of his life and should choose that most suitable to his personality.[13] Inevitably, in stressing the importance of individuality, the romantics sometimes took issue with Kant's and Fichte's ethics of duty. They contended that Kant's emphasis on universal laws as the heart of morality left no place for individuality in ethics. Fichte had once taken this aspect of Kant's ethics so far as to state that the moral ideal should be for everyone to be completely alike and to dissolve into a single person.[14] This was the romantic idea of hell, the *reductio ad absurdum* of the ethics of duty.

Reaffirming the classical neo-Platonic equation of the good with the beautiful, the early romantics interpreted their ideal of *Bildung* in aesthetic terms. To develop all one's human and individual powers, to form them into a single whole, was to create a work of art. Hence Schlegel, Tieck, and Novalis were fond of saying that the individual should make his life into a novel, a beautiful whole. There were two analogies sustaining this aesthetic concept of *Bildung*, two concepts upholding the connection between the ideal of self-realization and beauty. First, both the self-realized individual and a work of art are organic wholes, where conflicting forces (reason versus sensibility) are welded into an indissoluble unity. Second, both the self-realized individual and a work of art exhibit freedom, the absence of constraint or outside interference, since both appear to follow their own internal laws, their own inner dynamic, independent of external forces.

3. Romantic *Bildung*

Despite the central importance of *Bildung* to the romantics, and despite its distinctive place in late-eighteenth-century ethics, this concept was *not* unique to, or distinctive of, *Frühromantik*. The concept of *Bildung* was indeed a mainstay of the German tradition, common to *Sturm und Drang*, *Aufklärung*, and *Klassik* alike. Among the *Sturmer und Dränger*, the ideal of *Bildung* appears in Hamann and Herder; among the *Aufklärer*, it is found in Wolff, Mendelssohn, and Baumgarten; and among the *Klassiker*, its champions were Wieland, Schiller, Goethe, Wilhelm von Humboldt, and Winckelmann. Though these thinkers gave differing, sometimes even opposing, accounts of this ideal, they all affirmed, in one form or another, an ethics of perfection and self-realization. Even the aesthetic conception of *Bildung* came from a long tradition. Winckelmann, Wieland, Schiller, and Goethe all defined human excellence in aesthetic terms, seeing it epitomized in "the beautiful soul."[15]

One of the most common views about romanticism is that it was a rebellion against the narrow intellectualism of the Enlightenment, a defense of the rights of feeling against the hegemony of reason. But it is a mistake to regard the romantic defense of sensibility as characteristic of their ideal of *Bildung*. The defense of the rights of feeling was a battle waged decades before them by the *Sturm und Drang* or *Empfindsamkeit* movement of the 1760s and 1770s. This was the campaign led by Hamann, Herder, Möser, and Lenz, and popularized by the young Schiller and Goethe. By the time of the rise of *Frühromantik* in the late 1790s these *Sturmer und Dränger* had made their point, and it seemed necessary to temper their tempestuous claims by once again reinstating the role of rational restraint in ethics and aesthetics. This was indeed the role of the romantics: to correct both the sensibility of *Sturm und Drang* and the rationalism of the *Aufklärung* by emphasizing the equal importance of both reason and sensibility. The romantic commitment to a holistic ideal demanded nothing less: the rights of reason had to be affirmed and limited no less than those of sensibility. But in their commitment to a holistic ideal, it is again difficult to determine how the romantics differ from many of their contemporaries or predecessors, who are usually classified under the rubrics of *Klassik* or *Aufklärung*.

If the concept of *Bildung* is a *Gemeingut* of the German cultural tradition, it is necessary to be more precise if we are to determine the characteristic ideals of *Frühromantik*. Although we have found its genus, we still have to go further to get to its *differentia specifica*. This means taking a closer look at the romantic ideal of *Bildung*. There were at least two characteristic features of its ideal.

The first is the central role the romantics gave to the concept of freedom. The romantics insist that *Bildung* must arise from the free choice of the individual, that it must reflect his own decisions. The self realizes itself only through specific decisions and choices, and not by complying with general cultural norms and tradition. *Bildung* cannot be the result, therefore, of some process of education or conditioning imposed by a culture or state. It is in this emphasis on individual freedom that the romantics differ from the classical ideals of *Bildung* in Plato and Aristotle, and that they reveal themselves to be distinctively modern.

Of course, the central role of freedom in ethics had been stressed before the romantics by both Kant and Fichte. They had argued not only that freedom is the characteristic mark of subjectivity, but also that it lies at the root of all moral obligations. Moral duty is sometimes phrased in terms of autonomy: a person is obliged to act only on those principles that he could will as a universal law, or only those that he could impose on himself as a rational being. The romantics did not question the Kantian–Fichtean emphasis on autonomy and its central role in morality. But in an important respect they took this concept a step further than their predecessors. They interpreted autonomy not only in moral but also in personal terms. Their emphasis on the value of individuality means that sometimes decisions are right not because they fall under some universal law but simply because they are individual. They sought to determine a realm of ethics that does not fall under general moral laws but that concerns the ultimate values by which a person leads his life. These values will have no other sanction than personal decision, individual choice. They will be good or bad, right or wrong, simply because I have chosen them, with no expectation that anyone else will follow me.

The second distinctive aspect of the romantic ethic is that most romantic of all characteristics: love. Love was the cardinal principle of romantic ethics, and indeed as important for the romantics as the categorical imperative was for Kant. Schleiermacher in his *Monologen,* Schlegel in his lectures on *Transcendentalphilosophie,* Novalis in his *Glauben und Liebe,* and Hegel in his *Geist des Christenthums* all stress the importance of love as the central principle of ethics. The romantics saw the ethics of love as one of the characteristic doctrines of the modern age, one completely absent from classical ethics.

Here again it is of the first importance to understand the romantic doctrine of love in terms of their general ethic of self-realization. We realize our common humanity, and we develop our unique individuality, the romantics often insisted, only through love. It is through love that we unify our opposing powers—that we reconcile our reason and sensibility—because in loving someone I act on the rational principles of duty from, rather than contrary to, inclination. It is also through love that I fulfill my individuality because love derives from my innermost self, from my unique passions and desires, and it consists in a unique bond between myself and another. It is noteworthy that the romantic ethic of love has more classical than Christian roots; it has more affinities with Plato's *eros* than Paul's *agape*. In their youth Hölderlin, Schlegel, Schleiermacher, and Novalis were enthusiastic students of Plato, especially his *Symposium* and *Phaedrus.*

4. The Reaction to Modernity

Apart from its emphasis on freedom and love, there is something else that is new to the romantic ideal of *Bildung,* something that distinguishes it from the very similar ideals of *Aufklärung* and *Sturm und Drang.* This has less to do with the ideal itself than its context: the rise of modern civil society. It was the task of the romantic generation to revive and reaffirm the classical ideal of *Bildung* against some of the growing trends of modern civil society: atomism, alienation, and anomie. These trends had become especially apparent in the 1790s, the decade when most of the early romantics came of age. While these trends tended to divide the individual from himself, others, and nature, the romantic ideal of *Bildung* reaffirmed the value of unity with one-self, others, and nature. The goal of romantic striving and longing was essentially holistic: that the individual feel at home again in his world, so that he would feel part of society and nature as a whole.

For the young romantics, there was ultimately one fundamental malaise behind all forms of modernity. They gave several names to this malaise: alienation *(Entfremdung)*, estrangement *(Entäusserung)*, division *(Entzweiung)*, separation *(Trennung)*, and reflection *(Reflexion)*.[16] Whichever term was used, they all designated a predicament where the self should be at one with something that it now sees as opposed to itself. Where there should be unity, harmony, or wholeness, there is division, discord, and separation. The source of this division, discord, and separation—it is further assumed—does not lie in some alien force outside human beings but within human beings themselves, who are autonomous and ultimately responsible for their own fate. Seen from this angle, the problem of alienation was nothing less than *self-enslavement*, a paradox first pointed out by Rousseau in the provocative first sentence of his *Contrat social:* "Man is born free; but everywhere he is in chains."

For the romantics, there were three forms of alienation. There was first the division within the self. This form of division took two forms. First, the conflict between reason and sensibility, where the self could act on its duty only by repressing or eradicating its desires and feelings. Second, the one-sidedness of specialization, where the self developed only one of its powers at the expense of all the others. While the conflict between reason and sensibility arose from the growth of culture and manners, one-sidedness came from the division of labor within civil society, which emphasized the narrow development of one skill to perform a single routinized task.

The second form of alienation—what we might also call anomie or atomism—was the division between the self and others. This form of division arose from the decline of the traditional community—the guilds, corporations, and family—and the rise of the competitive marketplace, where each individual sought his self-interest at the expense of others. For the romantics, the epitome of such social alienation was social contract theory, according to which the individual entered a group only if it suited his self-interest.

The third form of alienation was the division between the self and nature. This too arose from two sources: first, the growth of modern technology, which made nature into an object of mere use, having no magic, mystery, or beauty; and second, mechanical physics, which made nature into a vast ma-

chine and the mind either a smaller machine within nature or a ghost standing outside it.

In the face of these ills of modernity, the romantics posed their ideals of
wholeness or unity. For each form of alienation or division there was a corresponding holistic ideal. The division within the self would be overcome in
the ideal of *the beautiful soul:* a person who acts according to the principles of
morality *from* rather than *contrary to* inclination, and who unites his thinking
and feeling, reason and sensibility, conscious and subconscious in one aesthetic whole. The division between self and other would be overcome in the
ideal of *community, free sociability,* or *the organic state;* here each person would
develop his individuality only through love and free interchange with others. Finally, the division between self and nature would be overcome only in
the ideal of *life* or *the organic concept of nature:* as a part of this organic whole
the self will realize that it is inseparable from nature as well as nature inseparable from it.

Although, in fundamental respects, the romantic ideal of *Bildung* was a reaction against modernity, it would be false to infer that it was nothing more.
For, in other basic respects, the romantic ideal was also an attempt to preserve modernity. All too often the romantic attitude toward civil society has
been portrayed as one of complete approval or total rejection, as if the romantics were either the champions or opponents of all forms of modernity.[17]
But both extremes are simplistic, failing to come to grips with the romantics'
much more complex ambivalence. The truth of the matter is that the young
romantics welcomed civil society in some respects but also feared it in others. They attempted to find some middle path between modernism and
antimodernism, radicalism and conservatism. Their *via media* was indeed
typical of the German moderate center in the late 1790s and early 1800s,
which attempted to reform society and the state according to liberal ideals
but also in a manner consistent with their historical development.

In three fundamental respects, the romantics were on the side of modernity, seeing themselves as champions of progress. First, despite their criticisms of the Enlightenment, the romantics placed the greatest importance
on the critical powers of reason, especially the right of the individual to
criticize all beliefs. Second, for all their misgivings about the consequences
of civil society, the romantics also valued its freedoms, especially the right
of the individual to think for himself, and to develop all his powers to
the fullest. Third, according to the romantic philosophy of history, the unity
and harmony of the past—whether it was in classical Greece or the Middle

Ages—had been lost forever by the advent of civil society and Enlightenment. Since there could be no going back, the problem was how to achieve
the earlier harmony and unity on a higher level in the future. What had
been given to the ancient Greeks had to be recreated on a higher level
through reason and effort. Hence the goal of romantic longing, the ideal of
its infinite striving, was not in the past but in the future. What Rousseau had
once placed in the state of nature—peace with oneself, others, and nature—
the romantics now saw as an ideal society in the future.[18]

It is only when we consider the romantic attitude toward modernity in all
its complexity and ambivalence that we can begin to appreciate the main
challenge confronting their generation. Their problem was how to preserve
the fundamental values of modernity—individuality, critical rationality, and
freedom—within their holistic ideals. The challenge was how to form a society and state that provides for community—a source of belonging, identity,
and security—but that also secured the rights of the individual. While there
could be no going back to the classical Greek polis, which did not appreciate
individual freedom, there also could be no going forward to a point where
society simply dissolved into a collection of self-interested atoms held together by a mere "watchguard" state. To use a hackneyed formula, the romantics' essential concern was how to achieve *identity-in-difference, unity-in-
opposition.* Such an agenda has often been ascribed to Hegel, as if it were his
distinctive virtue as a political philosopher.[19] But in this regard, as in so
many others, Hegel was simply a typical romantic.

5. Postmodernist and Marxist Interpretations

My account of *Frühromantik* lays special stress on its holism, seeing this as
its solution for the divisive wounds of modernity. Of course, there is nothing new in emphasizing the holistic dimension of romantic thought. A striving toward wholeness, a longing for completion, and the idea of organic
totality have often been said to be characteristic of *Romantik.*[20] Lately, however, this characterization of *Frühromantik* has come in for some heavy criticism on the grounds that romantic narrative and discourse is committed to
"nonclosure," the incomplete, incoherent, ironic, and fragmentary.[21] These
postmodernist scholars have explicitly rejected the older holistic interpretation of *Frühromantik,* claiming that it ignores its antisystematic, antifoundationalist, and antirationalist elements.

But this criticism is a singular instance of the failures of the literary approach to *Frühromantik.* It focuses on romantic "discourse" and "rhetoric" at the expense of its metaphysics, ethics, and political philosophy, where the romantics' holistic ideals and organic view of nature are abundantly in evidence. The postmodernist insistence on "nonclosure" in romantic writing ultimately rests on a simple confusion between the *esprit systematique* and the *esprit de systems.*[22] While the romantics opposed the *esprit de systems* because systems restrict our vision, stifle our creativity, and stop short enquiry, they still adamantly affirmed the *esprit systematique* because a complete system is a necessary, if unattainable, regulative ideal of reason. If romantic irony is indeed directed against any claim to completion or closure, that is only because its aim is to goad our striving, to intensify our efforts, so that we approach closer to the ideal of a complete system.

There is another important precedent for my own interpretation of *Frühromantik.* That *Frühromantik* must be understood in social and political terms, and that its reaction toward civil society is an essential aspect of it, are theses that can be found, if not always explicitly, in some Marxist authors.[23] In both respects I support their interpretation. Those who wish to banish Marxist views wholesale as remnants of a defunct ideology are, I fear, in danger of throwing the baby out with the bathwater. The great strength of the Marxist interpretation is that it places *Frühromantik* in its social and political context, allowing us to see the underlying purpose behind its only apparently autonomous art, religion, and metaphysics. These advantages are lost whenever we follow the conventional interpretation of *Frühromantik,* which all too often sees its literature as belonging to some *sui generis* realm, independent of all morals and politics.

That said, it must be added that there are serious problems with the Marxist interpretation. First, it is a great mistake to assume, as almost all Marxists scholars do,[24] that *Frühromantik* is essentially a reactionary movement, longing for a reinstatement of the medieval past. This fails to grasp the specificity of the early romantic political program, which was essentially reformist in intention, the forerunner of the Prussian reform movement of the early 1800s.[25] When the politics of *Frühromantik* are placed within the spectrum of political opinion of the 1790s and early 1800s, the differences from much more explicitly reactionary movements become immediately evident. Romantic politics were far to the left of the views of Haller and the *Eudämonisten,* who were intent on reviving divine right doctrine and the absolute power of the princes.[26] Second, it is no less an error to think that *Romantik* is in total opposition to *Aufklärung,* as if it wished to restore the irrational faith of Christianity against the forces of reason. Here again Marxist scholars have failed to see the specificity of *Frühromantik,* whose attitude toward the *Aufklärung* is complex and ambivalent. If the romantics broke with the *Aufklärung* in some respects, they radicalized it in others. The problem here is to specify precisely the respects in which *Frühromantik* endorsed and criticized the *Aufklärung.* Third, it is anachronistic, in the context of the 1790s, to equate the *Aufklärung* with democratic and liberal values. Some of the foremost *Aufklärer* in Berlin, such as Christian Garve, Friedrich Nicolai, and J. A. Eberhard, were staunch defenders of enlightened absolutism, a doctrine abhorrent to Novalis, Friedrich Schlegel, and Schleiermacher.[27] In this regard, then, the romantic reaction against the *Aufklärung* cannot be understood as reactionary but as progressive.

In seeing *Frühromantik* as a reactionary movement, Marxist scholars have never really gone beyond the political debates of the 1840s, when Heinrich Heine, Arnold Ruge, and Karl Marx were compelled to defend their progressive ideals against some of the later romantics. Their own characterizations of *Frühromantik* have been captive to the radical tradition, committing its basic fallacy—anachronism—by describing all periods of *Frühromantik* in the light of some of its last representatives.[28] However understandable this fallacy might have been in the context of the political struggles of the 1840s, it makes no sense to reassert it now. It is time to revive the historical spirit inaugurated by Haym—and excoriated by Marxists—over a century ago: to reconstruct *Frühromantik* in all its totality and individuality within the context of its time and place.[29]

6. Romantic Politics

The romantic attempt to reconcile classical holistic ideals with some of the central values of modernity is especially evident from their social and political thought. This should be apparent from a brief account of their theory of the state.

Contrary to the apolitical interpretation of *Romantik,* it is necessary to stress the exact opposite: that it was of necessity political, and indeed gave pride of place to politics. The romantics were indeed some of the first thinkers of the modern era to reaffirm the importance of the political, to make politics once again "the first science," as Aristotle once made it.[30] In the spirit of Aristotle, Friedrich Schlegel would write: "Political judgment is the highest of all viewpoints."[31]

The importance of politics for the romantics follows immediately from one of their central doctrines: that the individual is a social being who can realize himself only within the state. If self-realization is the highest good, and if self-realization is achieved only within the state, then politics, the doctrine of the state, becomes crucial. Politics becomes the preeminent science to tell us how to achieve the highest good. The romantics would have fully endorsed Aristotle's definition of the state in the *Politics:* "a community of equals aiming at the best life possible."[32] They rejected decisively, therefore, the modern liberal view of the state, which holds that its end is only to protect the rights of individuals to seek happiness by themselves.

The heart of romantic social and political thought is their ideal of community. Ultimately, this ideal goes back to classical rather than Christian sources, especially to Plato and Aristotle.[33] Romantic social and political thought was essentially a revival of the classical ideal of the *polis* against the modern individualistic tradition of Grotius, Hobbes, and Locke. The fondness for the *medieval* communitarian ideal is a later development, appearing first in Novalis's 1799 "Christenheit oder Europa." The *loci classici* of the romantic communitarian ideal are the final letter of Schiller's *Aesthetische Briefe*, Novalis's *Glauben und Liebe*, Schlegel's *Vorlesungen über Transcendentalphilosophie*, Schleiermacher's *Monologen*, and Hegel's *System der Sittlichkeit.*[34]

The romantic ideal of community has to be understood on at least two levels, one logical and the other normative. On a logical level, the romantic ideal goes back to Aristotle's dictum in the *Politics* that the state is a whole prior to its parts.[35] Very crudely, this means that the state is not reducible to a collection of individuals, each of which is self-sufficient, but that the existence and identity of the individual depends on its place within the community. Like Aristotle, the romantics stressed the social nature of a human being, insisting that he owes his identity to his education into society, apart from which he is nothing more than a beast or a god.

In going back to Aristotle, the romantics were taking issue with the modern liberal theory of the state, specifically social contract theory, which holds that the state is formed by a contract between consenting individuals, each of whom is self-sufficient. The problem with contract theory, in the romantic view, is that the concept of a self-sufficient individual is an artificial and arbitrary abstraction; apart from the social whole, of which he is only a part, the individual would not even have self-interest, let alone moral principles or a power to deliberate. The attempt to conceive a social whole out of a multitude of self-interested individuals is to square the circle, Novalis argued, because the individual will exempt himself from the rules whenever self-interest dictates.[36]

On a normative level, the romantic ideal of community claims that self-interest is not only logically but morally secondary to the common good; in other words, on certain occasions, the individual should act for the common good even when it is contrary to his self-interest. This moral claim upon the individual went hand-in-hand with a specific view about the purpose of the state: namely, its goal should be not only to protect the rights of individuals, but also to ensure the common good.

It is commonplace among liberal critics to interpret the romantics' communitarian ethic as a form of incipient totalitarianism. It seems that in putting the common good before the interests of the individual the romantics give the state reason to abrogate individual rights. But this criticism is anachronistic, failing to see that the romantics communitarian ideal was essentially republican. The common good was to be determined first and foremost by the people themselves, who were the sovereign power in the state. No laws could be imposed on them, then, that were not *self*-imposed. To be sure, the romantics sometimes stress the importance of self-sacrifice for the sake of the public good. But this derived not from totalitarianism but from the republican tradition of Montesquieu, which stressed the importance of virtue in a republic, the willingness to sacrifice self-interest for the public good.

The central idea or governing metaphor behind the romantic ideal of community is the organic or "poetic" concept of the state. This concept is best understood in contrast to its opposite, the "machine" state of the Enlightenment. There were two fundamental features of the machine state. First, like any machine, the machine state is directed from above and outside—whether by a revolutionary committee or a prince—so that the source of its motion does not come from within itself, that is, from its individual citizens. Second, again like a machine, the machine state is created according to an abstract blueprint, a design that is imposed on it from above. The organic state contrasts with both these features of the machine state. First, like any organism, the organic state consists in parts that are self-organizing and self-generating; that is, its life will derive from the active participation of free citizens and autonomous groups. Second, again like any organism, the organic state will evolve over time and adapt to local circumstance, so that its structure will be the result not of some artificial constitution imposed from above but from historical development and tradition from below.

So far I have stressed the essentially holistic dimension behind the romantics' social and political ideal. But it is also crucial to emphasize that the romantics also wanted to preserve the rights of the individual within their community. This should be clear not only from their ethic of individualism, but also from their adherence to some of the basic ideals of the French Revolution, such as the rights of man. To be sure, the romantics were not *radical* republicans—left-wing Jacobins intent on complete democracy and the abolition of all aristocracy and monarchy. Such a position was more the exception than the rule among them, and it occurred only for a short while in Friedrich Schlegel, the most radical among them. The romantics' political ideal was more for a mixed constitution, a synthesis of monarchy, aristocracy, and democracy.[37] Their organic state was meant to be a highly differentiated structure, with a plurality of sources of authority, so that power was always shared among many groups rather than monopolized by an elite.

To avoid some common misunderstandings of the romantics' organic state, it is of the first importance to stress its *differentiated* and *stratified* structure. A central aspect of this structure was its pluralism, the presence within the political body not only of different levels of government but also of autonomous groups independent of central control. The romantics were champions of the estates, local councils, and guilds. In this regard their thinking was indeed conservative, for they wanted to preserve some of the old corporate structure of the medieval past. But it is also important to note that one of the main points behind this corporatism or pluralism was to limit the powers of central authority, and so to minimize the danger of totalitarianism. The romantics saw such a danger not only in the old absolutism, but also in the new revolutionary governments, which were no less centralized in authority than the states of the *ancien régime*.

It was through the corporatist or pluralistic structure of the organic state that the romantics believed they could square the political circle of modernity: that is, provide for both community and individual liberty. The organic state would provide for community because its autonomous groups would ensure participation in political affairs and provide for a center of social belonging. It would also, however, ensure liberty because these groups would be not only channels for popular participation, but also bulwarks against central power. In stressing the role of independent groups in these respects, the romantics have anticipated more modern pluralistic doctrine, the ideas of, say, Durkheim or Kornhauser.

For the romantics, both the absolutist princes in Germany and the Jacobins in France had made the same fundamental mistake: they abolished autonomous groups, the old corporations and guilds, so that everything could be directed from above, whether that was by the will of a monarch or some revolutionary committee. In doing this they created a stark opposition between the ruler and the individual, so that there was nothing between them to restrain the rule of the despot or the mob. The only safeguard against despotism of the prince or the mob was the differentiated structure of the organic state.

It is precisely in this context, I believe, that we must understand the romantics' medievalism. This medievalism has been interpreted as an essentially reactionary sentiment and doctrine, and so indeed it eventually became in the later writing of Friedrich Schlegel. But in its inception and original inspiration the romantic fascination with the corporate structure of medieval society had more to do with their hatred of absolutism, and with their preference for pluralism, whose main aim is to find some bulwark against totalitarianism and centralization.[38] Far from a surrender of individual rights, their pluralism was intended as a means of protecting freedom while also providing the individual with some form of social belonging.

No one saw more clearly than the young Hegel that continuity with the medieval tradition did not mean a denial but an affirmation of freedom. In his 1799 *Verfassungsschrift* he writes that never had the rights of the individual been so strongly affirmed and protected than during the Middle Ages.[39] It was the unrelenting reign of absolutism, which did everything in its power to break down the estates and the guilds, that had made people forget their medieval heritage, which was the ultimate source of all the ferments of the revolutionary age.

7. Romantic Aesthetics

Our moral and political account of *Frühromantik* seems to come to grief in the face of one central, stubborn, and indisputable fact: namely, *Frühromantik* was essentially an aesthetic movement, one which gave supreme value to art. In the classical triad of truth, beauty, and goodness, the romantics saw beauty as *primus inter pares*. It is well-known that Schelling, Schlegel, Novalis, and Hölderlin made poetry the basis of metaphysical knowledge, moral goodness, and political legitimacy. But if this is so, then surely the moral, social, and political should be subordinate to the aesthetic.

The primacy and autonomy of the aesthetic has indeed been the central premise behind the apolitical and literary interpretations of *Frühromantik*. Because the romantics gave such importance to art, it seems as if they flee the reality of the social and political world, or at best as if they use the social and political only as a means or "occasion" to produce works of art.[40] Indeed, because they affirmed the autonomy of the aesthetic, its independence from all moral and political ends, it seems as if they should never allow aesthetic creativity to be compromised by morality and politics.

To avoid some very common misunderstandings, especially the all too common conflation of aestheticism with aesthetism, it is of the first importance to examine precisely the sense in which the romantics gave primacy to the aesthetic. This primacy does not mean that the romantics preferred beauty over goodness and truth, as if they would choose aesthetic values instead of moral and political ones (if they had to make the choice), or as if they would value appearances over moral and intellectual qualities (aesthetism). Since they defined beauty in moral and political terms, it is indeed impossible for them to separate these values, so that, for them, the question of preferring one to the other cannot arise. To be sure, the romantic account of the beautiful makes it, if only in one sense, secondary and derivative: beauty is the *appearance* or *manifestation* of the harmonious individual and state. The romantics gave importance to beauty because of its moral and political dimension; they did not give importance to the moral and political because of the aesthetic. To assume the converse is simply to confuse the defiendum, conditioned, or grounded with the defiens, condition, or ground. The romantics gave primacy to beauty only in the sense that they made beauty the *ratio cognoscendi*—the criterion or means of knowing—of the true and good; they did not think that it is the *ratio essendi*, the essence, basis, or ground of the good and the true.

However one interprets the meaning of aesthetic primacy, it is difficult to see how it provides any evidence for the apolitical interpretation of *Frühromantik*. That interpretation works only if one gives a very narrow interpretation of the aesthetic, so that it refers to works of art in the conventional sense. Usually, this phrase is understood to refer to some form of literature, whether poems, plays, or novels, though it could also denote works of music, sculpture, or painting. This interpretation is unduly narrow, however, because the romantics viewed not only poems, plays, and novels, but even the individual, society, and the state as works of art. Their aim was indeed to break down the barriers between art and life, so that the entire world becomes a work of art. If, however, the individual, society, and the state are also to be works of art, then it becomes difficult, in any straightforward sense, to sustain the thesis that romantic art is meant to be apolitical, of no relevance to the social and political world.

Rather than a doctrine of political indifference or escapism, romantic aestheticism is better understood as a kind of moral and political theory, specifically a holistic one that equates the good with the beautiful through the idea of an organic whole. The early romantics did not take beauty out of the moral and political world for the simple reason that they made it into the very touchstone, sign, or criterion of moral and political value. If a person unified their reason and sensibility—if they did their duty from inclination—then they would possess "grace" or become "a beautiful soul." Similarly, if the state unified all its citizens into a harmonious community, then it would be an "aesthetic" or "poetic" state. Hence romantic aestheticism is not only a theory about works of art in the narrow sense—plays, poems, and pictures—but also a theory about works of art in a very broad sense—the life of the individual, society, and the state.

Still, it might be asked: How does this social and political dimension of *Frühromantik* square with its belief in the autonomy of art? Notoriously, the young romantics were followers of Kant's doctrine of aesthetic autonomy, according to which aesthetic qualities have their value independent of moral principles and physical desires. They passionately rejected the utilitarian aesthetics of Gottsched, who had made art serve moral and political ends. But if this is so, how can we insist on the primacy of ethics and politics for the young romantics? This would seem to violate their own belief in the autonomy of art.

The solution to this problem lies with an apparent paradox: that the romantics insisted on the autonomy of art not in spite of, but precisely because of, their moral and political ends. Ironically, it is only by virtue of its autonomy that a work of art represents the highest moral and political value: freedom. A work of art signifies freedom just because it is autonomous, or just because it is not a means to other ends, whether these are moral or physical.

This paradox is already apparent in Schiller, whose aesthetic views had a great impact on the romantics.[41] While affirming Kant's doctrine of aesthetic autonomy, Schiller also contends that art plays a central role in the education of humanity. The solution to the apparent contradiction is implicit in his definition of beauty. According to Schiller, the essence of beauty consists in the appearance of freedom; and a work of art has its moral value precisely because it represents freedom, the very basis of morality.[42] To symbolize freedom, however, a work of art must have its own integrity and autonomy, its own freedom from external purposes. Ironically, then, art has its greatest moral significance precisely when it is not used for specific moral ends.

While the romantics never explicitly struggled with this apparent tension in their philosophy, their response to it follows along the lines suggested by Schiller. As A. W. Schlegel once commented on a moralistic but botched play: "Is there really no other way to improve humanity than spoiling its taste?"[43] Like his brother, he had always believed that moralistic art is bad art; yet a completely free taste improves humanity. So, ironically, art has its greatest moral significance when it is not used for moral ends. The autonomy of art has indeed a moral foundation. As Friedrich once wrote his brother: "The soul of my doctrine is that humanity is the highest end, and art exists only for its sake."[44] This simple statement alone might serve as the motto—and conclusion—for a moral and political interpretation of *Frühromantik*.

CHAPTER 3

Early Romanticism and
the *Aufklärung*

1. Romanticism versus Enlightenment?

For more than a century, it has been a commonplace to regard the birth of German romanticism at the end of the eighteenth century as the death of the *Aufklärung*.[1] Supposedly, romanticism was the reaction against the *Aufklärung*, its self-conscious opposition and antithesis. Hence the ascendancy of romanticism in the early 1800s spelled the demise of the *Aufklärung*, which accordingly should be relegated to the eighteenth century.

This commonplace has united both friends and foes of German romanticism. In the 1830s and 1840s German liberals and left-wing Hegelians condemned romanticism because they saw it as a reactionary movement opposed to the *Aufklärung*.[2] But, beginning at the end of the nineteenth century, and then reaching a crescendo in the 1920s and 1930s, German nationalists and conservatives embraced romanticism because they too believed it to be opposed to the *Aufklärung*; in their view, however, such opposition was a virtue rather than a vice, since the Enlightenment was an alien ideology imported from France and hostile to the German spirit.[3] After World War II the same entrenched attitudes reappeared, now reinvigorated by the reaction against fascism. Since romanticism seemed to be essential to fascist ideology, liberals and Marxists joined forces in attacking it.[4]

The secondary literature gives at least three reasons why romanticism broke with the *Aufklärung*. First, it attempted to replace the rationalism of the *Aufklärung* with aestheticism. Rather than making reason the highest authority, the ultimate standard of truth, as the *Aufklärung* had done, the romantics gave such authority to the intuitions and feelings of art, which transcend all conceptualization, judgment, and reasoning. Hence romanticism is

43

often accused of "antirationalism" or "irrationalism." Second, the romantics criticized the individualism of the *Aufklärung*, advocating instead an ideal of community in which the individual was subordinate to the group. While the *Aufklärer* tended to see society and the state only as instruments to ensure the happiness, and to protect the rights, of the individual, the romantics insisted that communal life was an end in itself, for which the individual should sacrifice his self-interest. Third, romanticism was an essentially conservative ideology, breaking with such liberal values of the *Aufklärung* as the separation of church and state, religious tolerance, and freedom of the individual. Hence some romantic thinkers, like Friedrich Schlegel, Adam Müller, and Zacharias Werner, converted to the Roman Catholic Church, while others, such as Ludwig Tieck and Novalis, flirted or sympathized with Catholicism.[5] In sum, then, we are told to contrast the antirationalism, communitarianism, and conservatism of romanticism with the rationalism, individualism, and liberalism of the *Aufklärung*.

Like so many generalizations in the history of ideas, this commonplace is a very misleading oversimplification. It is misleading, first of all, because German romanticism was a very protean movement, passing through several phases and undergoing several transformations. It is commonly divided into three periods: *Frühromantik*, from 1797 to 1802; *Hochromantik*, to 1815; and *Spätromantik*, to 1830.[6] Accordingly, the relationship of romanticism to the *Aufklärung* also underwent change. It is generally true that some romantics, especially Friedrich Schlegel and Müller, *became* more conservative, and therefore more hostile to some of the central values of the *Aufklärung*. But this generalization holds only for some thinkers of *Spätromantik*, and it does not apply to earlier phases of the movement. It is therefore very important to avoid the danger of anachronism, judging all of romanticism on the basis of its final incarnation. This fallacy has been the main flaw behind the liberal and left-wing interpretation.

This commonplace is misleading for another reason. It is not only that German romanticism underwent great change, so that what is true of one period is not necessarily true of another. The issue is even more complicated than that because, *within each period,* the attitude of the romantics toward the *Aufklärung* was never a simple and straightforward rejection but a much more complex and subtle ambivalence. If the romantics were the critics of the *Aufklärung*, they were also its disciples. The problem is then to determine, for each period, in what respects the romantics accepted and rejected the *Aufklärung*.

The task of this essay is to address this problem, though only in a preliminary and partial manner. I reexamine the complex relationship between romanticism and the *Aufklärung* in the early formative years of German romanticism from 1797 to 1802, the period known as *Frühromantik*. This is the most interesting and revealing period for an understanding of the romantics' relationship to the *Aufklärung*. For it was during these years that the young romantics took issue with, and developed their attitudes toward, the *Aufklärung*, which was still the reigning ideology in late-eighteenth-century Berlin. Although conclusions about *Frühromantik* do not necessarily apply to the later stages of romanticism, they will suffice for our purposes here: to determine whether the *origins* of romanticism represented a reaction to, and complete break with, the *Aufklärung*.

In undertaking this reexamination of the relationship between *Frühromantik* and *Aufklärung* I make no claims for originality. Since the 1970s many scholars have insisted on reconsidering this relationship, and they have shed valuable light on some of its complexities.[7] A consensus has been building that the old antithesis is no longer tenable and that the relationship between *Frühromantik* and *Aufklärung* is indeed ambivalent and complex.[8] This does not mean, however, that the issue has been solved. On the contrary, it is only now that the problem of investigation has become clear. For there is still much work to do in spelling out precisely the very involved, subtle, and multifaceted relationship between *Aufklärung* and *Frühromantik*. What follows is an attempt to explain only one very important aspect of that relationship.

2. The Crisis of the *Aufklärung*

To understand the relationship between *Frühromantik* and *Aufklärung* it is first necessary to have some basic idea of the beginnings, ideals, and members of the early romantic circle.

If we are to assign an official date for the beginning of German romanticism, then we would do well to choose the year 1797. It was in this year that some young poets, philosophers, and literary critics began to meet in the salons of Henriette Herz and Rahel Levin in Berlin. Later, and until 1802, they would meet at the house of A. W. Schlegel in Jena. The purpose of their meetings was to hold frank and free discussions about philosophy, poetry, politics, and religion. They would read one another their latest work, criticize one another openly, and collaborate on literary projects. This circle was called by contemporaries "the new sect" or "the new school," and it later became known to history as "the romantic circle."

The members of this circle were destined to become famous in German intellectual history. They were the brothers August Wilhelm (1767–1845) and Friedrich Schlegel (1772–1829), the novelist Ludwig Tieck (1773–1853), the natural philosopher Friedrich Wilhelm Joseph Schelling (1775–1854), the theologian Ernst Daniel Schleiermacher (1768–1834), the art historian Wilhelm Heinrich Wackenroder (1773–1801), and the poet and philosopher Friedrich von Hardenberg (1772–1801), who adopted the pseudonym "Novalis." On the fringes of this circle, though sharing many views with it, was the tragic and lonely figure Friedrich Hölderlin (1774–1843). Undoubtedly, the leading figure of the romantic circle was Friedrich Schlegel, who first formulated the group's aesthetic ideals, and who founded and edited its journal, the *Athenäum*.

When one first considers the young romantics' attitude toward the *Aufklärung*, one is immediately struck by their negative comments on it. When referring to the French *philosophes* or the Berlin *Aufklärer*, A. W. Schlegel, Novalis, and Schleiermacher almost invariably attack them.[9] They were critical of the *philosophes* for their hedonism, materialism, and utilitarianism, which seemed to reduce the world to a mere machine, leaving no place for the higher values in life, such as art and religion. They were also hostile to the Berlin *Aufklärer*—especially, Garve, Eberhard, and Nicolai—for their reactionary faith in enlightened absolutism, for their persistent adherence to a dogmatic metaphysics, and for their making common sense the final intellectual authority. Such doctrines seemed to be utterly antiquated after Kant's critique of knowledge, which had shown the untenability of the old metaphysics and the weakness of all appeals to common sense. In attempting to defend metaphysics against Kant's critique of knowledge, and in trying to vindicate enlightened absolutism against the French Revolution, the Berlin *Aufklärer* only demonstrated their obsolescence, their incapacity to adapt to the new order.

Such criticisms have led more than a few scholars to conclude that *Frühromantik* was implacably opposed to the *Aufklärung*. But such a generalization presupposes a much too reductivist view of the *Aufklärung*, as if it could be somehow equated with the materialism of the French *philosophes*, and with the absolutism and deism of the older *Aufklärer* in Berlin. This still leaves out of account some of the fundamental values of the *Aufklärung*: the right to think for oneself; the right to self-determination, to develop one's powers and individuality independent of external authority; and the value of education and enlightenment, the need to overcome prejudice, superstition, and ignorance.

It is precisely with regard to these fundamental values that the young romantics remained loyal to the *Aufklärung*. For all their criticisms of the *Aufklärung*, the romantics upheld at least two of its fundamental principles: radical criticism, or the right of the individual to think for himself; and *Bildung*, the education of the public.[10] Far from questioning these beliefs, their aim was to defend them in the 1790s, a decade in which the *Aufklärung* faced a severe crisis.

By the late 1780s it had become clear that the *Aufklärung* was in danger, not so much from its external enemies as from its own internal tensions. The most significant of these inner conflicts was that the radical criticism of the *Aufklärung* seemed to undermine its ideal of *Bildung*. While its criticism seemed to end *per necessitatum* in skepticism or nihilism, its ideal of *Bildung* presupposed a commitment to some definite moral, political, and aesthetic principles. But how is it possible to educate the public about the principles of morality, politics, and taste when reason casts nothing but doubt on them?

The problem here was a classical one. In the *Apology* Socrates claimed that only the examined life is worth living because it alone tells us about justice and virtue; yet he also claimed to be the wisest man of them all because he knew nothing.[11] How could the examined life lead to *both* complete ignorance and knowledge of justice and virtue? That, of course, was the question of Meletus and Anytus, Socrates' accusers. In late-eighteenth-century Berlin, some critics of the *Aufklärung*, most notably Hamann and Jacobi, were raising that very question all over again. Socrates had been the hero of the *Aufklärung*, its patron saint in the battle against enthusiasm, superstition, and barbarism. But had the *Aufklärer* not failed to learn the deeper lesson behind his trial? Hemlock, it seemed, could be the only answer to the *aporia* of the examined life.

3. The Context of Romantic Aestheticism

One of the most salient characteristics of early German romanticism—one its friends and foes immediately note—is the enormous importance it gave to art. Friedrich Schlegel, A. W. Schlegel, Schleiermacher, Schelling, Novalis, and Hölderlin all gave art a fundamental role in the revitalization of German culture. The painter, the poet, the composer, and the novelist were in the forefront of cultural reform, and were cast in the role of educators of the human race. We can put the young romantics' emphasis on art in its proper historical perspective by seeing it as the reversal of Plato's infamous doctrine in the *Republic*. While Plato wanted to banish the artists, the romantics wanted to enthrone them. What is the best prince, the young Novalis asked, but the artist of artists, the director of a vast drama whose stage is the state?[12]

Why, though, did the young romantics give such great importance to art? Why did they regard it as the key to social, political, and cultural revival? The answer to this question is crucial for understanding the young romantics' relationship to the *Aufklärung*. For their aestheticism was their means of executing the ideals, and resolving the outstanding problems, of the *Aufklärung*.

The aestheticism of the young romantics is comprehensible only in the context of their reaction to the French Revolution. The Revolution had a profound impact on the early romantics. It gave birth to their political consciousness, and it set much of the problematic of their early social, political, and aesthetic thought. With the exception of A. W. Schlegel, who was skeptical from the beginning, the young romantics greeted the French Revolution as the dawn of a new age. They were delighted by the collapse of the *ancien régime*, and they looked forward to a new era free of privilege, oppression, and injustice. Tieck, Novalis, Schelling, Schleiermacher, and Friedrich Schlegel affirmed the ideals of *liberté, egalité et fraternité*, and they insisted that true humanity could be realized only in a republic. What is most striking about their reaction to the Revolution is how long they retained their sympathies. Unlike so many of their compatriots, their loyalties were not affected by the September massacres, the execution of the king, the invasion of the Rhineland, or even by the Terror.[13]

Novalis, Schelling, Schleiermacher, and Schlegel became critical of the Revolution only around 1798. They then began to attack the egoism, materialism, and utilitarianism of modern civil society, which they believed had been encouraged by the Revolution.[14] They also expressed fears of ocholocracy and insisted on some measure of elite rule. The true republic, they believed, should be a mixture of aristocracy, monarchy, and democracy, because in any true state the educated must have power over the uneducated.[15] Such cautious and moderate doctrines were not reactionary, however, still less peculiar to the romantics. Rather, they were typical of the late 1790s, mirroring the trend of opinion in France itself, where the elections held in March 1797 resulted in the return of royalist majorities in the two legislative councils. Despite their increasing moderation and caution, the romantics did not abandon their republicanism, which they hoped to incorporate within a constitutional monarchy. As late as the early 1800s, we find Novalis and Schlegel reaffirming the ideals of liberty, equality, and fraternity.[16] If, then, we confine ourselves to the early romantics, it becomes absurd to speak of a "romantic conservatism." The young romantics were indeed more loyal to liberal and progressive ideals than many of the *Aufklärer*, who still clung to their faith in enlightened monarchy.[17] The connection of *Aufklärung* with progressive and democratic ideals is a much later development, which should not be read into the 1790s, the political context of the romantics.

Although the romantics were republicans in the 1790s, they were not revolutionaries. Though they endorsed the ideas of the Revolution, they renounced its practice. With the possible exception of Hölderlin, they did not believe that insurrection was feasible, or even desirable, in their native land.[18] The events in France made them fear that a revolution would result in incurable anarchy and strife, and hence they insisted on the need for gradual evolutionary change from above. Like so many of the *Aufklärer*, the romantics held that the principal danger in radical political change lay with the people themselves, who were not ready for the high moral ideals of a republic. A republic demanded wisdom and virtue, just as Montesquieu and Rousseau had always taught; but it was not possible to expect these in Germany, given the low level of education and the slow progress of the Enlightenment in most territories of the empire. The fundamental political problem facing the young romantics was therefore plain: to prepare the German people for the high ideals of a republic by giving them a moral, political, and aesthetic education. Their task as intellectuals in the Germany of the 1790s was to define the standards of morality, taste, and religion, so that the public would have some ideal of culture and some model of virtue. Thus, in their crucial formative years from 1797 to 1800, the romantics were neither revolutionaries nor reactionaries. Rather, they were simply reformers, moderates in the classical tradition of Schiller, Herder, Humboldt, Wieland, and a whole host of *Aufklärer*.[19]

It is in the context of this reformism that we must place the young romantics' aestheticism. They gave such enormous importance to art mainly because they saw it as the chief instrument of *Bildung*, and hence as the key to social and political reform. If the people were to be prepared for the high moral ideals of a republic, then it would be through an aesthetic education, which would be the spearhead of the new social and political order.

In assigning such importance to art, the young romantics proved themselves to be the disciples of Schiller, who had put forward this very thesis in his famous *Aesthetische Briefe* of 1793. They agreed with Schiller's analysis of the political problem: that *Bildung* was the precondition of social and political change, the only firm basis for a lasting republican constitution. They also accepted Schiller's solution to the problem: that an aesthetic education should be the core of *Bildung*. According to Schiller, it was art, and art alone, that could unify the divided powers of humanity, provide it with a model of virtue, and inspire people to action. In all respects, the romantics agreed. Nowhere was their agreement more apparent than in that mysterious document, "The Oldest System Program of German Idealism," where it is declared that poetry should again become what it once was at the dawn of civilization: the teacher of humanity.[20]

If, then, we place the young romantics' aestheticism in its original historical context, it turns out to be nothing less than their strategy for social and political reform. This reveals, however, how their main goals were continuous with the *Aufklärung*, insofar as the young romantics remained loyal to one of its fundamental aims: the education of the public, the development of its moral, intellectual, and aesthetic powers. Such, indeed, was the aim of their journal *Athenäum*, which was explicitly devoted to the goal of *Bildung*, like so many of the *Zeitschriften* of the *Aufklärung*. The young romantics' insistence on further education and enlightenment as the precondition for fundamental social and political change only reiterated a point frequently made by the *Aufklärer*. Indeed, in their attempt to make enlightenment serve the growing demands for social and political change, the young romantics seem to be nothing less than the *Aufklärer* of the 1790s. They appear to differ from the earlier generation of *Aufklärer* only in their disillusionment with enlightened absolutism and in their readiness to embrace republican ideals. So it is tempting to conclude that the romantics were the *Aufklärer* of the postrevolutionary age. But, as we shall soon see, the truth is much more complicated than that.

4. Radical Criticism and Its Consequences

If the young romantics were loyal to the *Aufklärung's* ideal of *Bildung*, they were no less faithful to its ideal of radical criticism. The *Aufklärung* had proclaimed the absolute right of criticism, the right of reason to criticize everything on heaven and earth. Neither religion in its holiness nor the state in its majesty, as Kant put it, could escape the tribunal of critique.[21] The young romantics did not dispute this principle but enthusiastically endorsed it. Novalis, Hölderlin, Schlegel, and Schleiermacher all greatly valued the power of criticism, which they regarded as indispensable to all philosophy, art, and science.[22] Indeed, if they had any complaint against the *Aufklärer,* it was that they betrayed their cause by not extending the authority of reason far enough in their willingness to compromise with the social, political, and religious *status quo.*

The value of radical criticism—of a thoroughgoing critique of religion, morals, and social conventions—was one of the guiding motifs of the *Athenäum.* "One cannot be critical enough," Friedrich Schlegel wrote, summing up the general attitude of the group.[23] The romantics' love of irony was another form of their devotion to radical criticism, for irony demanded standing above all one's beliefs and creations through relentless self-criticism. Nowhere is the romantic allegiance to the Enlightenment ideal of criticism more apparent, however, than in Friedrich Schlegel's admiration for Lessing, who was famous as the boldest *Aufklärer* of his day.[24] Schlegel venerated Lessing for his independence of mind, for his power to think for himself regardless of convention and orthodoxy. His ambition was to be nothing less than the Lessing of the 1790s.

The young romantics' attitude toward criticism was especially apparent in their reaction to the pantheism controversy, the true acid test for anyone's loyalty to reason in late-eighteenth-century Germany. During this controversy, which began in 1786, F. H. Jacobi argued that a consistent rationalism must end in the atheism and fatalism of Spinozism, and that the only way to rescue one's moral and religious beliefs was through a *salto mortale,* a leap of faith. Schlegel, Novalis, Hölderlin, Schelling, and Schleiermacher were, however, all critical of Jacobi's proposed leap. In their view, Jacobi's great mistake was in turning his back on reason when he saw that it threatened his cherished beliefs. It would have been better and more honest, they thought, for him to renounce his beliefs rather than his reason. Although the romantics themselves were not immune to the attractions of mysticism, they never approved of leaps of faith that were contrary to reason. Although it was permissible to hold beliefs lacking evidence, it was forbidden to hold beliefs that were contrary to it.

The young romantics greatly valued criticism because they saw it as the instrument by which the individual could liberate himself from oppressive social norms. Rather than wanting to subordinate the individual to the ends of the group, the romantics championed an ethic of individualism, of "divine egoism," according to which the end of life should be the development of each individual's unique and characteristic powers.[25] They stressed, however, that for such development to take place, the individual would have to learn to think for himself, to dare to use his own understanding. The sovereign rights of criticism were the instrument to maintain the sovereign rights of the individual.

Yet, for all their belief in the value of criticism, the romantics were also aware of its dangers. It was high time, the young Schlegel believed, that philosophers began to ask where their reason was taking them. If reason could criticize everything on heaven and earth, should it not also criticize itself?[26]

By the late 1790s, some of the most troubling consequences of radical criticism had become clear. First of all, it seemed as if criticism, if it were only consistent and thorough, would end in the abyss of skepticism. All moral, religious, political, and commonsense beliefs had been examined; but rather than revealing their underlying foundations, criticism had shown them to be nothing more than "prejudices." In the late 1790s the danger of skepticism seemed more acute than ever. Philosophers such as Solomon Maimon, J. G. Hamann, Thomas Wizenmann, A. W. Rehberg, H. A. Pistorius, G. E. Schulze, and Ernst Platner developed a form of neo-Humean skepticism, one that doubted Kant had a satisfactory answer to Hume. The specter of nihilism also arose when J. A. Obereit and F. H. Jacobi argued that the fundamental principles of Kant's philosophy ultimately result in *Nihilismus*, the doctrine that one cannot know the existence of anything except one's passing impressions.

Another disturbing consequence of radical criticism– understood in the general sense of scientific method—was that it had alienated man from nature.[27] Now that it had been the subject of scientific investigation, nature seemed to be nothing more than a mere machine, obeying laws with strict necessity and regularity. Modern technology had also disenchanted nature, depriving it of its beauty, magic, mystery. To the extent that reason subdued nature, it was a mere instrument or tool of human satisfaction; but to the extent reason could not control it, nature was only an obstacle to its efforts. In either case, whether nature was a means or obstacle to human ends, the self could not feel part of it; it was no longer at home in its world.

The most problematic result of radical criticism, in the view of the young romantics, was that modern man had lost his sense of community, his feeling of belonging to a group.[28] For all their insistence on the value of individualism, the romantics also stressed the value of participating in, and identifying with, the community. For they argued that human beings are essentially social creatures who realize their characteristic powers only within the group. But radical criticism seemed to undermine the possibility of self-realization within the community. By bringing all forms of social and political life under criticism, the individual began to regard them as a form of irrational authority, as a threat to his individual autonomy. If the individual should accept no belief or law until it agrees with the critical exercise of his own reason, then it seemed as if there could be as many sources of authority as there are individuals. Thus radical criticism seemed to lead to not only skepticism but anarchism.

The consequences of radical criticism raised some very serious questions, however, about the very coherence of the *Aufklärung*. For it seemed as if two of its most basic ideals—radical criticism and *Bildung*—were in conflict. For if criticism ends in complete skepticism, then according to what moral, political, and religious principles should we educate the people? If it destroys all the beauty of nature, then how can we develop or cultivate our sensibility, which is an essential part of our humanity? And if it results in complete anarchism, how can we expect people to play a responsible and productive role in society? Thus the moral idealism behind the *Aufklärung's* program of *Bildung* was undermined by its commitment to radical criticism.

The general problem facing the romantics in the 1790s should now be clear. How is it possible to fill the vacuum left by the *Aufklärung* without betraying reason? How is it possible to restore our beliefs, our unity with nature and society, without forfeiting individual autonomy? Or, in short, how is it possible to reconcile the *Aufklärung's* ideal of *Bildung* with its demand for radical criticism? The young romantics knew that they could not escape this problem by simply reaffirming the value of "prejudice" in the manner of Burke in England and de Maistre in France. For that reactionary strategy simply failed to recognize that the powers of criticism were as inescapable as they were invaluable.

5. An Ambivalent Solution

What was the romantics' path out of this dilemma? It lay with their faith in art. It was art, and art alone, they believed, that could restore belief and unity with nature and society. Only art could fill the vacuum left by the deadly powers of criticism. While reason was an essentially negative and destructive power, art was a positive and productive one. It had the power to create an entire world through the imagination. What had been *given* to early man on a naive level—moral and religious belief, unity with nature and society—had been destroyed by the corrosive powers of criticism; the task now was to *recreate* it on a self-conscious level through the powers of art.

Art could restore moral and religious belief through the creation of a new mythology.[29] It could regenerate unity with nature by "romanticizing" it, that is, by restoring its old mystery, magic, and beauty.[30] And it could reestablish community by expressing and arousing the feeling of love, which is the basis of all social bonds, the natural feeling joining all free and equal persons.[31]

This aesthetic credo was the romantics' response to the crisis of the *Aufklärung* at the close of the eighteenth century. The ideals of *Bildung* and radical criticism could coexist, in the romantic view, provided that the task of *Bildung* was left to the creative powers of art. A conflict arose only when reason presumed to play a more positive role in *Bildung;* for such a presumption did not square with the essentially destructive powers of criticism. Like many critics of reason at the close of the eighteenth century, the young romantics tended to limit reason to a strictly negative role: its task was merely to combat prejudice, dogmatism, and superstition. They seem to agree with one of the fundamental points behind Kant's and Jacobi's critique of reason: that reason does not have the power *to create* facts, but only the power *to relate* them through inference; the facts themselves must be given to reason from some other source. For the romantics, this source could only be the productive imagination.

There was, however, a deep ambiguity at the bottom of the romantics' program of aesthetic education, an equivocation reflecting their own uncertainty about the powers of reason. It was unclear whether they intended their program of aesthetic education *to replace* or *to support* the authority of reason. Was its task to establish the moral, religious, and political principles that reason seemed only to destroy? Or was its aim to provide only a stimulus or incentive for the moral and political principles that reason could create but not bring into practice?

Regarding this central question the romantics appear to have been ambivalent. In making aesthetic experience the criterion of moral and political value, and in insisting that such experience transcends articulation in conceptual terms, they made art the indispensable foundation for morality and politics. Sometimes, however, they seem to have held that reason does have the power to justify moral and political principles. For example, Schelling and Schlegel, following the example of Fichte's *Wissenschaftslehre,* gave a priori deductions of the principles of natural right and the state.[32] They seemed to concur with Kant and Fichte that, though reason could not demonstrate the *theoretical* principle of metaphysics, it could justify at least the *practical* principles of morality and politics. In this case, the role of art was only to help us *to act* on the principles of morality and the state by stimulating feelings and the imagination; it was not to discover or justify these principles.

This ambivalence is of the first importance in determining the romantics' relationship to the *Aufklärung.* For if the young romantics intended art to replace reason, then they were indeed going beyond the *Aufklärung.* If, however, they intended art only to support reason—to provide only an incentive or stimulus to action—then they remained within the limits of the *Aufklärung.* Like the *Aufklärer,* they were simply attempting to overcome the gap between thought and action, theory and practice, by realizing the principles of reason in public life. In the end, then, the problem of determining the young romantics' relationship to the *Aufklärung* depends on precisely ascertaining their attitude toward reason. But it is just here that the texts of the young romantics prove to be very elusive, vague, and, at best, ambivalent.

Whatever the young romantics' attitude toward the powers of reason, it is still difficult to regard them *simply* as the *Aufklärer* of the postrevolutionary age. For this rides roughshod over their own concern with the crisis of the *Aufklärung* at the end of the 1790s. While the older generation of *Aufklärer* attempted to refute the criticisms of Kant and Jacobi, the young romantics felt that they had no choice but to build on them. If the aesthetic program of the young romantics was their solution to the crisis of the *Aufklärung,* then we have no choice but to view *Frühromantik* as both the affirmation and negation of the *Aufklärung.* Like a phoenix, the *Aufklärung* was consumed by its own flames. From its ashes arose romanticism.

CHAPTER 4

Frühromantik and the
Platonic Tradition

1. *Romantik* as *Aufklärung*

According to a long and venerable tradition of scholarship, there was a radical break between early German romanticism *(Frühromantik)* and the Enlightenment *(Aufklärung)*.[1] Many reasons have been given for contrasting
these movements, but one of the most basic concerns their apparently conflicting views about the authority of reason. Regarding this fundamental issue, two distinctions have been made. First, the *Aufklärung* made the
concepts and judgments of reason, while *Frühromantik* made the intuitions
and feelings of art, the supreme intellectual authority, the ultimate criterion
and instrument of knowledge. Second, the *Aufklärer* affirmed, while the
Romantiker denied, the existence of universal standards of truth, that is, general criteria of knowledge and criticism that are valid for all human beings in
all cultures and epochs. Supposedly, the young romantics broke with the
tradition of natural law by affirming that all truth and value ultimately depend on personal decision.[2]

Lately, this tradition has come under some severe scrutiny.[3] The sharp antithesis between *Frühromantik* and *Aufklärung* has begun to crumble in the
face of more detailed historical research. The picture now emerging is that of
a more complex ambivalence where the early romantics broke with the
Aufklärung in some respects but followed it in others. Even where the romantics were criticizing the *Aufklärung* most severely, it has been pointed
out, they were still only taking its underlying principles to their ultimate
conclusion. In important respects, then, *Frühromantik* seems to be—to steal
an appropriate phrase—little more than *Aufklärung der Aufklärung*.[4]

The traditional antithesis between the "irrationalism" of *Frühromantik* and
the rationalism of the *Aufklärung* has been found problematic for at least

three reasons. First, the romantics not only accepted but radicalized the *Aufklärung's* program of critique. True to the legacy of the *Aufklärung*, the romantics insisted that reason should have the right to criticize all our beliefs. It is indeed noteworthy that the young romantics made no defense of prejudice and prescription in the manner of Burke or de Maistre. Rather than disputing the power of criticism, the young romantics wanted to take it a step further. They demanded that the radical criticism of the *Aufklärung* become its *self*-criticism.[5] Hence they were especially critical of those *Aufklärer*—Garve, Nicolai, Eberhard, and Mendelssohn—who, in their view, betrayed their own critical principles by not questioning the traditional metaphysics underlying religion and morality. Second, *Aufklärung* and *Frühromantik* shared the same fundamental ideal: *Bildung*, the education of the public. No less than the *Aufklärer*, the romantics believed that the goal of *Bildung* should be the development of all our human powers; first and foremost among them was that power most prized by the *Aufklärung*: *Selbstdenken*, the power to think for ourselves. It is indeed precisely in this context that we should understand the aestheticism of *Frühromantik*. The goal of art was to achieve one of the *Aufklärung's* most cherished ideals— namely, closing the gap between theory and practice so that the principles of reason could be realized in public life. The value of art was that it could inspire the people to act according to the principles of reason. Third, the medievalism of *Frühromantik* was not a reactionary ideology opposed to the *Aufklärung* because it had its sources in the *Aufkärung*, which latched onto medieval traditions as a bulwark against neoclassicism and despotism.[6]

2. New Wine in Old Bottles

Much has been gained, I believe, by these criticisms of the traditional interpretation. It is indeed the case that *Frühromantik* had a much more complex and ambivalent relationship to the *Aufklärung* than the conventional stereotype admits. Yet someone might well ask if these criticisms go that far toward undermining the traditional antithesis. For even if we admit them, there still seems to be a profound difference between *Frühromantik* and *Aufklärung* regarding the authority of reason. Consider the following points. First, it is still the case that most *Aufklärer* assumed, while some *Romantiker* questioned, the universal authority of reason. Thus Schlegel and Novalis were skeptical of universal standards of criticism;[7] and Hölderlin and Schleiermacher embraced the Fichtean doctrine that the choice of a philosophy is ultimately a matter of personal decision.[8] Second, it is also the case that most *Aufklärer* affirmed, while most *Romantiker* denied, that reason is the *ultimate* criterion and instrument of knowledge. This antithesis still holds at least if we understand reason in a *discursive* sense, that is, as the power of conceiving, judging, and inferring in the traditional sense of the Port Royal Logic. Although many *Aufklärer* would agree with the *Romantiker* that reason has no power to grasp the infinite or unconditioned, there were few, if any, *Aufklärer* who would admit that the intuitions and feelings of the artist succeed where the concepts and proofs of reason fail. For any *Aufklärer*, this would be nothing less than enthusiasm, *Schwärmerei* in aesthetic dress.

The traditional interpretation also seems to be supported by some very recent scholarship, more specifically by the careful studies by Dieter Henrich and Manfred Frank of classical German philosophy in Jena during the 1790s.[9] These studies have made very clear the profound extent to which this philosophy was *antifoundationalist*. The circle surrounding Immanuel Niethammer—which consisted of C. F. Schmid, Benjamin Erhard, P. J. A. Feuerbach, C. F. Diez, and F. K. Forberg—was extremely critical of the foundationalist program of Reinhold and Fichte, which attempted to build a complete and infallible system by deduction from self-evident first principles. The ultimate purpose behind this program was to uphold the authority of reason of the *Aufklärung*, to save it from the increasing attacks of skeptics and mystics. It is a clear sign of the growing weakness of the *Aufklärung*, therefore, that this program came under such searching criticism and was spurned by the young generation. The young thinkers of the Niethammer circle developed a subtle and sophisticated critique of Reinhold's and Fichte's foundationalism. They doubted the possibility of establishing indubitable first principles and creating a complete system of all knowledge. Applying Kant's regulative constraints on a metacritical level, they argued that the search for first principles, and the quest for a complete system, were at best regulative ideals that we could approach, but never attain, in the ceaseless striving for knowledge. In a very direct and immediate way, these criticisms were of fundamental importance for the early romantics. For Novalis, Hölderlin, and Friedrich Schlegel were closely connected with the Niethammer circle; and their fragments and notebooks in the 1790s show the influence of its critique of Reinhold and Fichte.

Though it is more by implication than by intention, Henrich's and Frank's account of the philosophical foundations of *Frühromantik* provides further support for the traditional interpretation. According to Henrich and Frank, the young romantics postulated a realm of being that transcends all re-flection, judgment, or rational cognition, and that is presentable only through the medium of art. Such a doctrine, they argue, is the inevitable re-sult of Hölderlin's, Novalis's, and Schelling's critique of Fichte's idealism. Al-though the three accepted Fichte's argument that the principle of subject–object identity is the fundamental condition of all knowledge and experi-ence, they denied that this principle could be identified with anything *within* the realm of knowledge or experience. For if this principle is the precondi-tion of all reflection—if it is the basic condition of all conceptualization—it cannot in turn be the object of reflection or conceptualization. Any at-tempt to know pure subject–object identity presupposes it, and so revolves in a vicious circle. Implicit within this argument, then, there is a distinc-tion between the aestheticism of *Frühromantik* and the rationalism of the *Aufklärung*, for both Henrich and Frank maintain that the romantics' first principle is suprarational and presentable only in art. It is indeed for reasons such as these that Frank has insisted on drawing a fundamental distinction between *Frühromantik* and idealism, especially the idealism of Kant, Fichte, and Hegel, which attempted *per impossible* to conceptualize the first condi-tions of conceptualization.[10]

3. New Problems

Once we consider all these points—the abiding differences between the *Aufklärung* and *Frühromantik* regarding the authority of reason, the roman-tics' debts to the antifoundationalism of the Niethammer circle, and the im-plications of the romantic critique of Fichte—it seems advisable to retain the traditional antithesis between *Aufklärung* and *Romantik*. To be sure, we must qualify this interpretation, specifying in what respects the romantics de-parted from the rationalism of the *Aufklärung*; but, ultimately, the funda-mental contrast between the rationalism of the *Aufklärung* and the irrational aestheticism of *Frühromantik* still seems to hold.

Yet this would still be too hasty a conclusion. The problem with the traditional interpretation, and indeed its recent variants, is that it neglects the deeper current of rationalism within *Frühromantik*, and more specifically its profound debt to the Platonic tradition. The Platonic inspiration behind *Frühromantik* is no great secret, and some scholars have even stated that *Frühromantik* is the greatest revival of Platonism since the Renaissance.[11] Still, if a few have appreciated this point, most have underappreciated it.

For once these Platonic origins are taken into account, it becomes impossible to sustain the antithesis between the aestheticism of *Frühromantik* and the rationalism of the *Aufklärung*. The Platonic legacy of *Frühromantik* shows that its aestheticism was itself a form of rationalism. The distinction between *Frühromantik* and *Aufklärung* is at best between two forms of rationalism; but it cannot be between aestheticism and rationalism *per se*.

The fundamental assumption behind the traditional interpretation and its later formulations is that the young romantics saw reason only as a *discursive* faculty that is limited to conceiving, judging, and inferring. Yet it is precisely this assumption that the young romantics' allegiance to the Platonic tradition forces us to question. Following that tradition, the early romantics saw reason as not only a discursive faculty but also as an intuitive one. Reason is not simply a formal power that conceives, judges, and draws inferences from facts, whatever these facts might be; rather, it is also a perceptive power that discovers a unique kind of facts not given to the senses. This perceptive power often went by the name of intellectual intuition *(intellektuelle Anschauung)*. While this concept had many meanings in late-eighteenth-century German philosophy, the historical evidence is overwhelming that, in the case of *Frühromantik*, its meaning and origins are essentially Platonic. Intellectual intuition was the "the vision of the forms" of the *Republic,* the "inner seeing" of the *Enneads.*[12]

So far were the romantics from regarding reason as only a discursive faculty that they sometimes made an explicit distinction between the discursive powers of the intellect or understanding *(Verstand)* and the intuitive powers of reason *(Vernunft).*[13] This distinction is usually ascribed to Hegel, who later employed it in his polemic against the romantics. But it is noteworthy that the distinction was already made by the romantics themselves. Their distinction follows roughly along the lines of Kant's contrast between the human and divine understanding in §§77–78 of the *Kritik der Urteilskraft,* which also has its precedents in the Platonic tradition.[14] According to the distinction, the understanding is *analytical:* it divides a whole into its separate parts, and it proceeds from the parts to the whole, or from the particulars to the universal; but reason is *synthetic:* it grasps the whole as a unity, and it proceeds from the whole to the parts, or from the universal to the particular. Rather than strictly opposing these faculties to one another, however, the romantics assumed that they are really complementary: it is the task of reason to provide hypotheses and suggestions to guide the detailed research of the understanding; conversely, it is the task of the understanding to confirm and elaborate the intuitions of reason, even if it cannot completely conceptualize or explain them. It is indeed more accurate to regard understanding and reason as distinct *functions* of a single faculty rather than distinct faculties; they are ultimately the same faculty because they have the same source and object, namely, the striving toward the infinite. It's just that they approach their object in different ways.

Whatever the precise distinction between reason and understanding, the crucial point to see here is that the romantics' aestheticism must be understood in the light of their Platonism. For them, aesthetic experience is not *suprarational,* still less *antirational;* rather, it is *hyperrational,* consisting in the act of intellectual intuition of reason. It was through the intellectual intuition of aesthetic experience, they believed, that reason could perceive the infinite in the finite, the absolute in its appearance, or the macrocosm in the microcosm. Such a perception was intellectual or rational chiefly because of its object: the idea, principle, or *arche* underlying all the particulars of sense experience.

Prima facie it might seem very odd to regard this identification of intellectual perception with aesthetic experience as Platonic, given Plato's notorious banishment of the artists in his *Republic.* But to understand its Platonic provenance we only have to keep in mind, of course, that other strand of Platonic thinking expressed in the *Phaedrus* and *Symposium:* that we have some knowledge of the forms in this life only through the perception of beauty. It was indeed no accident that the *Phaedrus* and *Symposium* were the favorite texts of the young Hölderlin, Schleiermacher, and Friedrich Schlegel.

It might be asked here: Why should any *Aufklärer* accept the Platonic concept of reason? It would seem that he should dismiss it as nothing more than *Schwärmerei,* pure mysticism concealed by an honorific name. Such, indeed, was Kant's attitude toward the Platonic mysticism of J. G. Schlosser.[15] Hence there still appears to be an antithesis between the rationalism of the *Aufklärung* and the aestheticism of *Frühromantik* after all: it is the difference between those who insist on a completely discursive concept of reason and those who also permit a mystical dimension to reason.

But any such dismissal of the Platonic concept of reason is all too quick and superficial, missing its underlying point. It is of the first importance to stress that, for the romantics, the object of reason is the whole: what reason intuits is the unity and indivisibility of an organic whole, a whole that is irreducible to its parts, and from which no part is separable. The purpose of the romantic concept of reason was to designate, therefore, a new form or kind of explanation—*holistic* explanation—which would understand each part by its place within a whole. To explain any particular or individual thing would be to show how it plays a necessary role within, and is inseparable, from an organic whole. Such explanation is not reducible to forms of *mechanical* explanation, according to which the cause of every event is some preceding event, and so on *ad infinitum*. It is important to see, however, that holistic and mechanical explanation still do not *oppose* one another. It's just that mechanical explanation is *subordinate to* holistic explanation, since there is now a reason for the infinite series of efficient causes, which realize in some form the idea of the whole. This emphasis on holistic explanation is again only in keeping with the Platonic tradition: one only needs to consider the primacy accorded to holistic and teleological explanation over mechanical in the *Timaeus*.[16]

Now it is in just this context that we must understand the romantics' emphasis on the primacy of the aesthetic. Art has priority over philosophy not because it symbolizes something transcendent and mysterious—"the mystery of being"*(das Rätsel des Daseins)*—which cannot be understood in discursive terms. Rather, it has such primacy because holistic explanation is prior to mechanical. Aesthetic intuition grasps the whole, the knowledge of which is prior to all its parts; philosophy, however, is limited by its discursive procedures to only a knowledge of the parts of the whole. The intimate connection between romantic aestheticism and its holism becomes immediately apparent when we consider that its aestheticism and organic concept of nature are really one and the same: to consider the universe as an organic whole meant for the romantics to view it as a work of art.

If we carefully examine those texts where the romantics first put forward their case for the primacy of the aesthetic, we find that it really amounts to an argument for the priority of holistic explanation.[17] A crude summary of the argument behind these texts takes the following syllogistic form. (1) Both philosophy and science presuppose the idea of an organism, that is, that nature forms a systematic whole. (2) The idea of an organism is also an aesthetic whole, that is, it has some of the defining characteristics of beauty, such as a holistic structure and freedom from constraint. (3) The unity and indivisibility of an aesthetic whole, that is, beauty, can be grasped only in the intuition of aesthetic experience.[18] It then follows from steps 1–3 that (4) all the sciences and philosophy presuppose aesthetic experience, which alone justifies their ideal of systematic unity.

If we consider the romantics' concept of reason as a form of holistic explanation, then the contrast between *Aufklärung* and *Romantik* takes a new form. It is not the contrast between irrationalism and rationalism but between two different models of reason: the mechanical paradigm of the *Aufklärung* versus the holistic one of *Romantik*. This reformulation of the difference between *Aufklärung* and *Romantik* is perfectly in keeping with the developments in philosophy in the late 1790s. For it is during that time that we begin to see philosophers defending a more holistic model of explanation against the mechanical model dominant in the physics of the late seventeenth and eighteenth centuries.[19]

4. Pitfalls and Objections

It might be objected here: pointing out the Platonic legacy of *Frühromantik* is not only unoriginal but obvious. What else could intellectual intuition be, someone might ask, other than Platonic mysticism? But such an objection not only underestimates the complex origins of *Frühromantik*; it also overlooks a serious pitfall in the interpretation of its mysticism. Let me explain why.

The complexity here derives from one underappreciated fact: that there were at least two competing traditions of mysticism alive in German philosophy in the late eighteenth century. Very crudely, there was the mysticism of the Platonic tradition, which understood mystical insight as *hyperrational*, and which made reason an intuitive power. There was also, however, the mysticism of the Protestant tradition, which saw mystical insight as *suprarational*, and which reduced reason to a strictly discursive power. The mysticism of the Protestant tradition ultimately had its roots in the *via moderna*, the nominalist tradition of late medieval thought, which traces its roots back to William of Ockham. According to this tradition, reason is simply a formal power of drawing inferences, and it has no insight into a world of universals or archetypes for the simple reason that there is no such world; the belief in universals results from hypostasizing the meaning of words. There is also no such thing as eternal natural laws that are somehow inherent in the very nature of things; for laws have binding authority only by virtue of the divine will, which always has the power to change them. It is indeed significant that the great reformers—Luther and Calvin—were schooled in the tradition of the *via moderna;* their distinction between the realms of reason and faith is the direct result of this schooling.[20] For Luther and Calvin, the only access to the supernatural realm is through faith, which consists not merely in belief but also in inner experience. However old, the tradition of the *via moderna* was far from dead in the late eighteenth century in Germany; its most powerful and persuasive spokesmen were the so-called *Glaubens-philosophen:* Hamann and Jacobi. The central theme of their critique of the *Aufklärung*—hypostasis, superstitious belief in *ens rationis*—came straight from the nominalist tradition.

The pitfall in interpreting the mysticism of *Frühromantik* arises from con-flating these mystical traditions. The confusion is easily made, since there is no denying that the young romantics were, in fundamental respects, also heavily influenced by the Protestant tradition. It is then very easy to con-clude that the mysticism of *Frühromantik* has its source in the suprarational-ism of the *via moderna* rather than the hyperrationalism of the Platonic tradi-tion.

This danger is not simply hypothetical; it is all too real. For it is the *pro-ton pseudos,* I believe, of Isaiah Berlin's reading of romanticism as a radical irrationalism. It is no accident that Berlin lays such stress upon the ances-try of Hamann, and upon the pietist influence upon the young romantics. Once the romantics are placed so firmly within the Protestant tradition, Berlin then reads them consistently along the lines of its suprarationalism. He comes to some of his most startling conclusions about the antirationalism of romanticism—that the romantics undermine all universal and necessary laws of reason and make personal decision the sole arbiter of truth and value—not least because he interprets it in the light of the voluntarism of the Protestant tradition. It is as if the romantics read Kant's and Fichte's doc-trine of the will in voluntaristic terms, so that there are no higher norms governing its decisions. The will of the romantic individual then becomes something like a modern secular version of Ockham's god: what it decides to do is good just because it decides to do it.

If, however, we interpret the mysticism of *Frühromantik* in terms of the Platonic tradition, we come to some very different conclusions about its gen-eral doctrines. It is then easy to see that the romantics do not deny the exis-tence of natural law, and still less the eternal structure of things. The object of their intellectual intuition is indeed the archetypes, the forms, or ideas underlying all phenomena. While the romantics are indeed skeptical of the powers of the intellect to know these forms, they still believe that they exist, and that we can have some intuition of them, however vague and fleeting.

Another stumbling block in appreciating the Platonic dimension of *Früh-romantik* comes from a popular misinterpretation of its Kantian legacy. According to this misinterpretation, the romantics were deeply indebted to Kant's Copernican Revolution, which marks a fundamental break with the Platonic tradition.[21] While the Platonic tradition assumed that reason *discovers* an order within things, which is given and eternal, Kant held that reason *creates* the structure of experience, which does not exist apart from its activity. Though seductive in its simplicity, this interpretation is very questionable, and for two very weighty reasons. First, it is false to assume that Kant is within the voluntarist tradition, as if he holds that the standards of truth and value simply depend on an act of will. For Kant is very clear that there is an a priori structure to reason, and that the decisions of the will have value only insofar as they conform to this structure. Kant lies far more within the Platonic tradition, I believe, than many scholars are willing to admit, especially those who interpret him as a kind of prescriptivist or constructivist in ethics.[22] Second, this interpretation presupposes a hard and fast distinction between creating and discovering the truth, a distinction alien to the Platonic tradition, and indeed to Kant. The Platonic tradition never held that the mind is simply passive in receiving the truth but always stressed the importance of the activity of mind in appropriating truth.[23] Furthermore, it never admitted a sharp distinction between creating and discovering the truth. When reason reflects upon itself to know the laws of its own activity, it discovers these laws through the act of recreating them. These laws are not created *ex nihilo*, of course, but they do have to be *reproduced* by the finite mind if it is to know them. The finite mind knows them only by making the implicit, inchoate, and potential into the explicit, organized, and actual; but in no respect is the object just given, as if it were lying perfectly formed before the perceiving mind. When our reason recreates its laws through knowing them, it shares or participates in—though, of course, only in a very meager and feeble way—the same creative activity by which the divine understanding once created the world itself.

If we take seriously the Platonic legacy of *Frühromantik*, then it is necessary to revise our present understanding of *Frühromantik* in several respects. One of the most important is recognizing that romantic aesthetic experience is not a kind of suprarationalism, a form of inscrutable awareness of the "mystery of being," which somehow presents the unpresentable only by virtue of the inexhaustible interpretability of a work of art. This assessment of romantic aesthetics, which finds its most powerful spokesman in Manfred Frank,[24] suffers from several fatal difficulties. It is blind to the Platonic concept of reason in *Frühromantik;* it neglects the close connection between romantic aesthetics and *Naturphilosophie*, where the romantics did attempt to provide holistic explanations of nature; and, most important of all, it injects an unnecessary element of obscurantism into *Frühromantik*, which makes it vulnerable to all the old charges of antirationalism. All these difficulties have their source in the basic inspiration behind Frank's reading of romantic aesthetics: the late Heidegger.[25] It should be clear by now, however, that such an interpretation is inaccurate and anachronistic.

Another important respect in which we must revise our understanding of *Frühromantik* concerns the purported distinction between *Frühromantik* and idealism.[26] I think that there are some perfectly sound points underlying such a distinction: we cannot assimilate the epistemology and metaphysics of *Frühromantik* to the subjective idealism of Kant and Fichte, which all too often has been taken as the foundation of *Frühromantik*. It is indeed correct that romantic epistemology and metaphysics is better understood as a reaction against Kant's and Fichte's idealism, and that it must not be conflated with the grand speculative systems of Fichte, Schelling, and Hegel. It does not follow from these points, however, that *Frühromantik* is a rejection of idealism *tout court*. Indeed, given the Platonic legacy of *Frühromantik*, it is possible, even necessary, to regard it as its own form of idealism. Following the usage of Schlegel and Schelling, we could call it an *absolute* or *objective* idealism.[27] It is idealism not in the sense that everything depends on some self-conscious subject, but in the sense that everything conforms to the idea, the purpose, or the *logos* of things.

Someone might object that my Platonic interpretation of *Frühromantik*, with all its emphasis on holistic explanation, is proto-Hegelian. But I am tempted to turn this objection against itself: it is more a romantic reading of Hegel than a Hegelian reading of the romantics, for it shows just another respect in which Hegel was indebted to the romantic tradition. Specifically, it shows how Hegel's absolute idealism grew out of the romantic tradition; it was indeed only the most obscure and cumbrous expression of the absolute idealism that had already been worked out by Novalis, Schlegel, Hölderlin, and Schelling. Here again we must imagine Hegel as Schelling and Hölderlin once did: *der alte Mann*, who ambled along on crutches. It is high time that Hegelians finally realize that their hero was a tortoise among hares, winning the race for posthumous fame only because he was a more sure-footed plodder.

Still, I admit that there is some point to this objection. Any proto-Hegelian reading of *Frühromantik* is problematic if it sees the romantics as system

builders like Hegel. One of the most striking cases of such a Hegelian interpretation of *Frühromantik* is Haering's *Novalis als Philosoph,* which treated
Novalis as a systematic thinker along Hegelian lines.[28] Still, despite these
dangers, I think that my Platonic interpretation of *Frühromantik* avoids this
pitfall. It still permits, indeed insists upon, a fundamental difference between *Frühromantik* and Hegel: namely, Hegel affirms, while the romantics
deny, that it is possible to create a complete system of philosophy. In other
words, Hegel affirms and the romantics deny that there is a single conceptual elaboration and demonstration adequate to the intuitive insights of reason. In the romantic view, which again only follows the Platonic tradition,
the discursive performance of reason will always fall short of, and never do
full justice to, its intuitive insights. The romantics deny, in other words, that
there is such a thing as the system of absolute knowledge; they read such a
system as only a regulative goal, which we can approach but never attain
through infinite striving.

It is indeed in *Frühromantik* skepticism about foundationalism that we
see once again its profound debt to the Platonic tradition. From a modern
perspective, it is somewhat difficult to understand how the hyperrationalism
of *Frühromantik* went hand-in-hand with its skepticism about systems and
first principles. When we think of rationalism nowadays what first comes to
mind are the grand systems and indubitable first principles of Descartes,
Leibniz, and Spinoza. But the ancient and medieval worlds did not see
things this way; not least because of the Platonic legacy, they often associated a hyperrationalistic mysticism with a skepticism about final systems
and ultimate foundations. It is the same combination of doctrines that we
find in *Frühromantik.* Scratch beneath the surface of Schlegel's and Schleiermacher's skepticism about first principles and complete systems and what do
we see? The ironic smile of Socrates. It is no great secret that it was Socrates
who inspired Schlegel's concept of irony as well as Schleiermacher's theory
of dialectic.

5. The Platonic Legacy

Since the Platonic dimension of *Frühromantik* is still underappreciated, and
since the consequences of recognizing it are so great, it is necessary to demonstrate in a little detail the Platonic influence on some of the leading romantics. As an addendum to my argument, I sketch some brief Platonic portraits of Friedrich Schlegel, Schleiermacher, Novalis, and Schelling.[29]

Before looking at these individuals, it is important to consider the general historical context: the Plato renaissance in late-eighteenth-century Germany.[30] The revival of interest in Plato in Germany began in the middle of that century, and then reached its zenith in the 1790s, the formative years for the romantic generation. In the early 1700s in Germany, however, Plato was almost forgotten, having been eclipsed by the Aristotelian scholasticism of the universities. The greatest German Platonist was, of course, Leibniz; but his Platonism was one of the more esoteric aspects of his teaching, and so it remained largely without influence. Interest in Plato began to appear only in midcentury, mainly due to the growth of classical philology. In the 1750s the classicists J. A. Ernesti and David Ruhnken did much to revive classical philology by insisting on reading Greek sources in the original. Admirers of Plato, Ernesti and Ruhnken delivered influential academic orations on his philosophy. It was in 1757 that Winckelmann read Plato, who became one of the central influences on his aesthetics. By the 1760s interest in Plato had grown enormously. It was then that the writings of Rousseau and Shaftesbury, which were filled with Platonic themes, began to have their impact. It was also in the 1760s that Hamann, Herder, Wieland, and Mendelssohn all wrote about Plato or Platonic themes. By the 1770s Plato had become a recognized author. New editions and translations of his writings frequently appeared. It was in the 1780s that the Platonic renaissance truly began. In Halle, F. A. Wolf began a more rigorous philological study of Plato, publishing several editions of some of his writings. From 1781 to 1787 the Zwiebrücker edition of Plato's writings appeared, making Plato more accessible than ever. It was also in the 1780s that writings of the Dutch Platonist Franz Hemsterhuis appeared in German translation.[31] They were one of the most important sources for *Frühromantik,* since the Schlegel brothers and Novalis were among his enthusiastic students.[32]

Now that we have considered the general context behind *Frühromantik* Platonism, let us see how it played out in some individual thinkers.

Friedrich Schlegel

It is in Friedrich Schlegel that the influence of Plato on *Frühromantik* is most visible and pervasive. Schegel himself was very keen to acknowledge the source of so much of his inspiration. In the preface to his 1827 *Philosophie des Lebens* he made a revealing statement about his main philosophical interest and its sources: "It is now thirty-nine years ago that I read through the complete works of Plato in Greek with indescribable curiosity; and since then . . .

this philosophical enquiry [metaphysics] has always been my proper main concern."³³

The Platonic sources behind Schlegel's rationalism first show themselves in an early dispute with his brother.³⁴ Sometime in 1793 August Wilhelm had been reading Jacobi, whose critique of the *Aufklärung* especially impressed him. But Friedrich did not approve, scolding his brother for a *Vernunfthaß*. Friedrich thinks that Jacobi is indeed guilty of irrationalism because he has a much too limited concept of reason. He has failed to distinguish between reason *(Vernunft)* and understanding *(Verstand)*, which consists in the power of conceiving, judging, and inferring. Reason is not simply a passive faculty for receiving facts, as Jacobi implied, but it is active and spontaneous. It is indeed not only one power in man but his fundamental power: the striving for eternity. Relying on the Platonic concept of *eros,* Friedrich then explains that there is really no distinction between reason and the heart, because reason is at bottom love.³⁵ Reason and love both consist in the striving for wholeness, the drive toward universality, the longing to become one with the infinite or the universe as a whole. After correcting his brother's confusion about reason, Friedrich then defends two other aspects of reason: the ideal and system. The ideal has its source in reason, in its longing after eternity; it keeps before us the fundamental goal of our life: the striving to be like God. A system is nothing less than an attempt to grasp through concepts the fundamental connection of things. It is what we call the soul of a poem, the spirit of a person, and the divine in creation. There is of course only one true system: the whole of nature. Friedrich insists, however, that a complete system is simply an ideal or goal that we can approach but never attain. Following Condillac, he distinguishes between the *esprit systématique* and the *esprit des système:* the former is the struggle to find greater unity in all knowledge, and is an essential function of reason; the latter is the attempt to create a system out of a few facts, which is then imposed on experience.

Throughout the 1790s and the *Athenäumszeit,* Schlegel continued to develop a philosophy fundamentally Platonic in inspiration. Beginning in 1796 the notebooks of the *Philosophische Lehrjahre* show how he was moving toward a doctrine he called—years before Schelling and Hegel—"absolute idealism." According to this doctrine, everything in reality conforms to reason, which consists in the forms, ideas, or purpose of things.³⁶ There is no fundamental difference between the objective and subjective because both are differing degrees of organization and development of a single rational activity, which acts through constantly dividing what is one and uniting what is divided. In the later notebooks Schlegel's concept of reason becomes much more complex. It is no longer simply identified with the Platonic eros, but is used in a bewildering variety of ways. Still, the Platonic provenance of his concept remains: reason is the intelligible structure of things, what we perceive in beauty through the power of intellectual intuition.[37] Schlegel's most systematic account of his absolute idealism appears in his 1801 lectures on transcendental philosophy. The basic Platonic inspiration behind these lectures is most explicit in the first of the disputation theses in which Schlegel defended them: *"Platonis philosophia genuinus est Idealismus."*[38] The enduring importance of Plato for Schlegel's thinking around 1800 is apparent from a notebook entry around the time of the lectures: "Plato contains properly wisdom, the whole spirit of philosophy is in him. He knew everything, namely the whole, that upon which everything rests."[39]

Schleiermacher

Of all the romantics, the one most influenced by Plato was probably Schleiermacher, who was perfectly explicit in acknowledging that influence: "There is no other writer than this divine man who has so effected me, and who has consecrated me into philosophy and the world of humanity . . ."[40] Such, indeed, was Schleiermacher's respect for Plato that he describes it as "inexpressible," "a religious awe."[41] Of course, Schleiermacher himself played a central role in the Platonic renaissance because of his translation of Plato's works, which is still used today.[42] Various aspects of Schleiermacher's philosophy have much of their origins in his study of Plato: his conception of dialectic, his organic view of nature, his skepticism about foundationalism, and his theory of religious experience. It is this final aspect of Plato's influence that is especially relevant here, however. If we carefully read Schleiermacher's analysis of religious experience in the second speech of the *Reden,* its Platonic roots soon reveal themselves. In a remarkable passage Schleiermacher explains that the intuition of the universe consists in a feeling of love, a longing to become one with it, where "I am its soul . . . and it is my body."[43] Such a longing is, of course, the Platonic eros. Yet it is not only the *act* of intuiting the universe that is Platonic; its object is no less so. What we perceive when we intuit the universe, Schleiermacher later explains in the same speech, is its intelligible structure. Hence he says that "we intuit the universe most clearly and in a most holy manner" when we grasp "the eternal laws according to which bodies are themselves formed and destroyed."[44]

"What actually appeals to the religious sense in its external world," he further argues, "is not its masses but its laws."[45]

Schelling

Plato's influence on Schelling is not as striking and dramatic as in the cases of Schlegel and Schleiermacher. There are no startling confessions, and there are only a few references to Plato in his early writings. Still, the Platonic legacy is there all the same. Schelling's love of Plato began in his early years in the *Tübinger Stift*, where he read Plato widely and deeply in Greek. His early interest in Plato is evident from two notebooks which he wrote in the early 1790s. One notebook, entitled "Vorstellungsarten der alten Welt," contains a long section on Plato; the other, "Ueber den Geist der platonischen Philosophie," is a commentary on the *Timaeus*.[46] Schelling's study of the *Timaeus* was important for his *Naturphilosophie*, which takes issue with Plato's ideas of the world soul and the demiurge.[47] The early influence of Plato on Schelling is apparent in two further respects: in his explanation of evil in *De malorum origine*, and in his account of intellectual intuition in his *Philosophische Briefe über Dogmatismus und Kriticismus*.[48] In both these works Schelling not only praises Plato but also borrows from him.

   Plato's influence on Schelling's thought becomes most evident, however, only after his break with Fichte, and during the development of his philosophy of identity (1800–1804). In *Bruno* and *Philosophie der Kunst*, Schelling sketches a *Weltanschauung* that would be best described as a synthesis of Plato and Spinoza; in other words, it is a form of Platonic monism or monistic Platonism. Schelling revives Plato's doctrine of ideas to explain the classic problem of how the infinite exists in the finite, the one in the many. He explains that particular things exist in the absolute only insofar as they reflect its whole nature, that is, only insofar as they are also in themselves the absolute; such particular things, existing entirely in the absolute, are the ideas.[49] Schelling's whole concept of the absolute, however, is Platonic. The single universal substance now becomes "the idea of all ideas," which is the single object of reason.[50] We know this absolute through an intellectual intuition, which is purely rational and yet irreducible to discursive reasoning.[51] True to the legacy of the *Phaedrus*, Schelling states that we know that there is a connection between the infinite and the finite, or that the infinite appears in the finite, first and foremost through the idea of beauty.[52]

Novalis

Prima facie Novalis might seem to be the least Platonic of all the early romantics. There are few references to Plato in his letters and writings, and he did not have the infatuation with things Greek of Hölderlin, Schelling, Schleiermacher, and Schlegel. Yet this impression is corrected by Friedrich Schlegel, who told his brother, after first meeting Novalis in 1792, that the *"Lieblingsschriftsteller"* of his new friend were Plato and Hemsterhuis.[53] The more closely we examine some of Novalis's early writings, the more we see the Platonic inspiration of his concept of reason. To be sure, in his early *Fichte-Studien* Novalis reveals himself to be a very severe critic of the pretensions of discursive thought, which falsifies the truth in the very act of trying to grasp it; but this should not be taken as evidence for his misology, and still less for an affirmation of suprarationalism. For Novalis does not see reason simply as a discursive faculty, whose only business is to conceive, judge, and infer. Rather, he regards it as an intuitive capacity, "an intellectual power of seeing," which is indeed "estatic."[54] Unlike Jacobi, he does not think that the only function of reason is to provide mechanical explanations; rather, he stresses that reason transcends the merely mechanical, and that its proper task is to grasp each thing in its necessary place in the whole.[55]

Novalis's debts to the Platonic tradition only become fully apparent later in his career. In the autumn of 1798 he makes a momentous discovery: Plotinus![56] He declares that no philosopher had penetrated so far into the sacred temple.[57] Writing under the influence of Plotinus, he now describes intellectual intuition as "inner light" or "ecstasy,"[58] and he interprets reason in terms of "the divine *logos*."[59] The main reason for this enthusiasm was that Novalis had been searching for some time for the right concept to unify idealism and realism. He now calls this concept *syncriticism,* a term that was once used to refer to the mystical tendencies of neo-Platonism.

All these facts about the young Schlegel, Schleiermacher, Schelling, and Novalis reveal the profound and pervasive influence of Platonism upon them. They alone warrant the interpretation of *Frühromantik* as a revival of Platonism. Once, however, we see *Frühromantik* as a Platonic renaissance, the consequences for any general interpretation of it are many. One consequence is that we must construe the mysticism and aestheticism of *Frühromantik* as a form of hyperrationalism. My only point here has been to explain this consequence alone.

CHAPTER 5

The Sovereignty of Art

1. Art as Metaphysics

One of the most remarkable traits of the early German romantics was their belief in the metaphysical stature of art. Almost all the young romantics—Wackenroder, Schelling, Schleiermacher, Novalis, the young Hegel, Hölderlin, and the Schlegel brothers—made aesthetic experience into the criterion, instrument, and medium for awareness of ultimate reality or the absolute. Through aesthetic experience, they believed, we perceive the infinite in the finite, the supersensible in the sensible, the absolute in its appearances. Since art alone has the power to fathom the absolute, it is superior to philosophy, which now becomes the mere handmaiden of art.[1]

Such a doctrine is remarkable for at least two reasons. First, it marks a radical break with the Enlightenment dogma of the sovereignty of reason, which made reason the highest intellectual authority. While the *Aufklärer* made reason—understood in a discursive sense as a faculty of conceiving, judging, and inferring—into the chief criterion, instrument, and medium of knowledge, the young romantics assigned such a role to the feeling and intuition of aesthetic experience. Second, it also departs from the dominant subjectivist trend of eighteenth-century aesthetics, which saw aesthetic perception as merely a sensation of pleasure in the spectator, and aesthetic creation as only an expression of feeling in the artist.[2] By disputing the objective element of aesthetic judgment, Kant's aesthetics did not challenge but simply completed this trend.

These striking characteristics of romantic aesthetics naturally raise some very interesting questions. What were the sources and influences on the young romantics that made it possible for them to break with the Enlightenment and the subjectivism of eighteenth-century aesthetics? What was the basis for, or rationale behind, their faith in the sovereignty of art? Of course, these questions have been raised before; no one can claim, however, that there has been anything like a definitive answer to them.

One of the most notable recent attempts to answer these questions is that of Manfred Frank in his rich and stimulating book *Einführung in die frühromantische Ästhetik*.[3] According to Frank, the romantic belief in the metaphysical status of art marks a fundamental break not only with the Enlightenment and eighteenth-century aesthetics, but with the whole of Western intellectual tradition since Plato.[4] This break consists in a rejection of a theory of truth as correspondence and its replacement with a theory of truth as creation or production.[5] As long as the conception of truth as correspondence prevailed, the artist had an inferior status to the philosopher, Frank argues, given that the artist's images and symbols could not represent reality with all the directness, clarity, and precision of reason. The end of the two-thousand-year reign of this conception of truth came, we are told, with the publication of the *Kritik der reinen Vernunft* in 1781.[6] With his Copernican Revolution, Kant replaced the conception of truth as correspondence with a conception of truth as production, according to which the subject does not merely reflect on a given reality but constitutes the very structure of reality through its activity. It was primarily this new conception of truth, Frank maintains, that allowed the romantics to give metaphysical status to art. Rather than being limited to the imitation of a given reality, the artist's creative activity was part of that general activity by which the subject creates its entire world.[7]

On Frank's account, then, the fundamental factor behind the development of romantic aesthetics came from the Kantian Copernican Revolution, more specifically from Kant's conception of truth in the first *Kritik*. Yet Frank does not limit the significance of Kant to the first *Kritik* alone. He also regards the *Kritik der Urteilskraft*, especially its first part, the "Kritik der ästhetischen Urteilskraft," as a central text for the young romantics. Accordingly, he devotes the first eight lectures collected in his book to a detailed analysis of Kant's theory of aesthetic judgment in the third *Kritik*.

In some respects, Frank's account represents the standard view of the rise of the romantic aesthetic. Usually, Kant's Copernican Revolution is taken as the starting point of the romantic aesthetic, and its crucial text is taken to be the *Kritik der Urteilskraft*. Frank's defense and elaboration of this view is notable for its depth and detail, providing the best possible case for it. In other respects, however, there is something new and important behind Frank's account of romantic aesthetics. He is one of the first to see—and to stress—that romantic aesthetics was not simply a poetic version of Kant's and Fichte's idealism, the standard view from Rudolf Haym to Hans-Georg Gadamer.[8] As we shall soon see, however, these two aspects of Frank's theory—the more traditional and the more innovative—are at odds with one another. Romantic aesthetics cannot both have its foundation in Kant's Copernican Revolution and break with the legacy of Kant's and Fichte's subjective idealism. For the Kantian conception of truth is the basis for that idealism.

In what follows my task is not only to expose the problems with Frank's theory but also to sketch an alternative account of the foundation of the romantic aesthetic. My own account will locate that foundation in a domain completely ignored by Frank: romantic *Naturphilosophie* and its organic concept of nature.

2. Expression and Imitation

Let me begin with Frank's central claim that the main premise underlying romantic aesthetic theory lay with its new Kantian conception of truth. There is something to be said in its behalf. Some of the young romantics did hold that the artist creates his standards of truth, and they denied that they are simply given to him in nature so that he must passively imitate them. Hence A. W. Schlegel and Schelling explicitly stated that nature does not provide the rule for the artist but that the artist provides the rule for nature.[9] Their statements seem to be little more than an aesthetic variant of Kant's Copernican Revolution.

It would be wrong to conclude from their statements, however, that the romantic aesthetic was inherently subjectivistic, a theory of the mind as a lamp rather than a mirror.[10] The romantics never completely rejected the theory of imitation, since they continued to hold that art has to be true to nature, or that the artist should represent the entire world around him.[11] The aesthetics of *Frühromantik* was never a simple doctrine of emotive expression, as if the value of a work of art lay solely in its capacity to express the feelings and desires of the artist. While the romantics did hold that the artistic genius has the power to lay down the rules of his art, they never claimed that these rules have only a subjective significance, referring to nothing but the mind of the artist. What is indeed most striking about early romantic aesthetics is its *synthesis* of the doctrines of imitation and expression. It holds that in expressing his feelings and desires, in fathoming his own personal depths, the artist also reveals the creative powers of nature that work through him. What the artist produces is indeed the self-production of the absolute through him, for the creative activity of art is the highest organization and development of all the creative powers of nature.

This synthesis of imitation and expression is just what we should expect from romantic metaphysics, whose fundamental principle was subject–object identity. According to this principle, the subjective and objective, the ideal and the real, the mental and physical are equal manifestations, appearances, or embodiments of the single indivisible reality of the absolute. The absolute itself is *both* subjective and objective, since both are its necessary appearances; but it is also *neither* subjective nor objective, since it is not exclusively either of them. This doctrine means that aesthetic experience, as the perfect incarnation of subject–object identity, should have both an objective and subjective manifestation; in each manifestation either the objective or subjective preponderates but neither exists without the other. When the objective side preponderates, the subject should conform to the object, so that the artist should imitate nature; and when the subjective side dominates, the object should conform to the subject, so that the object reveals itself only through the expressive activity of the subject.

It should be clear from this metaphysical theory that the Kantian Copernican Revolution, which claims that objects should conform to concepts (rather than conversely), grasps only one side of aesthetic experience. It does justice only to the subjective side, according to which the subject creates the standard for the object; but it fails to account for the objective side, according to which the object imposes the standard for the subject. In less schematic terms, the fundamental problem with a strictly Kantian reading of the romantic aesthetic theory is that it cannot explain its *objective* dimension. If the activity of the artist originates within the subject alone, then it is cut off from the absolute; it loses its metaphysical dimension, failing to be a revelation or manifestation of the absolute itself. For the romantics, the main reason that the creativity of the artist has a claim to metaphysical truth is that his activity is continuous with, and an integral part of, nature as a whole.[12] The activity of the artist is a revelation and manifestation of the absolute because it is nothing less than the highest expression and embodiment of all the powers of nature. Hence what the artist reveals is what nature reveals through him. To be sure, the artist does not simply mirror or imitate nature; it is his creative activity that determines the standards of aesthetic worth. Yet the crucial point to see is that the artist is a *co-producer,* indeed the final link in a chain of production running throughout the whole of nature. So it is not only the activity of the artist that is being expressed; it is also the activity of the absolute that expresses itself through him.

This objective dimension of romantic aesthetic theory is especially apparent in the romantics' growing fondness for Spinoza in the mid-1790s. For the romantics, Spinoza represented the very antithesis of the transcendental idealism of Kant and Fichte. If the Kantian–Fichtean philosophy made the ego its absolute, of which nature is only a modification, Spinoza made nature into his absolute, of which the ego is only a modification. By the late 1790s Schelling, Schlegel, Hölderlin, and Novalis had come to admire Spinoza, whose realism, they believed, should be the complement to the idealism of Kant and Fichte. This Spinozistic dimension of romantic aesthetics has often been overlooked; but it is explicit in no more central text than Schlegel's *Athenäumsfragmente,* where Schlegel not only defends Spinoza, but also regards a mystical feeling for his one and all as an essential element of aesthetics.[13] In the *Gespräch über Poesie* we learn that one cannot even be a poet "unless one honors, loves, and appropriates Spinoza."[14]

That this objective or Spinozistic dimension of romantic aesthetics has been underestimated or neglected for so long is chiefly due to the standard interpretation, which has stressed the romantics' dependence on Fichte's 1794 *Wissenschaftslehre.* According to this interpretation, the romantic belief in the metaphysical powers of art grew out of the Fichtian concept of imagination; the creative powers of the artist were simply a higher manifestation of the subconscious powers active in the production of experience. Romantic aesthetics then turns out to be nothing more than the poetics of the *Wissenschaftslehre.*

The chief premise behind this still very popular account of romantic aesthetics is that the romantics were disciples of Fichte's 1794 *Wissenschaftslehre.* Given the young romantics' admiration for Fichte, it is very easy to see why such an account is still popular. But the early fragments and notebooks of Hölderlin, Novalis, and Friedrich Schlegel tell a very different story— namely, they were not loyal disciples but sharp critics of Fichte. From 1795 to 1797, the formative years for the romantic aesthetics, they took issue with Fichte's foundationalism and idealism. They criticized his foundationalism on the grounds that it is not possible to establish infallible first principles and a complete system of all knowledge. They attacked his idealism for its subjectivism, more specifically for its conception of the principle of subject–object identity as residing in the ego or subject alone.[15] To overcome the one-sidedness of Fichte's subjective idealism, they insisted on complementing it with Spinoza's realism or naturalism. If the absolute were subject–object identity, they argued, then it should be possible to conceive it as both objective and subjective, as both real and ideal. This argument is most explicit in Schelling's 1800 *System des transcendentalen Idealismus;* yet it was already implicit in the fragments of Hölderlin, and in the notebooks of Novalis and Schlegel, as early as 1796.

No one has done more to expose the errors behind the traditional interpretation of romantic aesthetics as a poetic version of Fichte's idealism than Frank himself. Rightly, he has stressed that the romantics ceased to see the ego as the first principle of philosophy, and placed its foundation in an absolute transcending it.[16] The romantics' belief in the metaphysical status of art, he explains, derives from their argument that there is a ground of subjectivity that cannot itself lie within subjectivity itself.[17] But if all this is the case, then in what sense can we maintain that the source of the romantic aesthetic lay in Kant's subjectivist conception of truth? Frank himself seems to appreciate the force of this point when, recognizing that the aim of the romantics was to establish an *objective* theory of beauty, he concedes that Kant's philosophy was not such a *Wendepunkt* for romantic aesthetics after all.[18]

The most charitable interpretation I can give of Frank's Kantian interpretation of the romantic aesthetic is to admit that there is one sense in which it was very indirectly the *historical* source of romantic aesthetics. Kant's conception of truth was the ancestor of Fichte's principle of subject–object identity, which the romantics then reinterpreted by locating the source of such identity in nature, being, or the universe. But it is very important to make a distinction here between the *historical* source and the *logical* foundation for a doctrine. Obviously, these are distinct, since a theory might be influential but also contradicted or transformed by its successors. This is indeed the case for Kant's theory of truth. While Kant's theory was one historical source for the romantic aesthetic, it was never the logical foundation for it. What is so misleading about Frank's account, however, is that it is easy to mistake the historical ancestor for the logical foundation. It then seems as if Kant's theory is somehow the basis for the romantic theory when it is really only one-half of the story.

3. The Challenge of Kant's Third *Kritik*

If Frank goes astray in ascribing such importance to Kant's first *Kritik*, he is surely on safer ground when he stresses the significance of the third *Kritik*.

There can be no doubt that some of the young romantics were inspired by Kant's third *Kritik,* which most of them carefully studied in their early years.[19] While they often took issue with Kant, they were also profoundly indebted to him.[20] Kant's doctrine of the autonomy of art, his concept of an organism, his idea of the finality of nature, his definition of genius, and his suggestion that beauty is the symbol for morality were all crucial in one way or another for most young romantics.

Yet, as far as the romantic doctrine of the metaphysical status of art is concerned, it is necessary to admit that Kant's third *Kritik* had more of a negative than positive significance. Kant's denial of the cognitive status of aesthetic judgment, his insistence that aesthetic experience consists only in a feeling of pleasure, and his general restriction of knowledge to appearances posed serious obstacles to the development of a romantic aesthetic. It was one of the central goals of the young romantics to get beyond the Kantian regulative limits on aesthetic experience.[21] While they believed that Schiller had taken a step in the right direction by attempting to provide an objective aesthetics that made beauty into an appearance of freedom, they also held that he had not gone far enough. True to Kant's critical teachings, Schiller insisted that we could only treat beauty *as if* it were an appearance of freedom; the young romantics wanted to go that crucial step further: to hold that beauty *is* an appearance of freedom.

Of course, Frank himself is well aware of the challenge that Kant's regulative doctrine presented to the young romantics. On several occasions he raises the objection how the third *Kritik* could be so important for the romantics in the face of Kant's insistence on the purely regulative status of aesthetic judgment and experience.[22] It must be said, however, that the answer he gives to this question is half-hearted, as if he is not so convinced himself.[23] His reply is essentially to stress §59 of the third *Kritik,* where Kant makes beauty into a symbol of morality and suggests that it also signifies the supersensible ground joining the noumenal and phenomenal worlds. According to Frank, Kant's argument here was crucial for the romantics, because it suggested a way of unifying the Kantian dualisms, which had been one of their central goals. By suggesting that beauty is the symbol for morality, Kant had in effect made it the middle term between the noumenal and phenomenal worlds, and indeed between practical and theoretical reason.

Of course, there is something to be said for §59 of the *Kritik der Urteilskraft* as a source of romantic doctrine. There is some evidence that it, or similar sections, were important for Hölderlin and Friedrich Schlegel.[24] Yet, for two reasons, it is wrong to place much weight on these passages. First, Kant's statement that beauty is the symbol of morality is still far too hedged with regulative qualifications for it to support the romantic doctrine that art provides a sensible image of the absolute. Kant does not think that beauty *is* the appearance of the good but only that we must judge it *as if* it were so.[25] Second, Kant's statement also implies his doctrine that there cannot be any constitutive theory to explain the unity of the noumenal and phenomenal; he leaves their unity a mystery by stating that only an aesthetic symbol represents it. But in this respect too the romantics went further than Kant: they sought some model to explain the unity of the noumenal and phenomenal; they did not want only an aesthetic symbol for the mystery of their interaction. Let us now consider that model of explanation.

4. The Precedent of the Third *Kritik*

While Kant's third *Kritik* had *mainly* a negative significance for the romantic belief in the metaphysical status of art, this is not to say that it had *entirely* or *only* such a significance. There is still a sense in which it had a positive significance regarding this belief, for it was Kant himself who suggested how his own critical limits could be overcome. In this respect the most suggestive and influential part of the third *Kritik* was not the critique of aesthetic judgment, as Frank assumes, but the critique of teleological judgment. Let me briefly try to explain why.

If we closely examine some of the central texts of the early romantics—specifically Hölderlin's *Hyperion*, Schlegel's *Gespräch über Poesie*, Schelling's *System des transcendentalen Idealismus*, and some of Novalis fragments—we find one common tacit argument for their belief in the metaphysical significance of art.[26] Put very crudely, the argument goes as follows. (1) Both philosophy and science presuppose the idea of an organism, that is, that nature forms a systematic whole where the idea of the whole precedes all its parts and makes them possible. (2) The idea of an organism is an *aesthetic* whole, that is, it has some of the defining characteristics of beauty. An organism is like a work of art in two respects: first, it has a holistic structure, where the idea of the whole determines all its parts; and, second, it is autonomous, free from external constraints, because it is self-generating and self-organizing. (3) The idea of an organism, or an aesthetic whole, can be grasped only in aesthetic experience. This is because aesthetic experience consists in intuition, the direct perception of a thing as a whole, whereas the understanding explains each thing analytically, only by dissecting it into its distinct parts.

It follows from these premises that all the sciences and philosophy presuppose aesthetic experience, which alone justifies their ideal of systematic unity. Without aesthetic experience, it is impossible to justify the existence of an organic unity in nature, which is the ideal of all philosophy and science. This argument attempts to provide, then, something like a "transcendental deduction" of the aesthetic, that is, it tries to show how the aesthetic is a necessary condition of the possibility of science itself.

However much Kant himself would reject this argument, there are clear Kantian precedents for each of its premises, or at least for some of the assumptions behind them. Each of these premises appears either in the introductions or in the second half of the *Kritik der Urteilskraft*. All that Hölderlin, Schlegel, and Schelling did was add them together, drawing the inevitable conclusion.

Take the first premise. Kant had argued that the idea of an organism, more specifically of the finality of nature, is a necessary idea of reason. Since it assumes that everything in nature conforms to some intelligent design, or that it has been created according to a rational plan, this idea unifies the realms of the noumenal and phenomenal. Equally significantly, it is necessary to provide systematic order for the multiplicity of empirical laws, which could not be guaranteed by the categories of the understanding alone. In several passages of the third *Kritik,* and in the Appendix to the Transcendental Dialectic of the first *Kritik,* Kant went so far as to argue that the idea of the systematic unity and finality of nature is necessary for the very possibility of empirical truth.[27]

There is also a Kantian precedent for the second premise. In the third *Kritik* Kant had made the idea of an organism central to aesthetics itself. He saw a close analogy between the concept of an organism and a work of art.[28] Their *structure* is the same since both involve the idea of an organic whole, where the identity of each part is inseparable from the whole, and where the identity of the whole is inseparable from each of its parts. Their *genesis* is also similar because both are created according to some rational plan, a synthetic universal where the idea of the whole precedes its parts. Furthermore, both concepts also involve the Kantian idea of purposiveness without a purpose *(Zweckmäßigkeit ohne Zweck),* because both nature and the artist work according to some intelligent design even though they are not fully conscious of it.

Finally, there is also some Kantian precedent for the third premise, though it was only negative in significance. Although Kant challenged the romantics in denying that aesthetic experience could have a cognitive significance, he also aided and anticipated them by arguing that there could not be any discursive insight into an organism. In the second half of the third *Kritik* Kant had provided two arguments against any such insight. First, our discursive understanding is analytical, proceeding from the parts to the whole; it is not synthetic, proceeding from the idea of the whole to all its parts. Second, our reason knows only what it creates, what it produces according to a plan of its own; since it cannot create the infinitely complex structure of an organism, it therefore follows that it cannot know it.[29]

If we put all these Kantian precedents together, it is clear that we come very close to the romantic doctrine of the sovereignty of art. Nevertheless, it is not close enough. The romantics still went two significant steps beyond Kant: first, in ascribing a constitutive status to the idea of an organism; and, second, in claiming that there can be some form of intuitive or non-discursive apprehension of the idea of an organism. Of course, in both these respects, the Kantian regulative limits would act as a challenge to the romantics. Here again, then, we see the essentially negative significance of Kant's teaching.

To be sure, though, these Kantian precedents for the romantic argument do justify ascribing some positive significance to Kant's third *Kritik*. If this work did not provide the argument itself, it did provide most of its premises. Yet it is still necessary to qualify any claim for the importance of the third *Kritik* in this regard for the simple reason that it was not the only source of these premises. Many of the central themes of the argument—that the universe forms an organic whole, and that the idea of an organism overcomes the dualisms between the subjective and objective—had become commonplace by the 1790s. Kant's *Kritik der Urteilskraft* reflected this new thinking as much as it helped create it.

5. The Metaphysical Foundation for Romantic Aesthetics

Hölderlin's, Schelling's, and Schlegel's transcendental deduction of the aesthetic indicates where we should look for the foundation of the romantic aesthetic. Its *immediate* source was in the realm of epistemology, and indeed in a new concept of truth, as we have just seen. Yet its *ultimate* source lay elsewhere: namely, with its implicit metaphysics, and more specifically its organic theory of nature.[30] This theory appears throughout the fragments, notebooks, and lectures of Hölderlin, Novalis, and the Schlegel brothers; it was formulated systematically by Schelling in his 1798 *Von der Weltseele*, then defended vigorously by the young (and still romantic) Hegel in his 1801 *Differenzschrift*. The development of this theory is of course closely associated with *Naturphilosophie*, which dominated physiology and physics in Germany at the close of the eighteenth century. Some of the central figures in *Naturphilosophie*—J. W. Ritter, C. A. Eschenmayer, H. Steffans, Franz Baader, Alexander von Humboldt—were of course closely associated with the romantic circles in Jena and Berlin.

The rise of the organic theory of nature was one of the most remarkable events in natural science since the onset of the scientific revolution in the early seventeenth century. The emergence of this theory marked the decline of the mechanical physics of Descartes and Newton, which had dominated natural philosophy throughout the late seventeenth and early eighteenth centuries. It is no exaggeration to regard the new organic theory as a "paradigm shift" insofar as it involved completely new criteria of explanation from mechanical physics. While mechanical physics understood a phenomenon by placing it within a series of efficient causes, where each event had its cause in preceding events, and so on *ad infinitum*, the organic theory explained a phenomenon in holistic terms by seeing all events as part of a wider whole.

There is a persistent and prevalent tendency to stereotype romantic *Naturphilosophie* as a kind of a priori speculation and system building in opposition to the normal empirical science of its day. Yet this stereotype is deeply anachronistic. During an age without sharp boundary lines between science and philosophy, *Naturphilosophie* was nothing less than the normal science of its day. Rather than consisting in a priori speculation and system-building, it grew directly out of the latest advances in eighteenth-century physics and physiology.[31]

Summarizing very crudely, there were two fundamental sources for the organic theory of nature. First was the emergence of the new dynamic physics, which maintained that the essence of matter consists in active force rather than inert extension. The mechanical physics always had great difficulty explaining the forces of attraction and repulsion, which seemed to imply "action at a distance." But now the new experiments in electricity, magnetism, and chemistry seemed to suggest that the same forces were inherent in matter and omnipresent in nature. The second source was the decline of the theory of preformation, which maintains that living creatures are already entirely preformed in their embryos due to some supernatural cause, and the rise of the theory of epigenesis, which holds that creatures develop from inchoate embryos into organisms due to natural causes. Both these developments taken together point toward a unified conception of nature. If the first development seems to bring the inorganic world closer to the organic by making the essence of matter into energy, the second appears to draw the organic closer to the inorganic by banishing the need for a supernatural origin of life. Thus the two realms of nature join in the idea of living force *(Kraft)*.

Two philosophers toward the close of the eighteenth century saw this development with great clarity: J. G. Herder and K. F. Kielmeyer, both of them seminal influences on the *Naturphilosophen*.[32] They not only saw a fundamental continuum between the organic and inorganic realms, but also insisted that the laws governing them could not be reduced to mechanism alone. The grandfather of such an organic view of nature was, of course, Leibniz, whose day had finally come.[33]

Ironically, Kant too had played a powerful role in the development of the organic theory of nature. The best analysis of what the romantics mean by an organism is Kant's own analysis of a natural purpose *(Naturzweck)* in §65 of the *Kritik der Urteilskraft*. According to Kant, the concept of an organism involves two essential elements: (1) that the idea of the whole precedes its parts and makes them possible; and (2) that the parts are reciprocally the cause and effect of one another. The first element alone is not sufficient, Kant argued, because both a work of art and an organism are created according to some general concept or plan. It is also necessary to add the second element because what is distinctive of an organism is that it is *self*-generating and *self*-organizing.

The romantics agreed with Kant's analysis of the idea of an organism; but they then extended it on a cosmic scale and dropped the regulative constraints on it. According to the romantics' organic metaphor, the cosmos is one vast organism, one single living whole, a *Macroanthropos*. All of nature forms a hierarchy of levels of organization and development, where each lower level reaches its end only in a higher one, which organizes and develops all the living powers below it. Ultimately, there is only one living force behind all of nature, which manifests itself in different forms and levels, but which ultimately remains one and the same.

This concept of force provided the *Naturphilosophen* with their mediating concept between the mental and the physical, the ideal and the real, the subjective and objective. There is no longer a fundamental difference in kind but only one of degree between these opposites, since they are only different degrees of organization and development of living force. The mental is the internalization of the physical, and the physical is the externalization of the mental. As Schelling so poetically summed up this view: "Nature should be visible spirit, and spirit should be invisible nature."[34]

The organic theory involved a completely new account of the relationship between the mental and the physical from that prevalent in the mechanical physics of the eighteenth century. According to the mechanistic tradition, nature consists in a plurality of independent things, which are connected with one another through causal interaction alone. One body acts on another through *impact*—by striking against another body and changing its position—where impact is measured in terms of change of place in a given amount of time. Like all things in nature, the mind and body are viewed as independent entities, which interact with one another only causally. Since it is impossible to claim that mental events change place, mechanism had serious difficulties in explaining how the body acts on the mind by impact. It was indeed just these difficulties that motivated the search for non-mechanical models of explanation, and that ultimately led to the new dynamic physics.

According to the organic concept, the interaction between the mental and the physical is not between distinct entities or events; rather, it consists in the actualization, realization, or manifestation of a force. A force is not simply the cause of its actualization, as if it were logically distinct from it, because it becomes what it is only through its actualization, realization, or manifestation. In other words, the mind does not simply act on the body, which exists prior to it, but it becomes *what it is* through its externalizations in the body; conversely, the body does not simply act on the mind, which exists prior to it, but it becomes *what it is* only through its internalization in the mind.

It should be clear that it is impossible to explain the connection between a force and its manifestations with the usual models—the concepts of logical identity or of efficient causality alone. If the force is not the cause of its manifestations, it is also not simply logically identical with them. Rather, the force and its manifestation relate to one another as the *potential, universal,* and *implicit* do to the *actual, particular,* and *explicit*. There is clearly a logical tie between things describable in these terms, since they have the same underlying content; but the tie is not one of mere identity, since such things present different aspects of the same content.

Now to understand the romantic aesthetic, especially the extraordinary claims it makes in behalf of the metaphysical knowledge of the artist, we only need to apply the organic theory to the artist. This theory provides several reasons for thinking that the creativity of the artist will also be the *self*-revelation of nature itself. (1) Since in an organism the whole is inseparable from each of its parts, it follows that the work of the artist, as one part of nature, will reflect all of nature; in other words, it will be, as Novalis liked to put it, a "microcosm" of the universe. (2) Since there is a continuum and hierarchy in nature that reaches its highest level in human activity, the creativity of the artist will be the climax of all the powers inherent in nature itself. (3) Since the mental is the internalization of all the powers inherent in the material—since it is only the explicit and manifest form of all the forces implicit and latent in matter—the creativity of the artist will embody, express, and develop all the natural forces acting upon it. All these points mean that the creativity of the artist is nothing less than the *self*-realization and *self*-manifestation of the powers in nature; in other words, what the artist creates is what all of nature creates through him.

If we consider these implications of the organic theory of nature, it becomes clear that the ultimate source of the romantic aesthetic did not lie in its new epistemology but in its new metaphysics. While it is possible to describe the romantic aesthetic as the result of a new epistemology, and more specifically of a new account of the concept of truth, this epistemology has an essentially secondary importance because it has to be placed within the context of the romantics' general metaphysics. Their organic theory of nature had profound epistemological consequences, not the least of which was the production model of the truth. Since the subjective and objective no longer relate to one another as distinct entities but as expressions of a single force, it is no longer necessary to describe truth in terms of a correspondence between distinct entities; rather, the subjective is the actualization and embodiment of the objective, and so also its creation. The correspondence theory of truth was indeed more appropriate for the older (now *passé*) mechanistic concept of nature, where all entities are distinct from one another, and where they correspond to one another in terms of some formal resemblance.

The fundamental weakness of Frank's account of the romantic aesthetic is that it does not place it within the context of its metaphysics and *Naturphilosophie*. It is only when we so contextualize it, however, that we can fully understand the remarkable claims that the romantics make for the metaphysical powers of art. Ultimately, this is not very surprising. Given the close analogy between an organism and a work of art, the organic concept was virtually one with an aesthetic view of nature itself. When nature itself becomes a vast work of art, it stands to reason that the artist will have some privileged insight into it. Hence, in the end, romantic aesthetics was little more than the capstone of its *Naturphilosophie*.

CHAPTER 6

The Concept of *Bildung* in Early German Romanticism

1. Social and Political Context

In 1799 Friedrich Schlegel, the ringleader of the early romantic circle, stated, with uncommon and uncharacteristic clarity, his view of the *summum bonum*, the supreme value in life: "The highest good, and [the source of] everything that is useful, is culture *(Bildung)*."[1] Since the German word *Bildung* is virtually synonymous with education, Schlegel might as well have said that the highest good is education.

That aphorism, and others like it, leave no doubt about the importance of education for the early German romantics. It is no exaggeration to say that *Bildung*, the education of humanity, was *the* central goal, *the* highest aspiration, of the early romantics. All the leading figures of that charmed circle—Friedrich and August Wilhelm Schlegel, W. D. Wackenroder, Friedrich von Hardenberg (Novalis), F. W. J. Schelling, Ludwig Tieck, and F. D. Schleiermacher—saw in education their hope for the redemption of humanity. The aim of their common journal, the *Athenäum*, was to unite all their efforts for the sake of one single overriding goal: *Bildung*.[2]

The importance, and indeed urgency, of *Bildung* in the early romantic agenda is comprehensible only in its social and political context. The young romantics were writing in the 1790s, the decade of the cataclysmic changes wrought by the Revolution in France. Like so many of their generation, the romantics were initially very enthusiastic about the Revolution. Tieck, Novalis, Schleiermacher, Schelling, Hölderlin, and Friedrich Schlegel celebrated the storming of the Bastille as the dawn of a new age. They toasted the ideals of liberty, equality, and fraternity, and they swore that humanity would blossom only in a republic. Their enthusiasm was much more intense and persistent than many of their older contemporaries, such as Schiller,

Herder, and Wieland, who became disillusioned in 1793 after the execution of Louis XVI, when it became clear that France would not become a constitutional monarchy. The romantic fervor glowed unabated throughout the September massacres, the execution of the royal family, the invasion of the Rhineland, and even the Terror.

By the late 1790s, however, the romantic ardor began to dim. The constant instability in France, the readiness of the French to invade and conquer, and the onset of Napoleon's military dictatorship disillusioned them, as so many of their generation. The romantics became especially troubled by the anomie, egoism, and materialism of modern French society, which seemed to undermine all ethical and religious values. Their political views grew more conservative in the final years of the decade. They asserted the need for some form of elite rule, for a more educated class to direct and control the interests and energies of the people. Although they continued to affirm their republican ideals, they believed that the best state was a mixture of aristocracy, monarchy, and democracy.

The political problems in France soon crossed the Rhine, posing a serious crisis for the old Holy Roman Empire. It had become clear that Germany could not follow the path of France: the French attempt to introduce wholesale political reforms, without any prior change in attitudes, beliefs, and customs, had proven itself a failure. But it was also plain that there could be no going back to the past: the Revolution had raised hopes and expectations among the people that could no longer be satisfied by the old alliance of throne and alter. The people wanted to participate in the affairs of the state, to have some control over their own destiny, and they no longer could be pawned off with the reassurance that their prince loved them and ruled in their name. Yet how was it possible to satisfy the widespread demands for social and political change *and* not to slide down the path of perpetual chaos, as in France? That was the question every intelligent observer of the Revolution pondered, and the romantics were no exception.

The romantics' solution to this crisis lay with education. If all the chaos and bloodshed in France had shown anything, they argued, it is that a republic cannot succeed if the people are not ready for it. A republic has high moral ideals, which are worthless in practice if the people do not have either the knowledge or the will to live by them. For a republic to work, it must have responsible, enlightened, and virtuous citizens. If the people are to participate in public affairs, they must know their true interests and those of the state as a whole; and if they are to be responsible citizens, they must have the virtue and self-control to prefer the common good over their private interests. But such knowledge and such virtue are possible only through education, and indeed by a very deep and thoroughgoing one. Somehow, it was necessary to transform the obedient, passive, and benighted subject of an absolute monarchy into an autonomous, active, and enlightened citizen of a republic.

The romantic argument in behalf of education seems like common sense, and it had been advanced by almost every moderate thinker in the 1790s. Nevertheless, it was still controversial. The argument presupposes a classical doctrine that they inherited from Montesquieu: that "the principle" of a republic is virtue.[3] In his famous *Esprit des lois* Montesquieu had written, with the models of ancient Rome and Greece in mind, that the stability of a republic depends on the virtue of its citizens, their willingness to sacrifice their self-interest for the sake of the common good. This doctrine had been countered by no less than Kant himself, who contended in his essay *Zum ewigen Frieden* that a republic would be possible "even for a nation of devils." Kant's point was that even if everyone acted solely on their self-interest, they would consent to live according to a republican constitution, because it alone ensured that everyone could pursue their self-interest with a minimum of interference from others. Hence the diabolic Kantian republic required no education at all.

The romantics believed that education was indispensable, however, because they questioned one of the central premises of Kant's argument: that self-interest can be socially cohesive. To build a true community from the separate self-interests of individuals, they argued, is to square the political circle.[4] A self-interested agent would except himself from the laws when they could not be enforced, so that the only form of social control for a nation of devils would be repressive and authoritarian rule, a true Hobbesian Leviathan. There was no recourse, then, but to turn to education, which provided the only foundation for the state.

2. Education as the Highest Good

Although the social and political context explains why education became such a pressing issue for the romantics, it still does not account for why they regarded it as the highest good, the supreme value in life. To understand why they put education at the very pinnacle of their hierarchy of values, it is necessary to reconstruct their philosophical position regarding a classical philosophical problem.

The question of the highest good, of the supreme value in life, had been a central philosophical problem since antiquity, and indeed a major source of controversy among all schools of philosophy. This issue had lost none of its relevance and importance in eighteenth-century Germany, where it was a popular theme of religious and philosophical writing. Kant had posed it anew in his *Kritik der praktischen Vernunft,* and Fichte had made it a central issue of his influential 1794 lectures *Über die Bestimmung des Gelehrten.* The romantics simply continued with the tradition; the problem of the highest good appears often in the unpublished writings of Friedrich Schlegel, Novalis, Hölderlin, and Schleiermacher. There can be no doubt that, when he wrote his aphorism, Schlegel was taking a stand on this ancient question.

In the classical sense, first defined by Aristotle and then reformulated by Kant, the "highest good" has two meanings. First, it is a *final* end, a goal that does not derive its value from being the means to any other end. Second, it is a *complete* end, a goal that comprises all final ends, so that nothing can be added to it to give it more value.[5]

Prima facie the romantic view that education is the highest good appears very paradoxical, not to mention implausible. Surely, it seems, education cannot be the supreme value, since it is only the means for something else. After all, someone might well ask, what do we educate people for?

The paradox disappears, however, when we reconsider the German term *Bildung.* This word signifies two processes—learning and personal growth—but they are not understood apart from one another, as if education were only a means to growth. Rather, learning is taken to be constitutive of personal development, as part and parcel of how we become a human being in general and a specific individual in particular. If we regard education as part of a general process of *self-realization*—as the development of all one's characteristic powers as a human being and as an individual—then it is not difficult to understand why the romantics would regard it as at least a plausible candidate for the title of the highest good.

The romantics regarded self-realization as the highest good in both its classical senses. Self-realization is the *final* end, because it does not derive its value as a means to some higher end, such as the common good or the state. Although the romantics stressed the importance of education for the state, they did not value it simply as a means to that end; on the contrary, they insisted that self-realization is an end in itself, and they argued that the state should promote the self-realization of each of its citizens. Self-realization is also the *complete* end, since an individual who attains it lacks nothing, having achieved everything of value in life. In other words, a person who achieves self-realization attains the end of life itself, the very purpose of existence.

These were broad and bold claims, to be sure, yet they were rarely defended explicitly in the writings of the young romantics.[6] Nevertheless, we can begin to reconstruct their position when we consider their attitude toward the two competing theories of the highest good in the late eighteenth century. One of these was the hedonism of the English utilitarians and the French *philosophes,* who defined the highest good in terms of pleasure. The other was the moral stoicism of Kant, who regarded virtue as the final good, and happiness in accord with virtue as the complete good.

The romantics rejected hedonism because it did not encourage the development of those capacities characteristic of our humanity or individuality. Pleasure by itself cannot be the highest good since, in immoderation, it even harms us. If it has any value at all, then that is when it is the result of, or integral to, acting on our characteristic human powers.[7]

The romantic critique of hedonism is most explicit and emphatic in Schlegel's and Novalis's indictment of the lifestyle of modern bourgeois society. They use a very redolent term to characterize this way of life: *philistinism.*[8] The philistine, Novalis says, devotes himself to a life of comfort. He makes his life into a repetitive routine, and conforms to moral and social convention in order to have an easy life. If he values art, it is only for entertainment; and if he is religious, it is only to relieve his distress. In short, the sin of philistinism is that it robs us of our humanity and individuality.

If the romantics found hedonism too morally lax, they regarded Kant's ethics as too morally severe.[9] They saw two fundamental difficulties to the Kantian ethic. First, Kant had stressed reason at the expense of sensibility, ignoring how our senses are just as much a part of our humanity and just as in need of cultivation and development. It is not simply a purely rational being who acts morally, the romantics held, but the *whole* individual, who does his duty not *contrary to* but *from* his inclinations. Second, by emphasizing acting according to universal laws, Kant had failed to see the importance of individuality. The Kantian ideal of morality demanded that we develop a purely rational personality, which we all shared simply as intelligent beings, and so it endorsed uniformity. While such an ideal might be a sufficient analysis of morality, it could not be regarded as an adequate account of the highest good, which also demands the realization of individuality, that which makes me just this person rather than anyone else.

The ideal of *Bildung* was meant to rectify these shortcomings of Kantian ethics. A romantic education had two fundamental goals, each compensating for one of these flaws. One would unite and develop *all* the powers of a human being, forging all his or her disparate capacities into a *whole*. The other would develop not only our characteristic human powers—those shared by everyone as a human being—but also our individuality—those unique aptitudes and dispositions peculiar to each individual. These goals were, of course, closely linked: to develop all one's powers as a whole was inevitably and naturally to realize one's individuality, for individuality emerges in that unique synthesis, that special unity, of all one's human powers.

3. Aesthetic Education

To describe the romantic ideal of education in terms of human perfection, excellence, or self-realization, as I have done so far, is insufficient. This gives only its genus, not its *differentia specifica*. Perfection was not an ideal characteristic of romanticism alone, but it can be found in many strands of eighteenth-century German thought. The pietists (P. J. Spener, Johann Arndt), the classicists (C. M. Wieland, Goethe, Herder), and the Leibnizian–Wolffian school (Moses Mendelssohn, Alexander Baumgarten, Christian Wolff) all had their ideals of perfection. It is necessary to be more precise because, in basic respects, the romantics were critical of the ideals of their predecessors and contemporaries.

We come closer to a more accurate account of the romantic ideal if we describe it as *aesthetic* education. The term was first given currency by Schiller in his famous 1795 *Über die Ästhetische Erziehung des Menschen in einer Reihe von Briefen*, a work of seminal importance for the romantics. Much of the aestheticism of the romantic movement—its belief in the central role of art in cultural renewal—can trace its origin back to this work. The romantics followed Schiller in seeing art as the chief instrument for the education of mankind, and in viewing the artist as the very paragon of humanity.

Why did Schiller and the romantics give such importance to art? Why did they see it as the key to *Bildung?* We can reconstruct their reasoning only if, once again, we place it in their social and political context, specifically the social and political crisis of the 1790s.

Well before the 1790s, the leading thinkers of the *Sturm und Drang*—J. G. Hamann, J. G. Herder, Justus Möser, and eventually Schiller himself—had criticized the traditional *Aufklärung* for failing to provide a proper education for the people. The *Aufklärer* of the Leibnizian–Wolffian school had defined enlightenment in terms of imparting knowledge, of spreading clear and distinct concepts, among the public, as if education were only a matter of cultivating the intellect. But such a program of education—so it seemed to Herder and Möser as early as the 1770s—suffered from two serious short-comings. First, it did not encourage thinking for oneself, or spontaneity of thought, because it presupposed that someone else had already done all the thinking for one; the public were made into passive and unquestioning re-cipients of knowledge already acquired and concepts already clarified. Sec-ond, and even more problematically, it assumed that if people did under-stand the principles taught to them that they would be willing and able *to act* according to them; but such fatuous intellectualism ignored the classical problem of *akrasia:* that even if we know the good, we might not act accord-ing to it.

For all these thinkers, the Revolution provided striking confirmation of this diagnosis. The *philosophes* in France had been preaching the principles of reason to the people for decades, and they had proclaimed constitution after constitution. But all to no avail. The people were not ready for such high principles and lofty ideals. Rather than acting according to the principles of reason, they gave free reign to their own interests and passions. The result was plain for all to see: France was tumbling, sinking further into the abyss of chaos, strife, and bloodshed.

The lesson to be learned from the failure of the Enlightenment and the chaos of the Revolution, Schiller argued, is that it is not sufficient to educate the understanding alone. It is also necessary to cultivate feelings and desires, to develop a person's sensibility so that he or she are *inclined* to act according to the principles of reason. In other words, it was also essential *to inspire* the people, to touch their hearts and to arouse their imaginations, to get them to live by higher ideals.

Of course, in the past there had been a remedy for this problem. Religion, with its powerful myths and seductive mysteries, had provided a popular in-centive to morality because it could appeal directly to the heart and the imagination of the people. There was nothing like the image of a suffering Christ, a resurrected Lazarus, or an angry Jehovah to edify the virtuous and to chasten the sinful. But, by the late 1790s, this traditional source of moral authority was on the wane, and indeed on the verge of collapse. Here the *Aufklärung* had been only too successful. Its ruthless and relentless criticism of the Bible, of the traditional proofs for the existence of God, and of the authority of the clergy had left little standing of the old religion, which was now condemned as prejudice, superstition, and myth. Clearly, there was an enormous vacuum to be filled. The obvious failure of Robespierre's contrived and artificial cult of reason had made this all the more apparent.

Art became so important to Schiller and the romantics because they saw it as the only means to resolve this crisis. They argued that while philosophy cannot stimulate action nor religion convince reason, art has the power to inspire us to act according to reason. Because it so strongly appeals to the imagination, and because it so deeply effects our feelings, art can move people to live by the high moral ideals of a republic.

Ultimately, then, the romantics sought to replace the traditional role of religion with art as the incentive and stimulus for morality. Hence they developed ideas for a modern mythology, a new Bible, and a restored church. Now the artist would take over the ancient function of the priest.

This case for the power of art to educate humanity was first put forward by Schiller, but it soon became a *leitmotiv* of the romantic movement. It is a central theme of Novalis's *Heinrich von Ofterdingen*, of Friedrich Schlegel's *Ideen*, of Wackenroder's *Herzensergießungen eines kunstliebenden Klosterbruders*, and of Tieck's *Franz Sternbalds Wanderungen*. Nowhere does it emerge with more simplicity and clarity, however, than in a later work of high romanticism, Heinrich von Kleist's short story *Heilige Cäcilie oder die Macht der Musik*. According to the story, which takes place during the early Reformation in Holland, four brothers, who are fanatical Protestants, organize a mob to attack a convent; its despairing and defenseless nuns appeal to Saint Cecilia, the patron saint of music, who inspires them to sing. Such is the beauty of their *Gloria* that the plunderers fall on their knees, confess their sins, convert, and then finally go mad, spending the rest of their days in a sanitorium, singing every evening the *Gloria*. Of course, this was a myth all of its own; but there can be no doubt that it expressed the highest hopes, and most fervent wishes, of the romantic soul.

4. The Role of Art

It might seem as if the romantics only traded one form of naiveté for another—namely, the Enlightenment confidence in reason for their own faith in art. Both beliefs seem quixotic because they ascribe exaggerated power to the realm of culture. It is very idealistic, to say the least, to assume that we can become better people simply by listening to music, reading novels, and attending plays. If art does have that effect, one is tempted to say, that is probably because people are already predisposed to it, and so already educated for it. But then the whole case for art is caught in a vicious circle: art educates humanity only if people are already educated.

The charge of naiveté is one of the most common objections to Schiller's argument, and the reputation of the romantics for hopeless idealism is largely based on it. But this criticism rests on a very superficial understanding of the role of art in romantic education. When the romantics wrote of aesthetic education they were not simply referring to the effect works of art have on moral character. They had something more in mind. But what?

Exactly how the romantics understood aesthetic education becomes clear from a close reading of Schiller's *Briefe*. It is striking that, in the tenth letter, Schiller virtually concedes the whole charge of naivité.[10] He admits that art will educate only the virtuous, and he notes that the periods when art flourished were also those when morals declined. But, after accepting these points, Schiller then turns his argument in a new direction. The question for him is not whether art has an effect on moral character, but whether beauty is an essential component of human perfection itself. Schiller's argument is that if we perfect ourselves—if we form our various powers into a whole— then we will become like works of art. To perfect ourselves is to unify the form of our reason with the content of our sensibility; but the unity of form and content is what is characteristic of beauty itself. Hence aesthetic education does not consist in having our characters formed by works of art but in making our characters into works of art.

Schiller's most detailed account of how a person can become a work of art appears in his treatise *Anmut und Würde*.[11] Here he puts forward his ideal of "the beautiful soul" *(die schöne Seele)*, the person whose character is a work of art because all his or her actions exhibit grace. For Schiller, a graceful action is one that shows no sign of constraint—whether that of a physical need or a moral imperative—and that reveals the spontaneity and harmony of a person's whole character. Such an action does not stem from sensibility alone, as if it were the result of natural need, and still less from reason alone, as if it were the product of a moral command; rather it flows from the whole character, from reason and sensibility acting in unison. The beautiful soul does not act from duty contrary to inclination, or from inclination contrary to duty, but from inclination according to duty. Such a spontaneous inclination is not, however, the product of the desires and feelings that are given by nature, but the result of our moral education, the discipline and training of virtue. In a graceful action, then, our desires and feelings are neither repressed according to reason, nor indulged according to sensibility, but refined and ennobled, or, to use a modern term, "sublimated."

Schiller's ideal of the beautiful soul gives a completely new perspective on how art motivates moral action. It is not that contemplating works of art inspires us to do good deeds, but that there is an aesthetic pleasure inherent in human excellence, which serves as an incentive to attain and maintain it. The stimulant to moral perfection does not derive from any work of art but simply from the pleasure involved in the exercise of characteristic human activities. Like most moralists, Schiller maintains that virtue brings its own reward, a unique kind of pleasure; he simply adds that this pleasure is essentially aesthetic, because achieving human perfection is like creating a work of art.

Schiller's argument in behalf of aesthetic education ultimately depends on a theory of beauty as perfection. Such a theory could easily be generalized and extended to whatever is capable of perfection, whether it is an object in nature, an individual person, or the state and society itself. This was a temptation that neither Schiller nor the romantics could resist. They broadened their case for the primacy of the aesthetic in human life by also applying it to the state and society. They argued that the perfect society or state is also a work of art. In the final letter of the *Briefe,* for example, Schiller wrote of his utopia as an *aesthetic* state *(ästhetischen Staat),* which, like a work of art, unites the different members of society into a harmonious whole.[12] In his *Glauben und Liebe* Novalis imagined a *poetic* state in which the monarch is the poet of poets, the director of a vast public stage in which all citizens are actors.[13] And in his early manuscript *Versuch einer Theorie des geselligen Betragens* Schleiermacher imagined an ideal society in which individuals form a beautiful whole through the free interaction of personalities and the mutual exchange of ideas.[14] Schiller, Novalis, and Schleiermacher all assume that the perfect society or state is like a work of art because there is an organic unity between the individual and the social whole, which is governed neither by physical nor moral constraints but only free interaction.

The early romantic ideal of utopia was therefore the creation of a social or political work of art. This aesthetic whole would be a *Bildungsanstalt,* a society in which people would educate one another through the free exchange of their personalities and ideas. The romantic *salons,* in Berlin and Jena, were fledgling attempts to put this ideal into practice. If life were only one grand *salon,* one long learning experience in which everyone participated, the romantics believed, then society would indeed become a work of art, and this life "the most beautiful of all possible worlds."

5. Education and Freedom

We come closer to the *differentia specifica* of romantic education when we describe it as aesthetic. Yet we are still far from our goal. The problem is that even the ideal of aesthetic education—though central to the romantics— was not unique to, or characteristic of, them. There were many thinkers in eighteenth-century Germany who described human perfection in aesthetic terms and stressed the need to cultivate human sensibility as well as reason. This line of thought can be found in the Leibnizian–Wolffian school, and especially in the writings of its most outstanding aesthetician, Alexander Baumgarten.[15] By the early eighteenth century the connection of virtue with beauty had already become a venerable tradition: it was a favorite theme of Shaftesbury and Hutcheson, who had an enormous influence in Germany. Schiller's theme of the beautiful soul also had a proud ancestry, which could trace its origins back to pietism and that "German Voltaire," C. M. Wieland.[16]

This raises the question: What, if anything, is characteristic of a *romantic* aesthetic education? How, if at all, did it differ from the forms of aesthetic education so prevalent in the eighteenth century?

Although there are clear points of continuity between the Leibnizian–Wolffian tradition and the romantics, there is also a drastic and dramatic break between them. That break is made by Kant's critical philosophy, which had sundered the link between virtue and beauty so carefully forged and crafted by the Leibnizian–Wolffian school. In the *Kritik der praktischen Vernunft* Kant had argued that the basis and incentive for moral action must derive from pure reason alone, independent of all considerations of pleasure, aesthetic or otherwise. And in the *Kritik der Urteilskraft* he stressed that the pleasure of beauty is completely disinterested, having its characteristic qualities independent of all moral and physical ends. When we experience an object as beautiful, Kant contended, we take pleasure in the sheer contemplation of its form, but we do not consider whether it conforms to moral or physical purposes.[17] In both these works Kant attacked the worth of the concept of perfection—the keystone of the ethical and aesthetic thought of the Leibnizian-Wolffian school—as a criterion of morality or beauty.

The sheer prestige of the critical philosophy in the 1790s in Germany would seem to be sufficient to bury, once and for all, the seductive equation of virtue and beauty, morality and aesthetics, which had entranced so many thinkers in the eighteenth century. But the very opposite is the case. Paradoxically, Kant's critique led to Schiller's reformulation and transformation of this equation, which gave it a new lease on life. In his unpublished but seminal 1793 *Kallias oder über die Schönheit*, Schiller resynthesizes on a new basis the realms of art and morality, of beauty and virtue, which had been so disastrously divided by Kant.[18] He endorses some of the negative conclusions of the Kantian critique: that art must be autonomous, serving neither moral nor physical ends, and that the concept of perfection, understood in the classical sense as unity in multiplicity, is insufficient to explain beauty. Nevertheless, Schiller argues against Kant that beauty is more than simply a subjective quality, such as the pleasure of contemplation, and he insists instead that it is an objective feature of an object itself. Whether or not an object is beautiful, Schiller contends, depends on whether it is *self-determining*, that is, whether it is free from external constraint and acts according to its inherent nature alone. Since self-determination is equivalent to freedom, and since a beautiful object presents, exhibits, or reveals this quality to the senses, beauty is nothing more nor less than *freedom in appearance.*

In thus defining beauty, Schiller intends to give a new foundation to Kant's concept of aesthetic autonomy, its independence from moral and physical ends. But, ironically, such a definition also provides a new connection between art and morality. For the self-determination of the aesthetic object—its independence from all forms of constraint, whether moral or physical—means that it can serve as a symbol of freedom, which, according to the critical philosophy itself, is the fundamental concept of morality. Hence Schiller, quite self-consciously and deliberately, rejoins the realms of art and morality, though now the connecting link between these domains is provided by the concept of freedom rather than that of perfection.

This does not mean that Schiller completely rejects the old concept of perfection, which he continues to use and to describe in the traditional terms as a unity in multiplicity; but it is important to see that this concept now has a new underpinning: the concept of freedom itself. Perfection is now defined in terms of self-determination, acting according to the necessity of one's nature independent of all constraint.

The romantic concept of aesthetic education has its roots in Schiller's redefinition of the moral role of art. What is central to and characteristic of the romantic concept is the Schillerian thesis that the end of aesthetic education is freedom. Like Schiller, the romantics maintain that to become an aesthetic whole, to make one's life a work of art, it is necessary to realize one's nature as a spontaneous and free subject. Since beauty consists in freedom in appearance, we attain beauty only when our moral character expresses freedom itself.

That *Bildung* consists in the development of freedom is a point much stressed by both Friedrich Schlegel and Novalis. Schlegel simply defined *Bildung* as "the development of independence" *(Entwicklung der Selbständigkeit)*, famously arguing that what is characteristic of *Bildung* in the modern world, in contrast to the ancient, is precisely its striving for freedom.[19] The purpose of our lives, he maintained, is to realize our nature as self-determining beings, where self-determination consists in constantly attempting to determine what one is, and then realizing that one is nothing but the activity of constantly attempting to determine what one is.[20] Novalis was no less emphatic and explicit than Schlegel: "All education *(Bildung)* leads to nothing else than what one can call freedom, although this should not designate a mere concept but the creative ground of all existence."[21]

It is this emphasis on freedom, then, that separates the romantic account of aesthetic education from its historical antecedents in the Leibnizian–Wolffian school. But is this not what we should expect? The rallying cry of anyone who came of age in the 1790s was freedom. The problem with the old *Aufklärer* of the Leibnizian-Wolffian school, the romantics complained, is that they had abandoned their freedom by compromising with the social and political status quo. A romantic education would be one fitting for the 1790s: the liberation of the spirit from all forms of social and political oppression.

6. The Awakening of the Senses

The chief aim of aesthetic education, whether in the romantic or Leibnizian–Wolffian tradition, was the cultivation of sensibility. Normally contrasted with reason, sensibility was defined in a very broad sense to include the powers of desire, feeling, and perception. The underlying premise behind the program of aesthetic education was that sensibility could be developed, disciplined, and refined no less than reason itself. Long before the 1790s, the

Sturmer und Dränger had complained that the *Aufklärung* had failed to educate this faculty. Since their main task was to combat superstition, prejudice, and enthusiasm, the *Aufklärer* had naturally devoted most of their attention to the development of reason. But, the *Sturmer und Dränger* objected, this was to neglect one-half of our humanity.

The romantics shared this criticism of the *Aufklärung*, and in this regard their concern with sensibility was continuous with the tradition of the *Sturm und Drang*. Like Schiller and the *Sturmer und Dränger*, the romantics wanted to cultivate sensibility as an *aesthetic* faculty. Their aim was to educate the senses, specifically their power to perceive the beauty of the world. This faculty could be made more sensitive, refined, and acute, they believed, so that a person's life could be greatly enriched and ennobled.

It is important to see, however, that there was something else unique to, and characteristic of, the romantic program of aesthetic education, and that in an important respect they went beyond even Schiller and the *Sturm und Drang*. What is distinctive of their program is not *that*, but *how*, they wanted to educate sensibility. Their aim was, in a word, *to romanticize* the senses. But what does this redolent word mean?

The best clue comes from Novalis. To romanticize the world, he explains in an unpublished fragment, is to make us aware of the magic, mystery, and wonder of the world; it is to educate the senses to see the ordinary as extraordinary, the familiar as strange, the mundane as sacred, the finite as infinite.[22] The romantics wanted to break outside the confines of our ordinary and mundane perception of the world, where we automatically categorize everything according to common concepts, and where we see things only as objects of use. Their goal was to develop our power of *contemplation* so that we can see things anew, as they are in themselves and for their own sakes, apart from their utility and common meaning.

The romantics sought to romanticize not only our external senses—our powers of perception of the external world—but also our internal ones—our sensitivity to the world within. They attempted to direct our attention to our inner depths, to the hidden recesses of the self, no less than to the world without, the realms of society and nature. For the romantics, self-realization was essentially self-discovery, an exploration of one's inner depths. As Novalis puts the point: "We dream of a journey through the universe. But is the universe then not in us? We do not know the depths of our spirit. Inward goes the secret path. Eternity with its worlds, the past and future, is in us or nowhere."[23]

It was this conviction that later inspired Novalis to write *Heinrich von Ofterdingen*—the major *Bildungsroman* of the romantic school—as an antipode to Goethe's earlier work in the same genre, *Wilhelm Meisters Lehrjahre*. While Wilhelm's apprenticeship consists in his adventures in the wider world, his encounters with extraordinary characters and difficult situations, Heinrich's education comes from unraveling the secret of his own dreams. There are two ways to educate the soul, Heinrich explains: one of them "the path of experience," which is very indirect and leads to only worldly wisdom or prudence, while the other is "the path of inner contemplation," which is very direct and results in spiritual self-realization.

There was a grand ambition behind this program for the reawakening of the senses, whether internal or external. The romantics aim was to *reunify* man with himself, nature, and others, so that he would once again feel at home in his world. According to the romantic philosophy of history, early man had been at one with himself, with others, and with nature; this unity was purely natural, and did not depend on any efforts of his own. Inevitably and tragically, however, this primal harmony had been torn apart by the development of civilization. Man had become alienated from others as a result of the increasing competition of civil society; he had become divided within himself with the rise of the division of labor; and he had become estranged from nature after the sciences had demystified it, making it into an object to be dominated and controlled for human benefit. The task of modern man was to *recreate* on a self-conscious and rational level that unity with ourselves, others, and nature that had once been *given* to early man on a naive and intuitive level.

Such indeed was the vocation of the romantic poet, who would attempt to revive our lost unity with ourselves, with nature, and with others. The key to recreating that unity consisted in the *remystification* of the world, in romanticizing the senses, because only when we were reawakened to the beauty, mystery, and magic of the world would we reidentify ourselves with it.

Not surprisingly, this demand for a reawakening of the senses led to the reappraisal of mysticism among the romantics. This sympathy for mysticism appears in many works of the early romantic school, in Novalis's *Die Lehrling zu Sais*, Schleiermacher's *Reden über die Religion*, Friedrich Schlegel's *Ideen*, and Schelling's *System des transcendentalen Idealismus*. All these works argue that we have a spiritual sense, a power of contemplation or intellectual intuition, which transcends our discursive reason and brings us into direct contact with ourselves, others, and nature itself. They all praise the power of the artist to express these intuitions, and to revive our slumbering powers of contemplation.

Naturally, this new mysticism went hand-in-hand with a revival of religion in the romantic circle, which became especially apparent after the publication of Schleiermacher's *Reden* in 1799. Rather than regarding religion as a primitive form of metaphysics or morality, as the *Aufkärung* had done, the romantics saw it as a specific form of contemplation or perception of the universe. The essence of religion, Schleiermacher argues in his *Reden*, is the intuition of the universe. This religious reawakening has often been criticized as a relapse into the ideology of the *ancien régime*, but it is important to see it in the context of the romantics' general concern with *Bildung*. They valued religion chiefly as an instrument of aesthetic education, as a means of reawakening the senses.

7. The Power of Love

The romantic program for the education of sensibility involved not only the cultivation of the senses, but also, more importantly, the development of "the faculty of desire." Its aim was to educate not only our powers to perceive, but also those to feel and desire. For the romantics, to educate feeling and desire meant essentially one thing: to awaken, nurture, and refine the power of love.

What especially inspired the early romantics—what, more than anything else, gave them their sense of purpose and identity—was their rediscovery of the lost power of love. It was their view that this vital source of our humanity had been forgotten, repressed, or ignored for far too long, and that it was now time to remember, reclaim, and revive it. Owing to the rationalism of the *Aufklärung* and to the legalism of the Kantian–Fichtean ethics, love had lost its once pivotal role in ethics and aesthetics, the pride of place it once held in the Christian tradition. The romantics saw it as their mission to restore the sovereignty of love to the realms of morals, politics, and art.

The central concept of romantic ethics is love. The romantics gave it all the stature once accorded to reason in the *Aufklärung* and Kantian–Fichtean ethics. It is now love, rather than reason, that provides the source and sanction of the moral law. Love, Schlegel tells us,[24] is to the law as the spirit is to the letter: it creates what reason merely codifies. The power of love indeed transcends all moral rules: while love inspires, the law represses; while love forgives, the law punishes. Love is also a much more powerful "determining ground of the will" (as Kant would call it), a much more effective stimulant to moral action, than reason. The bonds that tie the individual to the community and state are not the universal norms of reason but the affection and devotion of love.

Love had a no less pivotal place in romantic aesthetics. It is the spirit of love, Schlegel writes, that must be "invisibly visible" everywhere in romantic art.[25] The artist could romanticize our senses only through the inspiring power of love. We can remystify the world—we can rediscover its lost beauty, mystery, and magic—only if we see all things in the spirit of love. It is through love that we see ourselves in nature and others, and so again identify with the world and become at home with it once more.

The romantic program of *Bildung*, of aesthetic education, stressed the cultivation of love, the development of the capacity of every individual to give and receive affection. This was essential to self-realization, to the development of our humanity and individuality, the romantics believed, because love is the very core of our humanity, the very center of our individuality. "Only through love, and the consciousness of love," Friedrich Schlegel wrote, "does a human being become a human being."[26] Love was indeed the key to reconciling and unifying the two warring sides of our nature, the intellectual and physical, the rational and the emotional. It was not simply a physical urge, but a much deeper spiritual desire: the longing to return to that golden age when we were at one with ourselves, others, and nature.

Although the romantic rediscovery of love was based on an reappreciation of its spiritual significance, it is important to see that they never neglected or debased its physical roots. The education of desire meant arousing and cultivating not only our spirituality, but also our sensuality. That we must learn to accept and enjoy our sexuality, that we must see sexuality as part of love, and that we must love someone sexually to be fulfilled human beings were the central themes of Friedrich Schlegel's novel *Lucinde*, which shocked the public of his day. There Schlegel protests against repressive social norms that view sexuality as legitimate only in marriage, and that regard marriage as a matter of domestic convenience. He could see nothing wrong with divorce and a *ménage à quatre* if it led to the development of one's individuality and humanity, and he could see nothing right with a marriage and chastity if it resulted in repression and indignity.

An essential theme of Schlegel's campaign for sexual liberation is his attack on sexual stereotypes. He criticizes the prevalent sexual norms that limit men to an active and aggressive role and women to a passive and submissive one. To better enjoy our sexuality, he advises couples to switch these roles. There is no reason within human nature itself why men cannot develop the passive, tender, and sentimental sides, and women develop their active, dominant, and rational sides. Masculinity and femininity are properties of each person, regardless of their sex.

8. A Final Paradox

The romantic philosophy of education ends with a paradox. We have seen that there was nothing more important to the romantics than *Bildung*, the education of humanity. This was the central theme and goal of their ethics, aesthetics, and politics. But, from a more practical perspective, there seems to be nothing less important to the romantics than education. When it comes to concrete suggestions about how to educate humanity—about what specific institutional arrangements are to be made—the romantics fell silent. There is very little in the writings of the romantics about the social and political structure to be created to ensure the education of humanity.[27]

Such silence, however, was more the result of principle than negligence. The reason for their taciturnity was their deep conviction that the self-realization of the individual must derive from his freedom, which must not be impaired by social and political arrangements. It is for this reason that Friedrich Schlegel would write: "Humanity cannot be inoculated, and virtue cannot be taught or learned, other than through friendship and love with capable and genuine people, and other than through contact with ourselves, with the divine within us."[28]

The paradox of German romanticism is its utter commitment and devotion to the education of humanity, and yet its recognition that it cannot and ought not do anything to achieve it. We are left, then, with a striking gap between theory and practice, which it was the very purpose of romanticism to overcome.

CHAPTER 7

Friedrich Schlegel:
The Mysterious Romantic

1. The Mystery

Scholars have often recognized Friedrich Schlegel's leading role in the development of early German romanticism *(Frühromantik)*. He has generally been given credit for formulating the concept of "romantic poetry" *(romantische Poesie)*, which became so characteristic of this movement. To be sure, Schlegel did not invent the concept, which had a long history in German aesthetics before him; but he did make it the defining aesthetic ideal of the romantic circle.[1] Thanks to him, *romantische Poesie* became the shibboleth of the early romantic movement.

But if Schlegel's role in the rise of *Frühromantik* is clear and uncontroversial, the opposite must be said about his own philosophical development. There has always been a deep mystery surrounding the origins of Schlegel's romantic aesthetic. Namely, it seems almost impossible to understand why Schlegel became a romantic in the first place. Schlegel's manifesto for romantic poetry in his famous 1798 *Athenäumsfragment* no. 116 seems to be a complete *volte face*, a radical reversal of his own neoclassical aesthetic, which he had defended passionately only a few years earlier in his neoclassical writings. In his 1795 *Über das Studium der griechischen Poesie*, the so-called *Studiumaufsatz*, Schlegel had already formulated, if only in crude outline, his later concept of romantic poetry.[2] Yet if in 1799 Schlegel embraced romantic poetry, in 1795 he repudiated it.

Whence this reversal in attitude toward romantic poetry? Why did Schlegel come to celebrate what he had once despised? Schlegel himself offers no explanation. And his extremely complex intellectual development presents a bewildering plethora of tantalizing clues and false leads. Yet there is a reward for trying to find one's way through the Schlegelian labyrinth.

For if we can determine why Schlegel reversed himself, we will also know something about the rationale for his romantic aesthetic. Given Schlegel's general historical significance, this should shed a little light on the genesis of *Frühromantik* itself.

Schlegel's conversion to romanticism has long been the subject of speculation and controversy. Roughly, there have been two opposing schools of opinion. One school stresses the *discontinuity* between the neoclassical and romantic phase, claiming that Schlegel's conversion must have been the result of some external influence.[3] Various candidates have been cast in the role of external agent: Goethe, Fichte, or Schiller, or some combination of them. The other school emphasizes the *continuity* between the early and later Schlegel, explaining the genesis of Schlegel's romanticism from entirely immanent or internal causes, such as his early fondness for romantic literature or the implicit logic of his philosophy of history. Sometimes these scholars stress the continuity of Schlegel's development to the point of denying that there was a *volte face* in the first place.[4] The emergence of Schlegel's romanticism, they maintain, was more a change of emphasis than a reversal in doctrine.

My task here is to reexamine the old debates about the sources of Schlegel's romanticism. My reasons for doing so are twofold. First, the availability of new sources, especially the publication of Schlegel's philosophical and literary notebooks, which appeared (respectively) in the *Kritische Ausgabe* of Schlegel's *Werke* only in 1963 and 1981.[5] These notebooks were not available when the battle lines of the old dispute were drawn; yet they hold the key to Schlegel's intellectual development from 1795 to 1798, the crucial years for his conversion to romanticism. Second, there has been much recent research on German philosophy in Jena during the late 1790s, the context in which Schlegel's conversion took place. This research program was first conceived by Dieter Henrich, but then developed in great detail by Marcelo Stamm, Wilhelm Baum, and Manfred Frank.[6] Their work has shed much light on Schlegel's formative years in Jena, and more specifically on how his romantic aesthetic grew out of a philosophical climate highly critical of foundationalism.

If we consider Schlegel's development in the light of his notebooks and his general intellectual context in Jena, it becomes clear that the decisive factor in his conversion to romanticism was his *critique* of Fichte's philosophy. This is the diametrical opposite of the traditional view, which maintains that Schlegel's romantic aesthetic was nothing more than a poetic application of

Fichte's *Wissenschaftslehre, "dichterisch übersteigerter Fichte."*[7] Contrary to this still common view, it was not Schlegel's adoption but his rejection of the *Wissenschaftslehre* that drove him toward his romantic aesthetic. Schlegel's shift from neoclassicism to romanticism parallels precisely—both chronologically and logically—his earlier endorsement and later repudiation of Fichte's foundationalism, the doctrine that it is possible to establish the first principles of all knowledge and to construct on their basis a complete system. While Schlegel's neoclassicism rested on his faith in Fichte's foundationalism, his romanticism grew out of his *critique* of Fichte's foundationalism. Once Schlegel became convinced that it is impossible to establish infallible first principles or a complete system of knowledge, he abandoned his faith in the possibility of an objective aesthetics, which was the fundamental article of faith of his neoclassicism. Romanticism began to seem more appealing to Schlegel precisely because it did not require the dogmatic faith in the attainability of first principles and a complete system of knowledge. Rather, the infinite longing and striving of the romantic aesthetic seemed entirely appropriate to an antifoundationalist epistemological doctrine that stressed the purely regulative status of first principles and complete systems. To be sure, the concept of romantic poetry was already in place in Schlegel's early classical writings; yet he reinterpreted and reappraised it in the light of his antifoundationalist epistemology. In a nutshell, Schlegel's romanticism was the aesthetics of antifoundationalism.

2. State of the Question

Before attempting to account for Schlegel's *volte face*, it is necessary to consider the precise problem in need of investigation. Since those scholars who stress the continuity of Schlegel's development sometimes deny that there was a radical reversal in Schlegel's views, they question whether there is really a phenomenon to be explained after all. It is of the first importance, then, to show that there is indeed a problem, and to explain in what precisely it consists.

The mystery of Schlegel's conversion arose from two apparent facts. First, the close affinity between Schlegel's early and later concept of romantic poetry. Second, Schlegel's radical change of attitude toward romantic poetry, which he first condemned and then celebrated. Those who defend the continuity of Schlegel's development emphasize the point that the concept of romantic poetry is already present in his early writings; but it is necessary to stress that this is not really the question at issue. This point is fully recognized even by those who stress the discontinuity of Schlegel's development.[8] The problem is to explain *a change in attitude* toward romantic poetry, not the development of a completely new concept. Those who insist on the discontinuity of Schlegel's development are not necessarily committed to the view that he created a completely new concept of poetry during his romantic phase.

But the question remains: Are these "facts" only apparent? Is the early concept of romantic poetry the same as the later one? And, if so, did Schlegel really change his attitude toward romantic poetry?

If we closely reexamine Schlegel's early concept of romantic poetry in the *Studiumaufsatz*, there is indeed a remarkable resemblance between his early and later concepts. Although in his early neoclassical writings Schlegel usually uses the terms "interesting" or "modern poetry," and only very occasionally "romantic" poetry,[9] these terms still signify, at least in *many* striking respects, what he later meant by "romantic" poetry. Schlegel ascribes the following characteristics to interesting poetry: (1) a constant confusion or mixtures of genres (I, 219); (2) an insatiable longing, an eternal striving (I, 219, 223); (3) the presence of persiflage or irony (I, 334); (4) a focus on the individual, the differences between things, at the expense of the universal, the similarities between things (I, 222); (5) a lack of concern with pure beauty and an attempt to make art serve the interests of morality and science (I, 220); (6) an absence of self-restraint, where goals are reached only to be transcended (I, 219–220, 230); (7) an attempt to portray a whole age, the culture of an epoch (I, 226–227); and (8) an attempt to fuse philosophy and poetry (I, 242–243). Notoriously, all these features of interesting poetry resurface, essentially unchanged, in Schlegel's mature account of romantic poetry in the *Kritische Fragmente, Athenäumsfragmente,* and *Gespräch über Poesie.*

All this does not mean, of course, that there are not some important differences between interesting and romantic poetry. While both reveal a concern with the individual, Schlegel later stresses how romantic poetry also strives for an ideal of totality, universality, and wholeness. Furthermore, Schlegel does not entirely reject his earlier concept of classical poetry; rather, he attempts to integrate elements of it into his new concept of romantic poetry, which would be a constantly evolving and infinitely elastic classicism.[10] Finally, Schlegel's later concept of romantic poetry is more philosophical than his earlier concept of interesting poetry, which has a more historical and aesthetic meaning.

It is equally clear that Schlegel also *reversed* his attitude toward romantic poetry. In his 1797 *Kritische Fragmente* Schlegel explicitly repudiated his earlier neoclassicism, and he even expressly disavowed his "early philosophical musicals."[11] Flatly contrary to the neoclassicism of the *Studiumaufsatz*, *Athenäumsfragment* no. 116 declares that *all* poetry should be romantic: "The romantic form of poetry is the only form that is more than a form and poetry itself; for in a certain sense all poetry is or should be romantic."[12] Schlegel now describes romantic poetry in the same terms as interesting poetry: it consists in the use of irony, the mixture of genres, the striving or longing for infinity, the attempt to fuse poetry and philosophy, and the attempt to portray the individual and a whole age. Yet now Schlegel casts all these characteristics in a positive light, portraying them as necessary elements of all true poetry.

3. Continuity and Discontinuity in Schlegel's Development

The similarities between Schlegel's early and later concept of romantic poetry, and his change in attitude toward it, provide sufficient warrant to talk about a reversal in Schlegel's development. Still, this is not the end of the dispute, for those who stress the continuity of Schlegel's development sometimes admit that there is a reversal in attitude. But, for two reasons, they tend to understate or downplay it. First, they point out that Schlegel's *predeliction* for romantic poetry, and not only his concept of it, was also present in his early neoclassical writings. Second, they also argue that Schlegel's classical aesthetic was inconsistent with many of his more fundamental doctrines, especially his philosophy of history. On these grounds, they conclude that there was not a radical or fundamental break in Schlegel's development after all. For when Schlegel later converted to romanticism he did nothing more than reveal his more basic preferences and draw the proper conclusion from his more fundamental doctrines.

Certainly, the young Schlegel did have a fondness for modern literature, which did not sit well with his professed neoclassicism. Nowhere is this predilection more apparent than in his judgment on Shakespeare in the *Studiumaufsatz*.[13] Although Schlegel regards Shakespeare as "the apex of modern poetry"—the very poetry he abhors—he also deeply, almost secretly, admires him. Thus he writes that Shakespeare unites "the most enticing blossoms of romantic fantasy, the gigantic greatness of the gothic heroic period, the finest traits of modern sociability, and the deepest and richest poetic philosophy" (I, 249). As if this were not enough, Schlegel then goes on to defend Shakespeare against narrow neoclassical critics, who fail to understand him by judging him according to narrow rules (I, 249–250). Schlegel also venerates that other great master of modern poetry, Dante, whose *Divine Comedy* he finds to be "sublime" (I, 233). Such, indeed, is Schlegel's fondness for modern literature that, in writing the retrospective preface to the *Studiumaufsatz*, he defends himself against the charge of a one-sided classicism by openly confessing his love for early modern literature (I, 208).

Doubtless, there are also some deep tensions in Schlegel's early writings, almost all of which arose from the conflict between his narrow and fanatical neoclassicism and his broad and liberal philosophy of history. While his neoclassical aesthetics claims *absolute* validity—the right to judge *all* works of art according to the criteria of order, harmony, and proportion—his philosophy of history limits these standards to the classical epoch alone. According to his philosophy of history, the two fundamental epochs of Western history—ancient and modern culture—are directed by completely opposed principles.[14] The basic principle behind ancient culture is nature or instinct *(Trieb)*, where the ends of action are set by nature and the understanding finds only the means for their fulfillment. The central principle behind modern culture, however, is freedom or reason, where the ends of action are set by our own spontaneous activity and where nature provides only the means for their fulfillment. Corresponding to these opposed principles, each culture developed its unique conception of history. While ancient culture had a *cyclical* view of history, because nature acts in cycles from birth to death, modern culture has a *progressive* concept of history, because complete freedom is an infinite ideal that we can only approach through endless striving.

The opposing principles of classical and modern culture seem to imply that it would be absurd to judge one culture, and its forms of literature, in terms of another. Sure enough, Schlegel himself sometimes draws just this conclusion. In his *Studiumaufsatz* he admits at one point that it would be inappropriate to expect the infinite striving of modern culture to end in the classical ideal of beauty (I, 255). Then, in an unpublished 1795 essay,[15] Schlegel is perfectly explicit in affirming the autonomy of each culture (I, 640). While he claims that the path toward reviving modern culture lies in imitating the ancients, he also stresses that all true imitation comes from "inner independence" and "free appropriation" (I, 638). We are warned not to live like beggars who live off the alms of the past (I, 640). Schlegel goes so far as to limit the role of ancient art to providing only examples for modern art. All that we receive from the ancients is the *materials* for a new culture, he explains, while from the moderns we learn the *direction* it should take (I, 638).

There are other passages from Schlegel's neoclassical writings where he states or implies that the principles of modern culture are even superior to those of classical culture. He defines *Bildung*, for example, as the development of human freedom, a definition that would limit all culture to the modern epoch alone (I, 230). While he praises the Greeks for attaining aesthetic perfection, he also stresses that they could do so only because their goals were so limited. Indeed, the very achievement of their goals meant that the eventual decline of their culture was inevitable (I, 35). The greatness of modern culture, however, consists in the fact that its goals are infinite, demanding nothing less than a constant striving (I, 640). Our shortcomings are our hopes, as he once put it, because even though modern man cannot achieve his ideals they are infinite.[16]

Given Schlegel's secret liking for Shakespeare and Dante, and given his statements about modern culture's independence from, and even superiority over, ancient culture, it would seem only natural for him to have a positive attitude toward modern romantic literature. The conversion to romantic poetry therefore seems entirely implicit in his early neoclassical phase. It arises less from a break with the past than from his immanent development. It seems as if all Schlegel did in proclaiming his romantic aesthetic is reveal his true colors and shed the pose or disguise of neoclassicism.

There can be no doubt, then, that, to an important extent, Schlegel's romanticism was already latent in his earlier views. It is worthwhile to stress the point if only because talking about Schlegel's break with his past tends to dramatize discontinuity at the expense of continuity. Nevertheless, it is also necessary to insist upon a break and a rupture. Even when we recognize Schlegel's secret fondness for romantic authors, even when we admit his celebration of modern culture, and even when we appreciate the inner logic of his philosophy of history, he still surprises us. For Schlegel deliberately underplays, restrains, and resists these elements of his earlier views because of his almost fanatical neoclassicism, his belief that all art should be judged according to the standard of beauty. It would be a mistake to regard Schlegel's neoclassicism as little more than a pose, as a shallow or lightly held opinion. It would be indeed a caricature to regard the young Schlegel as little more than a *crypto-* or *proto*romantic, for his neoclassicism also had its deep roots. Those who one-sidedly insist on the continuity of Schlegel's development do not see how far down these roots go.

The sources of Schlegel's neoclassicism were Winckelmann and Kant. From Winckelmann, Schlegel acquired two fundamental beliefs: that the purpose of all art should be to portray beauty, and that imitation consists not in copying individuals in nature but in reproducing the ideal form behind nature.[17] It was indeed Winckelmann who inspired all Schlegel's classical studies, since his ambition was to be the Winckelmann of Greek poetry. From Kant, Schlegel gained his belief in the autonomy of art, its independence from the claims of morality and science, and its intrinsic value as a realm of pure play and contemplation.[18] These Winckelmannian and Kantian doctrines coalesced in Schlegel's belief that the purpose of art is to create an ideal and completely autonomous realm of beauty.[19] Schlegel could not abandon his neoclassicism, then, without departing from such basic principles.

It was this Winckelmannian devotion to beauty, this Kantian insistence on autonomy, that motivated Schlegel's harsh verdict upon modern literature. If beauty demands restraint, conformity to universal forms, then modern literature goes astray in mixing genres and giving complete freedom to the artist. Furthermore, if beauty should be autonomous, then modern literature is corrupt in making art serve the interests of morality and science, and in pandering to the interests of its readers. Finally, if beauty consists in complete satisfaction, then modern literature is perverse in its incessent longing, its eternal striving toward infinite goals. Not content simply to damn modern literature from the higher standpoint of classical beauty, Schlegel develops an *immanent* critique of modern literature, which attempts to show how it will inevitably destroy itself by its own inner tendencies and values. He argues at length in the *Studiumaufsatz* that modern literature is heading toward a crisis that can be resolved only by the creation of a new classicism. The infinite striving and eternal longing of modern culture is leading to complete exhaustion and emptiness because it never ends in the complete satisfaction of beauty. Each writer strives to be more interesting than the last by creating novel effects to please the public (I, 238). Either this tendency will end in complete bankruptcy or it will correct itself when writers finally acknowledge the need for a new aesthetics of beauty.

Besides his Winckelmannian and Kantian heritage, there was another source of Schlegel's neoclassicism. This was his equation of classicism with another fervently held belief: the possibility of criticism. Like many in the neoclassical tradition, Schlegel identified the characteristics of classical beauty—order, harmony, proportion, and restraint—with the universal and necessary standards of all art. If these characteristics did not have an absolute authority, it seemed as if there could be no criticism at all. It was indeed in just this respect that the young Schlegel was eager to take issue with Kant. For all his debts to Kant, he still could not accept Kant's argument in the *Kritik der Urteilskraft* that there could be no rules for taste. To Schlegel, this was tantamount to the claim that there could be no objective criticism at all, for all criticism requires the application of universal standards and rules. Hence it was one of Schlegel's early ambitions to provide the foundation for just such objective criticism, a science of aesthetics. He duly sketched several drafts for a deduction of beauty, a proof of its universal and necessary qualities.[20]

It is precisely here that Fichte's foundationalism played a crucial role in Schlegel's neoclassical aesthetics. It was Fichte's *Wissenschaftslehre* that supported his belief in the possibility of establishing a science of aesthetics, a science that would provide the critic with universal and necessary rules of taste. Just as Fichte had discovered the first principles of reason, and so secured a firm foundation for Kant's critical philosophy, so Schlegel believed it would now be possible to determine the first principles of beauty, and so provide a sound basis for a science of aesthetics and criticism. Hence, at the close of his *Studiumaufsatz,* Schlegel states that, after Fichte's discovery of the foundation of philosophy, there cannot be any reasonable doubt about the possibility of an objective aesthetics (I, 358). Along with his studies of Greek poetry, Schlegel now planned to publish his own "Euclidean poetics" to develop his own science of aesthetics, which would provide the ultimate philosophical foundation of his neoclassicism.

The dependence of Schlegel's neoclassical aesthetic on Fichte's foundationalism is most apparent in the *Studiumaufsatz* when Schlegel stresses how all imitation of the Greeks ultimately requires knowing the universal standards of beauty (I, 347). Like Winckelmann, Schlegel denies the possibility of imitating Greek art simply by observing and copying particular works; one first has to know the universal laws of beauty itself. Hence Schlegel argues that to understand any particular work of art it is necessary to know the whole of Greek culture; but to know Greek culture, he writes, one must already have "an objective philosophy of history" and "an objective philosophy of art." In other words, if there could not be such an objective aesthetics, there could not even be imitation of Greek art, so that the whole neoclassical aesthetic would collapse.

It should now be clear that there was a deep tension in Schlegel's early philosophy that could not be removed without a radical upheaval. Whatever Schlegel's early liking for romantic art, and whatever the implications of his philosophy of history, he could not develop them without abandoning his classicism. But Schlegel could not disavow his classicism without surrendering his Winckelmannian devotion to beauty, his Kantian faith in the autonomy of art, and, worst of all, his belief in the possibility of criticism in the classical sense.

4. The Question of External Influence

Given the difficulties of explaining Schlegel's conversion to romanticism from the internal evolution of his classicism, and given that it involves some break in his philosophical development, it seems necessary to postulate some external influence as the source of his conversion. Hitherto the most popular candidates for this role have been Goethe and Schiller.

The case for Goethe's influence was first put forward by Rudolf Haym in his masterly *Die romantische Schule*.[21] Haym noted the remarkable resemblance between Schlegel's concept of *romantische Poesie* in *Athenäumsfragment* no. 116 and his description of Goethe's *Wilhelm Meister*. The key to understanding Schlegel's concept, Haym argued, is that *romantische Poesie* is the same as *Poesie des Romans,* where the paradigm of the *Roman* was Goethe's *Wilhelm Meister*. Though Haym's hypothesis is quite old and has been subject to some trenchant criticism, it has been revived very recently by Ernst Behler.[22]

Haym's thesis suffers from at least two difficulties. First, on sheer chronological grounds, it is unlikely that Goethe's work made Schlegel abandon his classicism. On the contrary, Schlegel admired it precisely for its classical virtues. In his *Studiumaufsatz* Schlegel had described Goethe's poetry as "the dawn of genuine art" because it seemed to achieve anew the classical ideal of pure beauty (I, 260). Schlegel continued to admire Goethe's work for its classical virtues as late as the summer of 1796, when he praised Goethe's poem *Idyll* because it was written in the classical Greek sense.[23] As we shall soon see, however, it was around just this time that Schlegel began his criticism of Fichte's philosophy, which would soon undermine the basis for his classicism. Second, as Körner and Eichner have argued, Schlegel's private views about *Wilhelm Meister* show that he did *not* regard it as the paradigm of a romantic work.[24] Thus, in mid-1797, when Schlegel most probably began his intensive study of Goethe's work, he wrote that "Goethe is not romantic," "Goethe has a poor idea of the *Roman*," and that Goethe has "no idea of romantic totality."[25] He was explicit that "A perfect novel must be much more of a romantic work than *Wilhelm Meister*," and he refused to call Goethe's work a *romantische Roman,* a tribute he would pay only to Cervantes's *Don Quixote*.[26] It is indeed significant that, in his published review of *Wilhelm Meister,* Schlegel refrained from ever calling it a *Roman.* While there cannot be any doubt that Schlegel admired Goethe's work, that was more because of its promise than its achievement. He saw romantic "tendencies" in Goethe's work, which, if they were only fully developed, could lead to a revival of the novel.[27] Yet because these were only *tendencies* it was not possible to maintain that *Wilhelm Meister* was the *"non plus ultra"* (Haym) of romantic art. Rather than deriving his concept of romantic poetry from *Wilhelm Meister,* as Haym and Behler assume, it is much more likely that Schlegel simply read his own already formed concept of romantic poetry into Goethe's work.

The case for Schiller's influence has been made most persuasively by Arthur Lovejoy in a celebrated 1920 article.[28] Since then, Schiller's seminal influence on Schlegel has become something of a dogma.[29] According to Lovejoy, Schlegel's conversion to romanticism arose from his reading of Schiller's *Über naive und sentimentalische Dichtung,* which was first published in the *Horen* in 1795, shortly after Schlegel finished the body of his *Studiumaufsatz* but before he wrote its preface. Supposedly, Schillers's treatise made him realize that much more could be said in behalf of modern poetry, and it led to an embarrasing recantation of his classicism in the preface to the *Studiumaufsatz.*

It is not difficult to understand how Schiller's treatise could have an impact on Schlegel. Schiller made a distinction between ancient and modern culture that corresponds roughly with Schlegel's own. Like Schlegel, Schiller assumes that ancient culture is governed by nature, whereas modern culture is ruled by reason.[30] While the ancients lived in immediate unity with nature, moderns strive to return to that unity, which they have lost with the growth of culture. Schiller's distinction between naive and sentimental poetry follows from his general distinction between ancient and modern culture. While the ancient poet *imitates* nature, because he lives in immediate unity with it, the modern poet *idealizes* nature, longing to return to the unity he has lost.[31] Like Schlegel, Schiller thinks that the ancient poet realized his goals because they are very limited, while the modern strives for an unattainable infinite ideal.[32] Unlike Schlegel, however, Schiller does not hesitate to draw the proper conclusions from his distinctions. He argues that since classical and modern poetry are governed by such distinct principles and goals, it would be absurd to judge one in terms of the other.[33]

It would seem, then, that Schlegel only had to read Schiller's treatise for him to draw the same conclusions from his own very similar principles. Since these conclusions were already implicit in his own work, and since he was already disposed to draw them, all that he needed to cast off the shell of his classicism was Schiller's example.[34] Sure enough, there can be no doubt that Schiller's work had an impact on Schlegel. No sooner had he finished his *Studiumaufsatz* than he read Shiller's treatise, which set him thinking for days. He describes its impact in a letter to his brother: "Schiller's theory of the sentimental has occupied me so much, that for a few days now I could do nothing more than read it and take notes. If you can read my treatise [the *Studiumaufsatz*] you will understand why it interests me so much. Schiller has really explained some things for me. When something cooks so much inside me, I am incapable of taking up anything else. The decision to work out a sketch of my poetics for publication is now firm."[35]

Given Schlegel's own admission of Schiller's influence, and given the strong similarity in logical structure between Schiller's and Schlegel's theories, the case for Schiller's influence seems beyond doubt. Still, a closer examination of the evidence shows that the kind of influence Schiller had on Schlegel was the very opposite of what is usually assumed: it inspired Schlegel not to abandon but to defend his classicism.

The evidence stated in behalf of Schiller's influence, apart from the (just cited) letter to his brother, is the preface to the *Studiumaufsatz*, which Schlegel wrote shortly after completing the main work and reading Schiller's treatise. Here Schlegel explicitly admits that Schiller's treatise has made him understand that much more could be said in behalf of modern poetry, and he begs the reader not to take his harsh verdict against modern poetry as his final word on the subject (I, 207, 209). These statements have been taken to mean that Schlegel now makes the interesting into the proper standard to judge modern works.[36] Yet Schlegel really says nothing of the kind. Considered in context, the passage where he concedes that Schiller has widened his view of modern poetry turns out to mean only that the concept of modern poetry is also applicable to the poets of late antiquity (I, 209). Hence Schlegel says only that there are elements of modern or sentimental poetry in the pastoral poetry of the Romans and in the erotic poetry of the Greeks (I, 209–210). Rather than making Schlegel doubt his verdict against modern poetry, Schiller's analysis of the forms of sentimental poetry has only confirmed his opinion that it is all interested poetry because it desires and believes in the reality of its ideal (I, 211). For Schlegel, this was tantamount to saying that sentimental poetry had forfeited the ideal of aesthetic autonomy, whose only goal should be free play, quite apart from the reality of its creation.

So far is Schlegel from abandoning his neoclassical aesthetic that he embarks on a new defense of it. The preface reaffirms the basis premises of his general argument: that (1) modern poetry is essentially interested, making poetry serve the ends of morality and knowledge, that (2) beauty should be disinterested, and that (3) beauty should be the sole ideal of all poetry (I, 211, 214). Schlegel is now willing to grant, however, that more could be said in behalf of modern poetry, and he proceeds to sketch a "deduction" of its necessity. It becomes clear from his deduction, however, that modern poetry has only a provisional or hypothetical validity. Its value is only that it prepares the ground for, or is a necessary stage toward, the rebirth of a new classical poetry. The conclusion of his deduction leaves no doubt about his abiding antimodernism: "According to this deduction, which is grounded on a proper science, applied poetics, the *interesting* is that which has a provisonal aesthetic worth. Of course, the interesting necessarily has a moral *content:* but whether it has *worth* I rather doubt. The good and true should be done or known, not exhibited or felt" (I, 214). There could not have been a more *anti*-Schillerian conclusion!

The most striking passage in favor of the traditional interpretation is where Schlegel seems to concede a merely hypothetical validity to all his own neoclassical judgments of modern poetry. He writes: "If there are pure laws of beauty and art, then they must be valid without exception. But if one takes these pure laws, *without further determination and guidelines in their application,* as the rule for the evaluation of modern poetry: then the judgment cannot be other than modern poetry, which almost completely contradicts these laws, has no worth at all" (I, 208). Such a conclusion, Schlegel then declares, is completely contrary to our feeling. One must admit this contradiction, he says, to discover the proper character of modern poetry, to explain the need for a classical poetry, and to provide "a striking vindication of the moderns."

Yet here again it is necessary to place this passage in its wider context. If Schlegel now casts his judgments of modern poetry in hypothetical form, that is not because he doubts them, and still less because he retracts them. Rather, Schlegel is conceding only that he still has to provide some justification for his principles, which he could only presuppose in a work of criticism whose task is *to apply* rules that have been demonstrated elsewhere. When Schlegel told his brother that he is now resolved to write his "sketch of my poetics" it is precisely because he now realizes he must defend the very laws Schiller has questioned. Hence Schiller's treatise has motivated him not to abandon but to defend his neoclassicism. Thus he later tells his brother in a letter dated March 6, 1796 that he wrote a long preface to his *Studiumaufsatz* because "I could not push this birth so naked into the world" (XXIII, 287). He then reaffirms his resolve to publish his *"poetischen Euklides,"* his rigorous a priori demonstration of the objective standards of criticism.

In sum, it could not have been Schiller who convinced Schlegel to abandon his neoclassicism. Even after the publication of the *Studiumaufsatz* and his reading of Schiller's treatise, Schlegel was as firm as ever in his neoclassicism; indeed, he was resolved to make a definitive defense of it.

Only one final point appears to stand in the way of this conclusion. In his retrospective July 20, 1796, letter to Schiller, Schlegel declared that his *Studiumaufsatz* filled him with *"Eckel und Unwillen"* and that he was on the verge of withdrawing it from publication (XXIII, 322). He then thanked Schiller for the instruction he received from his essay on sentimental poetry.[37] This letter could be read as a complete retraction of the *Studiumaufsatz* due to Schiller's influence. But such a conclusion, it is necessary to realize, would be anachronistic. When Schlegel wrote this letter he had already moved away from the foundationalism involved in his neoclassicism. He had renounced a position that he no longer held for independent reasons, having nothing to do with Schiller's influence.

What, then, were these reasons? What made Schlegel finally reject his neoclassicism, despite his resolve to defend it? The answer ultimately lies with Schlegel's complicated relationship to Fichte, which we must now explore.

5. Schlegel and Fichte, 1795–1797

Schlegel's first knowledge of Fichte goes back to his Dresden years (January 1794–June 1796). His initial opinions about Fichte were deeply flattering, revealing all the naivité and enthusiasm of youth. He wrote his brother August Wilhelm in August 1795 that Fichte was "the greatest metaphysical thinker now living," and that he was "the kind of intellectual Hamlet had sought in vain" because he had united thinking and acting (XXIII, 248).

Such, indeed, was the young Schlegel's admiration for Fichte that he placed him as a thinker above Kant and Spinoza, and as a popular writer above Rousseau.[38]

The reasons for Schlegel's admiration for Fichte were complex. They were in part philosophical. Like many in the early 1790s, Schlegel saw Fichte as the first thinker to complete Kant's Copernican Revolution. It was Fichte who had finally discovered the foundation of the critical philosophy, and who had created a complete and consistent system of idealism.[39] While Schlegel would soon voice his doubts about Fichte's idealism, he never ceased to regard it as an achievement of the greatest cultural significance. He wrote in a famous aphorism that Fichte's *Wissenschaftslehre*—along with the French Revolution and Goethe's *Wilhelm Meister*—was one of the greatest tendencies of the age.[40] Fichte's idealism had become "the central point and foundation of the new German literature," he wrote in 1802, because it expressed the spirit of freedom characteristic of the modern age, which was the heart and soul of the new romantic literature.[41]

There were not only philosophical but also political motives behind Schlegel's admiration for Fichte. Since 1793 Schlegel had allied himself with the Revolution in France, and his political interests became so strong that they eventually began to overshadow his classical studies.[42] In 1796 he published his most radical political essay, "Ueber den Begriff des Republikanismus," which defends a left-wing interpretation of republican principles, and which criticizes Kant for both restricting the franchise and denying the right of revolution.[43] Given his political commitments, it is not surprising that Schlegel admired Fichte, who was one of the most famous German spokesmen for the French Revolution. It is indeed no accident that when Schlegel praises Fichte so highly in his August 1795 letter he refers to Fichte's *Beyträge zur Berichtigung der Urtheile des Publikums über die französische Revolution*, a radical defense of the course of the Revolution.

There can be no doubt that, during his Dresden years, Schlegel completely endorsed the foundationalist program of Fichte's *Wissenschaftslehre*.[44] He seems to be fully convinced not only that there is a first principle in philosophy, but also that Fichte has discovered it. In his 1795 *Studiumaufsatz*, for example, he praised Fichte for establishing the foundation of the critical philosophy, and he stated that there could no longer be any reasonable doubt about the possibility of an objective system of aesthetics (KA I, 358). In his 1796 fragment "Von der Schönheit der Dichtkunst" he reaffirmed his faith in an objective aesthetics, which would be based on the fundamental principles of practical philosophy, whose foundation had been established by Fichte (KA XVI, 5, 17–18, 22). Finally, in "Ueber den Begriff des Republi-kanismus" he began his deduction of republican principles from the Fichtean postulate "The ego ought to be" (VII, 15–16).

If Schlegel were ever a disciple of Fichte, it was only for a short time, prob-ably at most for a year, from the summer of 1795 to the summer of 1796.[45] It was in the summer of 1796 that Schlegel began to have his first doubts about Fichte's philosophy. In late July he visited his friend Novalis, who might have imparted to him some of his reservations about Fichte's ideal-ism;[46] and in early August he went to Jena, where he associated with the Niethammer circle, whose antifoundationalism seemed to rub off on him.[47] Some of the notebook entries from the autumn of 1786 indicate a growing skepticism about, and disillusionment with, foundationalism. Thus Schlegel now wrote of skepticism: "There is still no consistent σκ [skepticism]; it is surely worthwhile to establish one. σκ [skepticism] = permanent insurrec-tion" (no. 94, XVIII, 12). He then complained about Reinhold's founda-tionalist program: "Reinhold, the first among the Kantian sophists, has or-ganized Kantianism and created misunderstanding.—He is a seeker after foundations *(Grundsucher)*" (no. 5, XVIII, 19). Referring to "the regressive tendency of the hypercritics" (no. 4, XVIII, 19), Schlegel also began to dis-tance himself from those Kantians who swore by the spirit of his philosophy (no. 191, XVIII, 36). These "hypercritics" could well have been Fichte and Schelling.[48]

Schlegel's doubts about Fichte's philosophy only intensified after his first meeting with Fichte in August 1796. After a conversation with Fichte he complained to C. G. Körner that Fichte had too little idea of things that did not directly concern him, and that he was especially weak in every science that has an object.[49] Schlegel was puzzled that physics and history simply did not interest Fichte. He then made an astonishing revelation: Fichte told him he would rather count peas than study history! These misgivings proved to be decisive, for one of the main reasons for Schlegel's later break with Fichte came down to the lack of realism and history in his system.

Schlegel began an intensive study of Fichte's philosophy sometime during the winter of 1796. He began to write down some of his criticisms and obser-vations, which he hoped to publish in the form of an essay provisionally en-titled "The Spirit of the *Wissenschaftslehre*."[50] The result of his investigations, he told Körner January 30, 1797, is that he had not only come to clarity about some fundamental points, but that he had also "decisively separated himself from the *Wissenschaftslehre*" (XVIII, 343). Though the essay was never written, the notes for it remain, revealing many of Schlegel's early reservations about Fichte's philosophy.

Many of his doubts concern the form and method of the *Wissenschaftslehre*. Schlegel is especially critical of Fichte's foundationalism, casting scorn on Fichte's claims to have a complete system and irrefutable first principles. It is easy simply to deny some of his fundamental first principles (no. 126, 31),[51] which themselves stand in need of proof. Why not say, for example, that the *non*-ego posits itself absolutely? (no. 51, 510). It is futile to think, however, that these principles could be proven because there is never an end to deduction, given that any proposition can be proven in myriads of ways (no. 129, 30; nos. 9 and 12, 518). Furthermore, Fichte's system is far too mathematical and abstract, leaving out the positive reality of experience; all his deductions can at best only derive abstractions, not the individual facts of experience (no. 141, 152). Given such doubts about Fichte's foundationalism, it is not surprising to find Schlegel treating the *Wissenschaftslehre* as a work of literature rather than philosophy. The *Wissenschaftslehre* is Fichte's *Werther* (no. 220, 38), and as rhetorical as Fichte himself, "a Fichtean exposition of the Fichtean spirit in Fichtean letters" (no. 144, 33). All Fichte's bluster and seriousness makes him a comic figure: he is like the drunk who tirelessly climbs atop his horse and, "transcending it," only falls down again (no. 138, 32).

Besides his notes for the "Geist der Wissenschaftslehre," Schlegel had several other collections of fragments in his notebooks that also focus upon Fichte.[52] These too show how much Schlegel had completely broken with Fichte's philosophy. One central theme of these collections is that Fichte is a mystic, and that like all mystics he begins his philosophy by postulating something absolute (no. 2, 3). This makes everything too easy, however, because once we postulate the absolute we can explain everything; but the real question is what gives us the right to postulate it in the first place (no. 71, 512). Schlegel thinks that in relying on a mystical experience—he has in mind intellectual intuition—Fichte has forfeited the demands of criticism, which do not allow us to appeal to some infallible experience (no. 52, 93; nos. 8–9, 12). Another basic theme of these notes is that Fichte has ignored the whole realm of history, which is vital to show the necessity of his own system. To justify the *Wissenschaftslehre* we should see how it arose, why it was necessary to solve the problems of its historical context; but that means we cannot separate the *Wissenschaftslehre* from the history of philosophy itself (no. 20, 520). Although it is indeed necessary to distinguish between the transcendental and empirical ego (no. 135, 31), Fichte's philosophy is still guilty of a kind of "empirical egoism," Schlegel argues, because it limits the experience of the subject to the eternal present, ignoring the historical dimension of self-consciousness that links us to the past and the future (no. 31; 508).

If we were to summarize the positive recommendations deriving from Schlegel's critique, it would be that philosophy must become completely regulative regarding its claims to first principles and a complete system. The only dimension of Fichte's philosophy that Schlegel wants to maintain are the doctrines that the ego consists in activity, and more specifically the activity of infinite striving. It is with striving, he insists, that philosophy should begin and end (no. 18, 101; no. 5, 13). But this very Fichtean theme is turned against Fichte himself, because it is made to apply to first principles and complete systems, which are now made into regulative ideals. Thus Schlegel reads Fichte's first principle "The ego posits itself absolutely" as an imperative: "The ego *ought* to be absolute"(no. 187, 36). This strategy of reading Fichte's foundationalism in strictly regulative terms was virtually a commonplace among the Niethammer circle, and it shows the profound extent to which Schlegel was indebted to the philosophical atmosphere in Jena.

6. An Antifoundationalist Epistemology

In the course of his reflections on Fichte's philosophy in the winter of 1796–1797, Schlegel sketched the outlines of an antifoundationalist epistemology that would ultimately transform his aesthetic doctrines. This epistemology appears chiefly in Schlegel's notebooks; but it also emerges in published form in the *Kritische* and *Athenäumsfragmente*. We can best summarize the antifoundationalist epistemology contained in these writings by stressing the following themes.

First Principles

Schlegel criticized the classical foundationalist doctrine, reaffirmed by Reinhold and Fichte, that philosophy must begin with a self-evident first principle and then derive all other beliefs by a chain of deduction from it. Schlegel made two objections against it. First, that any proposition, even the apparently self-evident, can be doubted; it too must be demonstrated, so that there is an infinite regress of justification. Second, that there is an infinite number of ways of proving any proposition, such that we can continue to perfect our proofs *ad infinitum*.[53] For these reasons, Schlegel concludes: "There are no first principles that are universally efficient companions and guides to truth" (no. 13, XVIII, 518).

Schlegel's skepticism about first principles is also apparent in his attitude toward the geometric method, which had for so long been the model for foundationalist epistemology. In his *Athenäumsfragment* no. 82 he laughs at its pretensions, claiming that defining and demonstrating a proposition is pointless. There are an infinite number of real definitions for any individual, and any proposition can be demonstrated in all kinds of ways. The main point is to have something interesting to say and then just to say it, following the "thetical method" where we set down "the pure facts of reflection without concealment, adulteration, or artificial distortion" (II, 178).

Critique

Schlegel accepts the fundamental demand of the critical philosophy: that *all* beliefs submit to criticism. However, he insists on applying this demand to the critical philosophy itself, so that it becomes *metacritical*. This demand for a metacritical philosophy appears constantly in the notebooks where Schlegel calls for a "philosophy of philosophy." The same theme emerges in the *Athenäumsfragmente:* "Now that philosophy criticizes everything that comes before it, a critique of philosophy would be nothing better than a justified reprisal" (no. 56, II, 173) Of course, the radicalization of criticism into metacriticism involves skepticism; but Schlegel does not shirk from this conclusion, insisting on the value of a real skepticism that "begins and ends with an infinite number of contradictions" (no. 400, II, 240–241).

True to such skepticism and his rejection of first principles, Schlegel questions the possibility of criticizing all claims to knowledge prior to making any such claims. We cannot bracket all claims to knowledge, and then evaluate them before we make them; for not only does the application of a standard of knowledge imply a claim to knowledge, but also we know the powers and limits of our cognitive powers only by using them. This means that we should be critical of our cognitive powers not *before* but *while* using them. In other words, criticism must be integrated with the process of enquiry and cannot stand apart from it.[54]

The Myth of the Given

Schlegel is as critical of empiricism as rationalism regarding the possibility of providing a secure foundation of knowledge. He questions the given hard data of senses no less than the infallible first principles of reason. This is the message of *Athenäumsfragment* no. 226 where Schlegel maintains that we can do history only with the guidance of hypotheses (II, 202). He argues that we cannot state *that* something happens unless we can say *what* happens; but to determine what happens we first must use concepts. Hence facts are such only through the concepts we use to identify them. Schlegel explains that this does not mean that anything can be a fact nor that we can use any concept to determine them, for among the large number of possible concepts only some can be used to identify a fact. Still, he insists that it is the task of the critical philosopher to be aware of which concepts he uses; otherwise, he will simply accept them according to chance or caprice. The main mistake to guard against, he warns, is the pretension that one has "pure solid empirical facts [*Empirie*] entirely a posteriori," for this is only to sanction "an extremely one-sided, highly dogmatic and transcendent a priori view."

System

Schlegel's antifoundationalism makes him ambivalent about the ideal of a system.[55] He both affirms and denies this ideal. He denies it in the classical rationalist sense of a body of knowledge derived from, and organized around, a single self-evident first principle. There is no perfect system, in his view, because there are so many ways of organizing knowledge, and no single one can claim to be the sole truth. But Schlegel also affirms the ideal of a system because the only criterion of truth now left to him is internal coherence. Following the Kantian tradition, he abandons the standard of truth as correspondence and replaces it with coherence. Rather than correspondence with some unknowable realm of being, and rather than deduction from some indubitable first principle, the only standard of truth is now the mutual support of propositions in a whole *(Wechselerweis)*. The proper form of a system is not *linear*, where we derive all propositions from a single principle in a unique deductive chain (no. 16, II, 22; no. 518, II, 521), but *circular*, where we can begin from any proposition and return to it because all propositions are interconnected.[56]

Schlegel's ambivalent attitude toward the possibility of a system is perfectly summarized by a fragment from the *Athenäum:* "It is equally false for the spirit to have a system, and not to have one. It therefore must decide to unite them both" (no. 52, II, 173). Both horns of the dilemma are inescapable. On the one hand, it is dangerous to have a system, because it sets arbitrary limits to enquiry and imposes an artificial order on the facts. On the other hand, it is necessary to have a system, because unity and coherence are essential to all knowledge and it is only in the context of a system that a proposition is justifiable.

If we both must and cannot have a system, all that remains is the persistant *striving* for one. For Schlegel, the ideal of a system takes on purely regulative status, as a goal that we should approach but cannot ever attain. Of course, there is no perfect system; but that does not mean that all systems are on the same footing, for there are better and worse ways of organizing our knowledge. The ideal system is that which combines the greatest unity with the greatest multiplicity, or which organizes the most data according to the fewest principles.

7. The New Criticism

Schlegel's critique of Fichte's foundationalism had a profound effect on his aesthetic thinking, which was very much in evolution in the winter of 1796–1797. The immediate and general effect was the collapse of Schlegel's classicism. If there are no universal and necessary standards of reason—or at least none that we can know—there is no tribunal of critique that has absolute authority for all works of art. Schlegel himself explicitly drew this conclusion when, in a review of Niethammer's *Philosophische Journal,* he doubted the possibility of criticizing philosophical works according to some objective standard of truth: "How should there be a scientific judgment when there is still no science? . . . In philosophy nothing is certain, just as appearances teach us. Here there are no grounds or foundations" (KA VIII, 30). If there were no objective standards for criticizing philosophical works, there were *a fortiori* none for appraising works of art. Schlegel drew a close connection between his critique of foundations and his rejection of neoclassicism when he wrote in his *Kritische Fragmente:* "The revolutionary rage for objectivity of my earlier philosophical musicals had a little something of that rage for foundations [*Grundwut*], which had become so virulent during Reinhold's consulate in philosophy" (no. 66, II, 155).

Now that Schlegel rejected that "rage for objectivity," the problem was to determine what was left for aesthetic criticism. In his notebooks around 1797 we find him struggling for an answer. He first seems to despair entirely of the possibility of criticism, doubting whether there can be any objective basis for aesthetic claims: "All proper aesthetic judgments are by their very nature fiats [*Machtsprüche*] and cannot be anything else . . . One cannot prove them, but one must legitimate one's right to make them" (no. 71, XVI, 91). Since all one can do is demonstrate one's right to make these judgments, the question of aesthetic value is ultimately only moral: "The pure aesthetician states 'Thus I *love* this poem,' the pure philosopher 'Thus I understand it.' The question of worth is ultimately ethical" (no. 1053, XVI 172). Accordingly, in a series of fragments devoted to the question of the foundation of philology, Schlegel doubts that philology can ever be a science (no. 117, XVI 40), insisting instead that it is only an art (no. 2, XVI 68;no. 35, XVI 40). To understand a poet, he now claims, one must be a poet (no. 168, XVI 49).

Yet Schlegel did not resign himself to a complete skepticism. He did not conclude from the lack of objective foundations that all aesthetic judgments must be completely subjective, as if they rest on nothing more than feeling. Instead, we find him paraodying the radical subjectivist view: "If mystical lovers of art, who regard all criticism as dissection and all dissection as destructive of enjoyment, thought consistently, then 'I'll be damned' would be the best judgment on the most worthy of works. There are also critics who say nothing more than this, although at much greater length" (no. 57, II, 154). Struggling to find some middle path between absolute standards and arbitrary feelings, Schlegel finally found something of an answer in his 1797 notebooks. The answer is what he called *characteristic*, or what now goes by the name of "immanent critique." Rather than judging a work by some purported universal standard, characteristic judges it in the light of the author's own standards; in other words, the critic must compare the author's achievement with his intention. Thus Schlegel writes in his notebooks: "Critique should judge a work not according to some universal ideal, but should seek the *individual* ideal of each work" (no. 197, XVI 270). In the same vein: "Critique compares the work with its own ideal" (no. 1149, XVI 179). To judge a work by its own internal standards requires a full knowledge of the author's aims and context. In other words, philology had to become profoundly historical. Schlegel himself insists on this point, stressing that the foundation of philology must be found in history. If in his early foundationalist days he stated that criticism must be based on a mixture of philosophy and history, he now gives pride of place to history alone (no. 18, XVI 36).

Schlegel's new conception of criticism could not fail to have a profound effect on his attitude toward romantic literature. It now followed that he would have to evaluate romantic literature in its own terms, according to its own goals and ideals. This would mean trying to understand how all the features of romantic poetry—its mixture of genres, its lack of constraint, its use of irony, its longing and striving—derived from its central aspiration: the desire for the infinite. Schlegel would now—but only now—have to admit the force of Schiller's point that romantic literature has equal rights to classical. Both had their distinctive ideals, and it was idle to measure one in terms of the other.

Yet Schlegel's reappraisal of romantic literature went much further than simply giving it equal rights to classical literature. There was something about romantic literature that now gave it a claim to superiority over classical.[57] Romantic literature had become *the* proper vehicle for epistemology. The central characteristic of romantic poetry—Schiller had insisted and Schlegel had agreed—is its *eternal striving*, its *constant longing* for the ideal or the infinite, which consists in complete unity with nature. Yet this very striving, this very longing, was also the central theme of Schlegel's new antifoundationalist epistemology, which held that absolute truth is only a *regulative* ideal, a goal that the enquirer could approach but never attain in an infinite progression. Since we can never know the first principles nor create the perfect complete system, Schlegel claimed that all we can do is to strive to attain such principles and such a system. Hence Schlegel now made an *epistemological virtue* out of the romantic writer. If only vaguely, implicitly, and subconsciously, the romantic writer had the proper methodology and attitude to approach the truth. Schlegel now read his epistemological views back into romantic literature, making romantic poetry into his philosophical ideal rather than merely an historical concept.

8. Romantic Irony

The connection of Schlegel's aesthetics with his antifoundationalist epistemology is especially clear in the concept of irony that Schlegel developed in his *Kritische* and *Athenäumsfragmente*. This concept was Schlegel's response to the apparent *aporia* of his antifoundationalist epistemology. Although there are no first principles, no perfect demonstrations, no criteria of criticism, and no complete systems, we must not despair. We are still left with the *progression* toward the truth, the constant *approximation* to our ideals, provided that we forever strive to overcome all our limits on the path to perfection. Irony consists in the recognition that, even though we cannot attain the truth, we still must forever strive toward it, because only then do we approach it. Of course, the greatest master of irony in the history of philosophy was Socrates, who now became Schlegel's model.[58] Although Socrates was the wisest man because he knew that he could know nothing, he was also a perpetual gadfly who spurred his friends into deeper investigations.

Schlegel gives his best characterization of what he means by irony in the 1797 *Kritische Fragmente*. He explains irony by two kinds of predicament encountered in the attempt to know the truth. The first kind consists in "the feeling of the irresolvable conflict between the unconditioned and conditioned" (no. 108, II, 160). The ironist feels a conflict between the unconditioned and conditioned because any attempt to know the unconditioned would falsify it by making it conditioned. The whole truth is the unconditioned, because it completes the entire series of conditions; but any form of conceptualizing and explaining the unconditioned makes it conditioned, either because it applies the principle of sufficient reason, laying down a condition for anything, or because it applies some determinate concept, which assumes its meaning only by negation.[59] The second kind of predicament consists in "the impossibility and necessity of a complete communication." The ironist feels that complete communication is *impossible* because any perspective is partial, any concept is limited, and any statement perfectible; but he also sees that complete communication is *necessary* because we can approach the truth only if we strive to attain such an ideal; only if we presuppose and strive toward the ideal of a complete communication do we achieve a deeper perspective, a richer concept, and clearer statement of the truth.

The ironist's response to these predicaments consists in "the constant change from self-creation to self-destruction"(no. 37, II, 151).[60] In other words, the ironist creates forever anew because he always puts forward a new perspective, a richer concept, a clearer formulation; but he also destroys himself because he is forever critical of his own efforts. It is only through this interchange between self-creation and self-destruction that he strives forward in the eternal search for the truth. Schlegel's *via media* between this self-creation and self-destruction is *self-restraint:* limiting our creative powers, and adopting a critical distance toward them, so that they do not completely expend themselves in the heat of inspiration. Yet here the restraint is not that of classicism, which is imposed on the artist; it is rather *self*-restraint, the autonomous creation and imposition of rules.

In fundamental respects, Schlegel's concept of romantic poetry is also the result of his antifoundationalist epistemology. Romantic poetry, as stated by Schlegel in the famous *Athenäumsfragment* no. 116 (II, 182–183), is essentially the aesthetic version of the philosopher's eternal striving for truth. The romantic poet cultivates the same ironic attitude as the philosopher. Both the poet and philosopher are engaged in endless enquiry, an eternal striving, to provide the best description of their object. Hence Schlegel states in no. 116 that the "characteristic essence" of romantic poetry is that it is forever in the process of becoming and is never complete. Furthermore, both poet and philosopher vascillate between self-creation and self-destruction because they are critical of all their efforts to describe their object but always create anew. Thus Schlegel also says in fragment no. 116 that the romantic poet "hovers in the middle on the wings of poetic reflection between the object depicted and the act of depicting it." Still further, both poet and philosopher realize that there is no end to self-criticism, and that there are no objective rules of criticism that somehow stand above criticism itself. And so Schlegel writes again in no. 116 that the romantic poet multiplies reflection *ad infinitum*, as if in an endless series of mirrors. Finally, both poet and philosopher refuse to acknowledge any final rules in their search for the truth, because these serve as artificial and arbitrary limits upon the creative process. Thus Schlegel declares in no. 116 that the romantic poet will not be bound by any definite rules of genre, and that he recognizes no laws limiting his own free will.

It should be obvious that much more could be said about the antifoundationalist epistemology behind Schlegel's romantic aesthetic. The role of such central romantic concepts as wit and analogy can also be explained on the same basis. Yet it is beyond the purpose of this chapter to explore these points. My main contention has been that Schlegel's romanticism arose not from the influence of Goethe, Schiller, or Fichte, but from Schlegel's disillusionment with Fichte's foundationalism.

CHAPTER 8

The Paradox of
Romantic Metaphysics

1. A Strange Wedding Plan

By the late 1790s, some of the leading romantic thinkers in Germany had already sketched the basic outlines of their new metaphysics, the *Weltanschauung* that would later become so characteristic of the romantic school. From 1795 to 1797 Hölderlin, Novalis, and Friedrich Schlegel drafted the rudiments of this metaphysics in various fragments; Schelling later gave it more systematic formulation in his 1800 *System des transcendentalen Idealismus* and 1801 *Darstellung meines Systems*. In the formulation of this doctrine there are some important differences between these thinkers; but there are also some striking similarities, some common characteristics. Just one of these characteristics will be our special concern here. This was the attempt of romantic metaphysics to synthesize idealism and realism, and more specifically the idealism of Fichte and the realism of Spinoza.[1]

Prima facie this characteristic is puzzling and problematic. Without doubt, Fichte and Spinoza were the philosophers who had the greatest influence on the romantic generation. But they were also, in fundamental respects, completely incompatible: Fichte's idealism, indeterminism, and dualism clash with Spinoza's realism, determinism, and monism. Though perfectly aware of these incompatibilities, the romantics still wanted to join them. Nothing less than marriage would do because, in their view, each had captured but one half of the truth. Just like ideal wedding partners, Fichte and Spinoza were perfect complements in an indissoluble whole.

The first reaction anyone is likely to have about this project is that it is a quixotic absurdity, another romantic *Schnappsidee* that, fortunately, never came to fruition. Fichte's idealism and Spinoza's realism are so contradictory, so fundamentally opposed in both purpose and content, that it seems

131

any attempt to unite them is doomed to failure. One might as well try to square the circle. Surely, it does not bode well that Kant and Fichte themselves ruled out any prospect of a liasion with Spinoza. Explicitly and emphatically, they conceived their idealism as the *antithesis* of Spinoza's realism and naturalism.[2] The only remedy against his fatalism, they warned, lay with their transcendental idealism.

Such suspicions pose questions. How did the romantics attempt to unite Fichte and Spinoza? And could such a synthesis be coherent? Any attempt to understand the romantic *Weltanschauung* must, I believe, eventually come to terms with these questions. All too often romantic metaphysics is understood as a poetic form of Fichte's idealism or of Spinoza's naturalism, as if it were one or the other. But these common interpretations are too one-sided, missing what is the most striking characteristic of romantic metaphysics: its attempt to wed Fichte and Spinoza. If this marriage is not understood, the most characteristic feature of romantic metaphysics remains a cipher, a paradox.

Dated though it might seem, there is still something of abiding interest in the romantic project of synthesizing Fichte and Spinoza. Nowadays philosophers often write of the bankrupty of the Cartesian tradition, whose epistemology ends in a complete subjectivism, the limitation of knowledge to the circle of consciousness; they see the antidote to such subjectivism in a naturalistic or a Heideggerian ontology, which makes the self one part of nature or history. But such a remedy is problematic, not least because it does not answer the skeptical problems that motivated Cartesian epistemology in the first place: How do we *know* that there is a nature or history beyond consciousness? We are then left with a dilemma: either skeptical epistemology or dogmatic ontology. It is one of the most intriguing aspects of romantic metaphysics that it attempted to escape these extremes. The young romantics knew this dilemma all too well: it was present for them in the choice between Kantian criticism or Spinozian dogmatism. The point of their synthesis of Fichte and Spinoza was to surmount this dilemma, avoiding the extremes of both subjectivism and dogmatism, and combining the virtues of a critical epistemology with a naturalistic ontology.

What follows is an attempt to unravel the paradox of romantic metaphysics, to explain their attempt to surmount this apparently eternal dilemma. Romantic metaphysics is perfectly comprehensible and coherent, I argue, once we place it in the context of its underlying organic concept of nature. It was this concept that allowed the romantics to join Fichte's idealism with Spinoza's naturalism, Fichte's belief in the primacy of the self and Spinoza's faith in the priority of nature.

Of course, there is nothing new in stressing the importance of the organic concept for romanticism. For generations, scholars have emphasized its crucial role, seeing it as a central characteristic of the romantic *Weltanschauung*.[3] It must be said, however, that this traditional view does not agree with the most recent trend of *Romantikforschung*, which has questioned the old emphasis on the organic concept, and stressed instead the lack of completeness and closure in romantic thought.[4] We shall soon see, though, that this organic concept is indispensable in unraveling the paradox of romantic metaphysics, and more specifically in understanding its apparently quixotic attempt to wed idealism and realism. This will help to vindicate the older scholarly tradition and to restore to its rightful place the organic in romantic thinking.

2. Profile of a Mismatch

Before I explain the romantic project, it is necessary to have a more concrete idea of the challenge facing them. What, more precisely, are the incompatibilities between Fichte and Spinoza?

There are several basic issues dividing them. First, they are at odds concerning the reality of the external world or nature. Fichte's philosophy is *idealistic:* it denies the reality of the thing-in-itself, that is, anything that exists independent of our awareness of it; and it maintains that everything exists for some actual or possible consciousness. In contrast, Spinoza's philosopy is *realistic:* it affirms the reality of the whole of nature, which exists independent of, and prior to, awareness of it. Rather than existing only for some subject, subjectivity is simply a mode, appearance, or part of nature as a whole. Second, Fichte and Spinoza clash concerning the scope of natural explanation. Fichte's philosophy is *antinaturalistic:* it limits the realm of nature to experience, and it postulates a realm of reason and freedom beyond experience. Spinoza's philosophy, however, is *radically naturalistic:* it places everything within nature, so that nothing escapes its laws. Following from this second difference, Fichte affirms, and Spinoza denies, the reality of human freedom in one very important sense: the power of choice, the capacity to do otherwise independent of external causes. For Spinoza, human volition and action are parts of nature, and so occur of necessity according to its laws; for Fichte, however, human volition and action transcend nature, so that it is possible for them to be otherwise.

The conflict between Fichte and Spinoza appears at its most extreme when we consider the third issue dividing them: their opposing visions of ultimate reality or the absolute. Fichte makes the ego his absolute, proposing to explain all of nature as its product; Spinoza makes nature his absolute, attempting to explain the ego as its product. We cannot combine Fichte and Spinoza, then, anymore than affirm the existence of two absolutes, two infinite realities. We cannot both "make the self everything and the world nothing *and* the world everything and the self nothing."[5]

Our suspicions about the romantics' synthesis only grow when we ponder what they saw in Fichte and Spinoza. What attracted the romantics to Fichte was his radical concept of human freedom, according to which the self posits itself, making itself what it is. It was this concept of the self-positing self that rationalized the French Revolution, giving to the self the right to remake laws and institutions according to the demands of reason. As supporters of the Revolution in France, the young romantics could only embrace the concept behind it. What the romantics admired in Spinoza was his synthesis of religion and science. Spinoza's pantheism seemed to resolve all the traditional conflicts between reason and faith. It had made a religion out of science by divinizing nature, and a science out of religion by naturalizing the divine. But it is precisely in these respects that Fichte and Spinoza seem utterly irreconcilable. If nature is divine, then it is infinite, and everything should fall under its laws; hence there cannot be any transcendental realm of freedom above and beyond nature. Rather than creating itself, the self simply realizes of necessity the essence given to it by the natural order of things.

Given all these incompatibilities, a successful marriage of Fichte and Spinoza appears hopeless. We cannot wed them anymore than we can pair idealists and realists, dualists and monists, indeterminists and determinists. If marriages between opposites sometimes do succeed, it is only because of some deeper underlying affinity. But here we find none. Why attempt to wed enemies?

3. Subject–Object Identity

Ironically, it was Fichte who first inspired the matchmaking efforts of the romantics. Despite all his bluster against Spinoza, Fichte virtually forced the romantics to embrace his nemesis as his necessary complement. This was the inevitable result of one of the fundamental principles of the *Wissenschaftslehre*, the principle that Fichte sometimes called *subject–object* identity. According to this principle, the subjective and objective, the ideal and real, are ultimately the same. Taking their cue from this principle, the romantics used it to rationalize their move beyond Fichte. They took the subjective or ideal pole to represent Fichte's idealism, the objective or real pole to stand for Spinoza's realism.

Why did the romantics feel compelled to interpret Fichte's principle in such an anti-Fichtean manner? The answer lies in the inherent difficulties of Fichte's own interpretation of this principle.

In the Jena *Wissenschaftslehre* Fichte interpreted subject–object identity essentially in terms of self-knowledge. Since knower and known are the same in self-knowledge, it has the required identity of subject and object, ideal and real. Fichte believed that this fact alone should entitle self-knowledge to be the paradigm of all knowledge. Since all knowledge presupposes some identity of knower and known, and since such identity is demonstrable in self-knowledge, self-knowledge should be the basis for all knowledge. If we can somehow show that all knowledge is a form of self-knowledge—even if subconscious self-knowlege—then we will provide a foundation for it.[6]

The inspiration behind Fichte's principle was nothing less than the guiding idea behind Kant's "new method of thought": that we know a priori only what we create.[7] Kant had claimed that the innate activity of the mind is transparent to itself, so that whatever it creates it knows.[8] Since the self embodies or reveals its activity in its objects, its knowledge of them amounts to a form of self-knowledge, so that self-knowledge is the paradigm of all knowledge. This paradigm of knowledge plays a basic—if not entirely explicit—role in the Transcendental Deduction of the first *Kritik* in the form of the unity of apperception, the "I think" or self-awareness that accompanies all representations. Such self-awareness amounts to the self's awareness of its own creativity, whose products are the various forms of a priori synthesis—namely, the categories of understanding and forms of space and time of sensibility.

In fundamental respects the romantics adopted Fichte's principle of subject–object identity. They agreed with Fichte that the principle of subject–object identity amounts to some form of self-knowledge, and that self-knowledge should be the basis of all knowledge. But they took issue with him regarding his *one-sided* subjectivist reading of this principle. Fichte's reading of this principle is subjectivist, in their view, insofar as it locates subject–object identity in the self-awareness of the transcendental subject, in the *"Ich denke"* of the unity of apperception or the *"Ich bin Ich"* of the *Wissenscahftslehre*. For Fichte, subject–object identity essentially consists in transcendental self-knowledge, the subject's awareness of its spontaneous activity. He insisted that such identity must be *immanent,* lying within the realm of possible consciousness; to place it outside this realm, as Spinoza had, was *transcendent,* nothing less than hypostasis, "the fallacy of pure reason."[9]

The romantics made two fundamental objections against Fichte's subjectivist interpretation of the principle of subject–object identity. First, the very concepts of the subjective and objective make sense only in contrast to one another; they have their specific meaning only within the realm of experience; but the principle is supposed to be transcendental, explaining the very possibility of experience, and so cannot be within experience; in that case, however, it cannot be either subjective or objective.[10] Second, such a reading makes it impossible for the principle to perform its function of explaining the possibility of knowledge. If it is a constitutive or theoretical principle, such as "I am" or "I think," then it cannot derive the dualism between the subject and object in experience, let alone the content of empirical knowledge. If, however, it is a regulative or practical principle, which expresses nothing more than the striving of the ego to control nature, then we are caught in a dilemma. Insofar as the ego dominates nature, the object is nothing more than a product of its activity, a mere noumenon; but insofar as it does not dominate nature, the object is an unknowable=X. We therefore have to choose between self-knowledge or a thing-in-itself. Toward the close of the 1794 *Wissenschaftslehre* Fichte admitted that this dilemma was unavoidable for any finite knower. For the young Schelling and Hegel, this was tantamount to an admission of failure.[11]

The essence of the romantics' critique of Fichte's principle is that it does no justice to the reality of experience, the existence of the external world. Fichte's principle of subject–object identity is subjectivist because it does not accommodate the experience of the objective world. *Prima facie* this objection seems unfair because Fichte intended his transcendental idealism to be a form of *empirical realism,* which explains the reality of things in space independent of the conscious subject. It was indeed the very purpose of the *Wissenschaftslehre* to explain the feeling of necessity accompanying our representations, the fact that they appear to come and go independent of our will and imagination. But the romantics were very well aware of Fichte's intentions; their point against him is twofold. First, empirical realism is insufficient, and second, Fichte does not even guarantee that. Empirical realism is insufficient because, although it allows objects to exist independent of the empirical self, it does not permit them to exist independent of the transcendental self, who is the lawgiver of nature. The romantics wanted to go further than Fichte in giving an independent reality to nature; they demanded a "higher realism," which would give reality to nature independent of the self, whether empirical or transcendental.[12] This higher realism was both a ground for, and result of, their sympathy for Spinoza. Second, Fichte could not establish even his empirical realism because he admitted that the first principle of the *Wissenschaftslehre*—"the ego posits itself absolutely"—cannot derive the reality of the non-ego, which is opposed to itself. All the immensely subtle and sophisticated reasoning of the first part of the 1794 *Grundlage der gesammten Wissenschaftslehre* finally came to the conclusion that the self-positing ego cannot limit itself by positing a non-ego opposed to itself. The failure of Fichte's deduction program in the 1794 *Grundlage* was crucial in convincing the romantics to go beyond the limits of his own subjectivist principles.

4. The Organic Concept of Nature

It was the need to explain the reality of the external world, to do justice to the sheer otherness of the non-ego, that eventually forced the romantics to abandon the one-sidedness of Fichte's idealism and to complement it with the "higher realism" of Spinoza. Somehow, they would have to find an interpretation of the principle of subject–object identity that would accommodate our experience of an external world. This was an inherently paradoxical undertaking, since the principle of subject–object identity postulates the identity of subject and object, but ordinary experience seems to show that they are distinct from one another. Somehow, there would have to be an identity of subject–object identity and subject–object nonidentity. But merely in formulating this desideratum one seems to contradict oneself. Another formulation—no less paradoxical—is to claim that there must be some unity of Fichte's idealism and Spinoza's realism.

For the romantics, the path out of this impasse lay with their organic conception of nature. This conception was developed in greatest detail and rigor by Schelling, first in his 1799 *Von der Weltseele* and then in his 1798 *Entwurf eines Systems der Naturphilosophie.* But the same idea also appears in the note-books of Friedrich Schlegel, Novalis, and Hölderlin.

The fundamental concept behind the romantic concept of nature is that of a natural purpose *(Naturzweck).* Kant had defined this concept very specifically in §65 of the *Kritik der Urteilskraft,* a crucial text for Schelling and the romantics. Something is a natural purpose, Kant wrote, only if it satisfies two essential conditions. First, it must have *organic unity,* where each part is inseparable from the whole, and where the idea of the whole determines the place of each part. Second, it must be *self*-generating and *self*-organizing, so that all parts are reciprocally the cause and effect of one another, having no outside cause. Kant argues that this second condition is the specific characteristic of a natural purpose as opposed to a work of art. Both works of art and natural purposes have in common that they are produced according to some idea of the whole; but only a natural purpose is *self*-productive. Its design and structure arise from within according to some internal principle; they do not arise from outside, as in a work of art.

The organic concept of nature arose from generalizing or extending Kant's idea of a natural purpose, so that it held for nature as a whole. The organic concept means that nature as a whole is one vast natural purpose, each of whose parts are also such purposes, so that nature is an organism of organisms. This concept postulates a single living force throughout all of nature, so that all the different species of minerals, plants, and animals, and even all the different kinds of matter, are simply so many different degrees of its organization and development. All of nature then forms one huge hierarchy, which consists in the various stages of organization and development of living force. Living force first manifests itself in the most simple forms of matter; it then passes through the more complex minerals, vegetables, and animals; and finally it ends with the most sophisticated forms of life, such as the self-consciousness of the transcendental philosopher and the creativity of artistic genius itself. Such self-consciousness is nothing less than the highest organization and development of all the powers of nature. This means that the artist's or philosopher's awareness of nature is also nature coming to its *self-awareness* through them.

The most important implication of the organic concept of nature is that there is no distinction *of kind,* but only one *of degree,* between the mental and physical. The mind and body are no longer heterogeneous substances, but are only different levels of organization and development of the single living force throughout nature. The mental is simply the highest degree of organization and development of the living forces active in matter; and matter is merely the lowest degree of organization and development of the living forces present in the mind. We can therefore regard mind as highly organized and developed matter, matter as less organized and developed mind. As Schelling put the point: "Nature should be visible spirit, and spirit invisible nature" (II, 56).

5. The Rationale for Organicism

No doubt, Schelling's organic concept of nature is daring and imaginative, and it has duly been condemned by positivists and neo-Kantians for careless and excessive speculation. But such judgments fail to consider the context of *Naturphilosophie*, specifically the crisis of physics and physiology at the close of the eighteenth century. While Schelling could not—and did not—claim final experimental proof for his concept, he did believe it to be warranted by the latest scientific results of his day. More important, however, Schelling developed his concept in the first place because he saw it as the only solution to the persistent problems facing physiology and physics. The main argument for the organic concept was more conceptual than empirical: it alone seemed to resolve the crises inherent in eighteenth-century natural science.

Schelling proposed his concept first and foremost as a solution to an apparently inescapable dilemma that had troubled physiology since the early seventeenth century: dualism versus mechanistic materialism. These extremes seemed to be the only possibilities if one adopted the Cartesian concept of matter and its paradigm of mechanical explanation. According to that concept, the essence of matter consists in extension, and it is inherently inert, moving only if it is moved by some external force. According to that paradigm, we explain all events as due to the impact of one body on another, where we measure impact in terms of how much a body must change its place within a given amount of time. If we adopt this concept and paradigm, then we have to choose between two unwelcome alternatives: either we place life outside nature—and so become dualists—or we reduce life to matter in motion—and so become mechanists. But both alternatives are unsatisfactory. While the mechanist upholds the principles of naturalism, he seems to ignore the characteristic qualities of life; and whereas the dualist recognizes such qualities, he transports them into a mysterious *sui generis* realm where they cannot be explained according to the methods of science.

It was the purpose of Schelling's organic concept to provide some middle path between the horns of this dilemma.[13] Schelling agreed with the dualist that mechanism could not explain the *sui generis* characteristics of life; but he also sympathized with the efforts of the materialist to explain life according to natural laws. The organic concept of nature alone, he believed, could avoid the problems of both dualism and materialism by providing a *naturalistic yet nonreductivistic* account of life and the mind. Since an organism is not reducible to a mechanism, it does not reduce life to a machine; but since it also acts according to natural laws, there is no violation of the principles of naturalism. Hence the organic concept calls into question the common premise behind dualism and materialism: that all natural explanation is mechanical. Rather than accounting for natural events by external causes acting on them, it explains them by their necessary place in a systematic whole. The paradigm of explanation is now holistic rather than analytical or atomistic.

Schelling's organic concept was dictated not only by a crisis in physiology, but also by one in physics. In the late eighteenth century the main challenge to physics came essentially from the fact that the mechanical paradigm, which had dominated physics ever since Descartes, no longer seemed to account for matter itself. The source of the problem lay with Newton's law of gravity. No one could doubt Newton's law, which had been confirmed time and again by observation and experiment; yet it postulated a force of attraction between bodies that seemed to operate through empty space. Hence arose the troublesome issue of "action at a distance." This was a serious problem for the mechanical physics, which insisted that one body acts on another only through impact, by one body striking another. Stubbornly but desperately, some physicists attempted to explain gravitational attraction by postulating subtle media or fluids between bodies; but experiments failed to detect their presence.[14]

The research on electricity, magnetism, and chemistry at the close of the eighteenth century seemed to ring the death knell for mechanism. The problem of explaining action at a distance became even more critical because the latest findings in these various areas of research seemed to suggest that matter itself consisted in forces of attraction and repulsion; the forces Newton postulated for the macrocosm now seemed to hold for the microcosm itself. The essence of matter no longer seemed to be inert extension but dynamic force. But if this were so, then not only life but matter resisted mechanical explanation. Such, at any rate, was the main conclusion of Schelling's first work on *Naturphilosophie*, his 1797 *Ideen zu einer Philosophie der Natur.*

We are now in a much better position to understand the general intellectual forces driving Schelling toward his organic concept of nature. If it is necessary to extend the naturalistic worldview so that mind and life were part of nature; and if, furthermore, there could not be a mechanical explanation of matter, let alone life and mind; then the only step forward lay in extending the organic paradigm so that it held for all of nature itself. The great promise of the organic paradigm is that, after the collapse of mechanism, it guaranteed the principle of the unity of nature, a single form of explanation for both life and matter. The *lex continui* was finally upheld. Mind and matter, the organic and inorganic, were no longer divided but simply different manifestations of living force.

The great ancestor of this organic concept of nature was that old *Erzfeind* of Cartesianism: Leibniz. It was not the exoteric Leibniz of the preestablished harmony, who made the mental and physical distinct realms; but the esoteric Leibniz of the monadology, who made matter only an appearance of vital force. It was no accident that Herder and Schelling, self-consciously and explicitly, revived Leibniz.[15] Ironically, the arch-dogmatist, so recently interned by Kant, had now been resurrected. Leibniz's hour had finally come; despite that baroque peruke, he had become a darling of the romantic age.

6. Revitalized Spinozism

Of course, that other sweetheart was "the sacred Spinoza," to whom Schlegel, Novalis, Schelling, Hölderlin, and Schleiermacher would all pay tribute. It was in the ether of Spinoza's substance that one had to learn to philosophize, Hegel later said, summarizing the conviction of an entire generation.[16] It would be a serious mistake, however, to see romantic metaphysics as little more than a revivification of Spinoza. For the romantics profoundly reinterpreted Spinoza, and indeed in ways that would have made Benedictus turn in his grave. It was only by reinterpreting Spinoza, of course, that they could integrate his naturalism and realism with the idealism of Kant and Fichte.

The romantics were especially attracted to two aspects of Spinoza's system. First, his monism, his belief that there is a single universe, of which the mental and the physical are only different attributes. Spinoza's monism was the antithesis to the dualistic legacy of the Cartesian tradition, which had created so many problems in physiology. Second, his pantheism, his identification of the divine with nature. The romantics rejected the all too common interpretation of Spinoza as an atheist, which simply confused *natura naturans* with *natura naturata*. Rather than an atheist, Spinoza was *"der Gott betrunkener Mensch"* because he saw everything as a mode of the divine. This identification of the divine with nature seemed to be the only way to keep religion alive in an age of science. The old theism had collapsed under the strain of modern biblical criticism; and deism had faltered in the face of Humean and Kantian criticism. Only Spinoza's pantheism was not vulnerable to rational criticism or scientific advance. The slogan *deus sive natura* seemed to make a science out of religion by naturalizing the divine, and a religion out of science by divinizing the natural.

Despite the attractions of Spinozism, the romantics believed it suffered from insuperable problems. The central drawback to Spinoza's system was that it was still limited by the antiquated dogmas of Cartesian physics. Spinoza not only accepted the Cartesian concept of matter as extension, but he also endorsed the mechanical paradigm of explanation. But in these respects Spinoza had shown himself to be a child of his time. If Spinoza's system were to stay alive, it would have to be reinterpreted according to all the latest advances in electricity, magnetism, and chemistry. For the romantics, this could mean only one thing: reinterpreting Spinozism according to their new organic paradigm of explanation.

Such an organic interpretation involved several profound changes in Spinoza's system. First, it introduced a notion of development into his frozen, rigid universe. Spinoza's substance was now nothing less than living force, *die Urkraft aller Kräfte*. Such a substance was no longer static and eternal, but active and temporal, undergoing development from the inchoate to the organized, from the indeterminate to the determinate, from the potential into the actual. Although Spinoza himself understood substance in terms of force,[17] he never understood force in organic terms along the lines of Leibniz's *vis viva*. Furthermore, his force never acted in time but eternally since substance related to its modes purely logically.

Second, the organic interpretation injected an element of teleology into Spinoza's system. If the divine substance is an organism, then it too is a natural purpose, whose aim is to realize its potentiality throughout nature. Notoriously, Spinoza banished teleology from his system on the grounds that it is anthropomorphic and anthropocentric, implying that nature were designed by God for human ends. But the romantics believed that Spinoza's rejection of teleology was far too hasty. They too rejected the old physio-theology of the past, which understood nature as if it were only an instrument created by God to serve man. But this was an "external teleology," which sees purpose as imposed on things; it is not an "internal teleology," which sees purpose as inherent in a thing, as the very idea or concept of the whole. An internal teleology has no necessary reference to human ends, because it assumes that the purpose of a thing derives from its own inherent concept or essence.

Third, the organic interpretation also involved the idea of a pyramid or hierarchy in nature, the idea of "the great chain of being." Spinoza had placed all modes on the same footing; a rock, a vegetable, or a human being are equal manifestations of the infinite, which is completely present in all things. The romantics organic concept meant, however, a return to the old hierarchic concept of nature. If the universe is a living force, then, like all such forces, it develops in degrees and stages, through levels of increasing organization. For the romantics, the highest degree of organization and development of the divine force was nothing less than the creativity of the artist, philosopher, or saint. Their creativity was the culmination of all the organic powers of nature. What the artist created is what the divine created through him, so that his work was nothing less than a revelation of the divine.

Fourth, the organic interpretation also meant a new account of Spinoza's attributes, his doctrine that the mental and physical are simply different attributes of a single indivisible substance. Indisputably, this doctrine is one of the most difficult to understand in Spinoza's system. How we interpret it depends on whether an attribute is something purely subjective—simply the way in which the intellect explains or understands substance—or whether it is something objective—a property of the divine that follows of necessity from its nature. But however we understand Spinoza's doctrine, and however close our interpretation brings him to the romantics, there is still one respect in which the romantics *reinterpreted* it. Namely, they understood Spinoza's attributes in organic terms as different degrees of organization and development of living force. The mental and the physical are not simply different properties or perspectives on substance but different degrees of organization and development of living force.

It is fair to say that, by organizing Spinoza's universe, the romantics reinterpreted it along Leibnizian lines. Their reinterpretation of Spinoza was essentially a synthesis of Spinoza and Leibniz. The romantics fused Leibniz's *vis viva* with Spinoza's single infinite substance, creating a vitalistic pantheism or pantheistic vitalism. If they accepted Spinoza's monism, they rejected his mechanism; if they rejected Leibniz's pluralism, they accepted his vitalism, his organic concept of nature implicit within his dynamics. It was with this remarkable fusion of Leibniz and Spinoza—the two greatest dogmatic metaphysicians of the seventeenth century—that the romantics would attempt to solve the *aporiae* of the post-Kantian age.

7. The Happy Nuptial Bonds of Idealism and Realism

It is in terms of this revived Spinozism that we must interpret the romantics' attempt to fuse idealism and realism. The wedding of Leibniz and Spinoza was the basis for the marriage of Fichte and Spinoza. A vitalistic monism, or monistic vitalism, seemed to be the best way to preserve the truths and negate the errors of Fichte's idealism and Spinoza's realism.

The romantics' attempt to fuse idealism and realism must be understood first and foremost as an attempt to revive Spinoza's doctrine of attributes. According to that doctrine, we can view the entire universe, the single infinite substance, under the attribute of thought or extension. The mental and the physical are no longer distinct substances but simply different attributes—either properties or perspectives (or both)—of one and the same thing. Since the mental and physical are no longer heterogeneous things, there is no longer a problem of explaining the interaction between them. The single infinite substance—the entire universe—remains undivided since one can explain everything under the attribute of either thought or extension.

On at least one interpretation of Spinoza's difficult doctrine, it seems to give equal weight to the claims of idealism and realism. If we interpret everything under the attribute of thought, we proceed idealistically, as if everything that exists is mental or ideal; and if we explain everything under the attribute of extension, we account for everything materialistically or realistically, as if everything that exists is only an appearance or manifestation of matter. Whatever the merits of such an interpretation, the romantics endorse it, taking it as their cue for the synthesis of idealism and realism. They now reinterpret Fichte's principle of subject–object identity along Spinozian lines. The identity of subject and object is not located in the self-knowledge of the transcendental subject but in the single infinite substance, which remains one and the same whether interpreted subjectively (idealistically) or objectively (realistically).

Of course, the romantics gave an organic twist to Spinoza's doctrine, so that the synthesis of idealism and realism must be understood in organic terms. We can interpret the entire universe in idealistic terms insofar as we see everything from top to bottom, viewing matter as nothing more than the lowest degree of organization and development of the living forces in the mind. We can also understand it in realistic terms insofar as we see everything from bottom to top, viewing mind as nothing more than the organization and development of the living powers already potential and inherent in matter. If nature is nothing more than visible mind, and if mind is nothing more than invisible nature, then both idealism and realism have been correct. The point is not to privilege one form or explanation over the other; both are independent and equally valid perspectives on a single reality, namely, living force.

It would be naive to think that this synthesis of idealism and realism accommodates both viewpoints without remainder, as if all their claims could be accepted. If their insights are to be preserved, their illusions are to be negated. It was an insight of idealism to think that nature can be understood in teleological terms, to assume that everything can be explained in terms of self-consciousness or subjectivity. Self-consciousness is indeed nothing less than the purpose of nature, the highest organization and development of all its powers. But the idealists went astray, the romantics believed, in confusing the *teleological* with the *ontological;* in other words, if self-consciousness and subjectivity are the *purpose* of all of nature, it does not follow that everything *exists* only in some self-consciousness or subject. If subjectivity is the purpose of things, that does not mean that only subjectivity exists. Fichte's principle that everything is for the ego is correct, then, but that should not mean that everything *exists* in the ego, but only that nature achieves its final purpose in the ego. The idealists failed to observe an old but fundamental point of Aristotle: what is first in the order of explanation is not necessarily first in order of being. Although the mind is the purpose of nature—although everything comes into existence for its sake—it does not follow that the mind creates all of nature.

Regarding the realistic perspective, it is correct in thinking that there is a nature that exists independent of subjectivity, in assuming that nature exists apart from and prior to human awareness of it. If subjectivity is first in order of explanation, objectivity is first in the order of being. It is indeed correct that human self-consciousness is only the manifestation and development of the powers that are implicit, inchoate, and potential within matter. The realist goes astray, however, in thinking that nature is a thing-in-itself that is indifferent to the human, subjective, or ideal. If human self-consciousness is the highest organization and development of all the organic powers of nature, nature only becomes fully actualized and determinate through it. If, for some reason, there were no such self-consciousness, nature would not fully realize itself. It would indeed continue to exist; but only in some potential, inchoate, and indeterminate form. It would be like the sapling that never became the mighty oak.

It will be readily seen that the romantics' accommodation of idealism within their organized Spinozism grants it an essentially teleological significance. The romantics sought an understanding of the universe no longer indifferent to the self; and they avoided this harsh implication of Spinozism by again recrowning the self as the culmination of creation. It might well be objected that this was simply a relapse into anthropomorphism and anthropocentrism, the very vices that Spinoza had once descried in teleology. It is important to see, however, that this is a new kind of anthropomorphism and anthropocentrism, one never within the purview of Spinoza. As we have already seen, the romantics claimed that the target of Spinoza's polemic was the *external teleology* of the old physico-theology, which saw everything existing only for man, as only a means to his ends. This was the teleology that explained the existence of cork trees from man's need for stoppers for wine bottles. The romantics' anthropomorphism and anthropocentrism grew out of an *internal teleology*, however, according to which everything in nature is an end in itself. It was in following the inherent laws of *its* development, the romantics claimed, that a natural purpose prepared the ground for the formation of human self-consciousness.

It is noteworthy in this context that the romantics' organic concept of nature implies that everything is reciprocally both means and ends. Depending on our standpoint, we can see each part of an organism as an instrument for the development of the whole, and the whole as an instrument for the development of each part. This means that it is possible to say both that man develops for the sake of nature as well as nature develops for the sake of man. If the romantics so often stress one implication rather than the other—the more anthropomorphic or anthropocentric aspect—that is only because they are so concerned to blunt the bitter edge of Spinoza's indifferent substance, its complete independence from all human concerns. For the romantics, such a belief was only one more troublesome legacy of the mechanical physics, whose demise could now be foreseen thanks to the organic concept of nature.

8. Revamping and Revitalizing Epistemology

In fundamental respects the romantics' organic concept of nature broke with the Cartesian epistemological tradition, which had analyzed knowledge according to some of the fundamental assumptions of its mechanical physics. One of these assumptions is that the subject and object of knowledge, like all substances in nature, interact with one another only through efficient causality. The subject and object are both substances, self-sufficient and independent entities, which are connected with one another only through relations of cause and effect. Either the subject is the cause of the object, as in idealism, or the object the cause of the subject, as in realism, or both are cause and effect of one another, as in some combination of realism and idealism. Whatever is the case, there is only a causal interaction between the subject and object that leaves the identity of both terms unchanged. Another assumption was Cartesian dualism. Since mechanism could not explain *res cogitans*, it placed it in a *sui generis* realm beyond the order of nature, which consisted entirely in the *res extensa*. This dualism meant that knowledge of the external world would have to consist in two very different terms: a mental representation and an extended object. This correspondence was usually understood as a kind of resemblance or isomorphism.

Of course, these assumptions created insuperable difficulties in explaining the possibility of knowledge. If the representation belongs in the mental realm, and if its object belongs in the physical realm, then how is there any correspondence between them? How is it possible to attribute a resemblance between such heterogeneous entities? The second assumption of the Cartesian model undermines the first, since the first assumes that the correspondence is effected through causal interaction; but the second makes it impossible to conceive of cause–effect relations between the mental and the physical. While the mechanical model presupposes that one object acts on another through impact, where impact is measured by the amount of change of place in a given time, the mental–physical dualism means that the *res cogitans* occupies no space, so that it is impossible to conceive how a physical cause has a mental effect. Although the mechanical model works fine between extended objects in the natural world, it does not apply to objects that are not extended, such as the thinking substance that is the locus of knowledge. Hence the net result of the Cartesian conception of nature is that knowledge becomes an utter mystery. It is impossible to explain in what the resemblance between representation and its object consists, and indeed how it comes into being.

If we replace the mechanical model of nature with the organic, these mysteries of traditional epistemology disappear. First, there is no dualism between the mental and the physical since both are degrees of organization and development of living force. Hence there is no problem in explaining the correspondence between heterogeneous entities. The subject's representation of the object does not stand in a different world from the object but is only the higher degree of organization and development of the living powers within the objective world. Second, there are not only accidental causal relations between the subject and object, but closer ties of identity where each realizes its nature only in and through the other. According to the organic model, everything in nature is part of an organic whole, where each part is inseparable from the whole, and where the whole is inseparable from each of its parts. No part has a self-sufficient or independent nature where it retains its identity apart from everything else; rather, each part reflects the identity of the whole. Like all parts of an organic whole, the subject and object are internally related to one another in this manner. The subject's awareness of an object develops and realizes the powers of the object, so that its awareness of the object is nothing less than the *self*-realization of the object. Since artistic creativity and philosophical contemplation is the highest organization and development of all the powers of nature, the artist's and philosopher's awareness of nature is nothing less than the *self*-awareness of nature through the artist and philosopher.

The organic concept of nature essentially involves a completely different model of the connection between the mental and physical from that prevailing in the Cartesian tradition. The connection is no longer simply causal, where each term retains its identity independent of the interaction; rather, it is teleological in the sense that each term realizes its nature only through the other. Each term becomes what it is only through the other, so that it becomes organized, actualized, and determinate only through the other, so that without the other it remains inchoate, potential, and indeterminate. As long as the analysis of knowledge remains stuck with the causal model it becomes impossible to explain the possibility of knowledge, because the activity of the subject on the object, or of the object on the subject, will affect the representation of the object, so that it gives us knowledge only of how the subject affects the object or the object affects the subject, but no knowledge of the object in itself apart from and prior to the interaction.[18] Hence the inevitable result of the mechanical model of interaction was the idea of an un-knowable thing-in-itself.

On the basis of this new organic model of nature, the romantics believed that they had finally overcome the traditional antithesis between idealism and realism. They held that idealism and realism are one-sided perspectives, which are both true and false: they are true about one aspect of the whole but they are false about the whole itself. If nature is an organic whole, it is not possible to say with idealism that it is completely *inside* consciousness nor with realism that it is entirely *outside* consciousness. Rather, it is both and neither.[19] The organic whole is inside consciousness because conscious-ness is the highest organization and development of *all* its living powers; the philosopher's and artist's awareness of nature is all of nature coming to its self-awareness through them, so that all of nature culminates within artistic creativity and philosophical contemplation. The organic whole is also out-side consciousness, because human consciousness is only one part of nature, which exists apart from and prior to us. Without humanity nature does not realize its purpose; it remains inchoate, unorganized, and indeterminate; but it does not follow that it does not exist. From this perspective, then, the idea of a thing-in-itself proves to be an absurdity. While it is true that nature exists apart from our awareness of it, it is false that nature has a complete and self-sufficient nature apart from the awareness of it; that idea would be simply an artificial abstraction from the idea of an organic whole.

9. The Question of Freedom

The question remains: How did the romantics square their new metaphysics with their belief in freedom? There seems to be an irreconcilable conflict be-tween that belief and their pantheism, which holds that everything happens of necessity according to the laws of nature. The fact that these laws are tele-ological as well as mechanical ultimately makes little difference. In this re-spect, their pantheism seems identical to that of Spinoza; but Spinoza was notorious for his fatalism as well as his atheism. How, then, did the roman-tics avoid the charge of fatalism? This was a problem that deeply troubled Friedrich Schlegel, Schelling, and Novalis, who dealt with it in their lectures, notebooks, and drafts from the late 1790s to the early 1800s.[20]

The romantics' organic concept of nature made it impossible for them to accept Kant's and Fichte's solution to the problem of freedom. Central to that concept is the firm belief in the unity of nature, in the oneness of the subjective and objective, the ideal and real. Kant's and Fichte's solution to the problem of freedom presupposed, however, a dualism between these realms. To save freedom, Kant and Fichte postulated a noumenal realm above and beyond the phenomenal realm of nature; while the noumenal realm complies with moral laws imposed by reason, the phenomenal realm is governed by strict necessity according to the laws of nature. The romantics rejected such a solution essentially because of its dualistic implications. They also questioned the underlying basis for the dualism: that the realm of nature is governed strictly by mechanical laws. If nature does not follow only mechanical laws, the whole question of freedom and necessity had to be rethought.

True to their antidualism, the romantics placed the self within nature, insisting that it is one mode of the single infinite substance, one part of the universal organism. They were no less naturalistic than Spinoza: they too affirmed that everything is within nature, and that everything in nature conforms to law. Contrary to one popular image of romanticism, they did not allow for caprice, arbitrariness, or chance in nature. Rather, they maintained that everything that happens in nature happens of necessity, such that it could not have been otherwise. The romantics also did not question that everything that happens must occur according to mechanical laws, so that for every event there will be some prior causes determining it into action. Where they differed from Spinoza is not in exempting events from mechanical necessity but in bringing mechanical necessity itself under higher organic laws. It is not that there are special organic laws, which are somehow beyond the jurisdiction of mechanism; rather, it is that mechanism is subordinate to organicism. The mechanical is simply a limited case of the teleological, deriving from a partial perspective that considers only the parts in their immediate relations to one another, but not in their relation to the whole. Mechanism considers what happens for determinate events under certain initial conditions; but it does not ask for the whys and wherefores of these initial conditions in the first place; instead, it allows the series of causes to regress *ad infinitum.*

Because of their committment to monism and naturalism, the romantics could not allow freedom in the radical sense intended by Kant and Fichte. They questioned the possibility of freedom in two senses championed by Kant and Fichte: first, Kant's concept of freedom as *spontaneity*, according to which the self initiates a causal series without determination by some prior cause; second, Fichte's concept of *self-positing*, according to which the self makes itself what it is, having no essence given to it by nature. Since both concepts exclude determination by natural causes, they presuppose the noumenal–phenomenal dualism, which the romantics reject.

Given their naturalism and monism, and given their rejection of transcendental freedom, it would seem that the romantics had no place for freedom. In what sense were they ready to admit freedom at all? Their own agenda was to reconcile freedom and necessity, to show that true freedom and necessity are not opposed but ultimately only one. They saw this unity first and foremost in the divine nature itself, which is free in Spinoza's sense: it acts from the necessity of its own nature alone. It is striking that while Schlegel and Schelling refuse to attribute freedom to any part of nature, they are happy to attribute it to the whole of nature, the infinite divine substance itself.[21] This substance is free in the sense that it is *causi sui,* both self-causing and self-making. Since it includes everything, there is nothing outside it, so that there are no external causes to compel it into action. For anything less than the whole, however, there will always be other parts outside it that determine it into action according to the laws of necessity. It is noteworthy, however, that even Spinoza's infinite substance is not free in the sense of Kantian spontaneity or Fichtean self-positing; for both concepts assume that the self can act otherwise, that it can choose a different series or causes or have a different nature. For Spinoza, the divine nature cannot be or act otherwise without contradicting itself.

Although Schlegel and Schelling attribute *absolute* freedom only to nature as a whole, they still attempt to dodge the implication of fatalism. While they deny the self is free as a part of nature, they affirm that it is free in its unity with nature as a whole. They make a distinction between two perspectives or standpoints: the self considered in its relations to other things, which is the self as individual, as one finite thing opposed to others; and the self considered in itself, apart from these relations, which is the universal self, the self as identical with everything else. If the individual self falls under the sway of necessity, the universal self shares in the divine freedom. Its identity is not limited to one part of the whole, where everything is determined by extenal causes; but it extends to the whole of all things, which acts with freedom, according to the necessity of its own nature alone. True freedom then arises from sharing or participating in divine necessity, in seeing that in all my actions the divine acts through me. This was the freedom of Spinoza's intellectual love of God, the freedom that reconciled the self to necessity when it recognized its identity with the whole universe.

While there was always this Spinozist dimension to the romantic reconciliation of freedom and necessity, it would be wrong to limit it to this dimension alone. Its unique and characteristic element came from their organic concept of nature. This concept gave a greater place for freedom than Spinoza's system chiefly because it made humanity the *telos* of nature itself. "Man is free," Friedrich Schlegel wrote, "because he is the highest expression of nature."[22] If the self is the highest organization and development of all the powers of nature, then nature ceases to be some external power outside the self, an external cause that compels it into action. Rather, nature becomes part of the self because its intrinsic ends are achieved only through it. If the self is the highest expression of nature, then nature contracts to the limits of the self as the self expands to the whole of nature. The reciprocity of means and ends means not only that the self is a means for the ends of nature but also that nature is only a means for the self. All of nature then becomes the organic body of the self. Once the self finally grasps its identity with nature, it then regards determination by nature as another form of *self-determination*.

If the romantics had succeeded in salvaging some sense of freedom in their organic universe, it also must be said that it was no longer the radical freedom with which many of them began. They had to abandon freedom as spontaneity and self-positing. In Fichte's dramatic choice between criticism and dogmatism, they had taken the plunge with dogmatism, affirming a universal necessity. There was indeed a remarkable change in the romantic ethos as the revolutionary ardor began to fade. The parole was no longer to change the world according to the demands of reason but to perceive the reason already within nature and society, reconciling oneself with its necessity.[23] In moral and political respects the romantic marriage of Fichte and Spinoza, of idealism and realism, was lopsided, to the disadvantage of Fichte's titanic striving and to the advantage of Spinoza's beatific stoicism. Like all marriages between incompatible partners, someone had to lose something. It was the price to be paid for an otherwise very remarkable alliance.

CHAPTER 9

Kant and the *Naturphilosophen*

1. A Relapse into Dogmatism?

Probably no other aspect of romantic *Naturphilosophie* has more aroused the wrath of its neo-Kantian critics than its organic concept of nature. These critics have dismissed this concept as a relapse into the worst kind of dogmatic metaphysics. They charge that it violates the *regulative* constraints that Kant so wisely placed on teleology. Supposedly, the romantic *Naturphilosophen*—thinkers like Schelling, Hegel, Friedrich Schlegel, and Novalis —naively and dogmatically gave the idea of an organism a constitutive status. True to their penchant for grand speculation and a priori reasoning, the romantics recklessly assumed that nature really *is* an organism, thus failing to observe Kant's critical teaching that it must be investigated only *as if* it were one.

Were the romantics really so naive and so careless? Or did they have some rationale for transgressing the Kantian limits? And, if they did, how plausible was it? These are the main questions I wish to discuss here. Part of my task is simply exegetical and historical: to reconstruct Kant's arguments against the constitutive status of teleology and the romantic replies to them. In doing so, I hope to show not only that the romantics were aware of the need to justify their new metaphysics, but also that they developed a rather sophisticated defense of it.[1] Another part of my task is more philosophical: to assess the romantic case, to determine whether they had an adequate response to Kant. While I contend that the romantics had a more plausible case than their neo-Kantian detractors think, I also hope to show that their response to Kant is ultimately inadequate, incapable of matching the deeper skepticism underlying Kant's regulative doctrine. Still, it will become clear that this gives the neo-Kantians no grounds for complacency and "I told you sos." The problem is that *Naturphilosophie* grew out of a deep *aporia* in the Kantian system: namely, its failure to explain the interaction between the intellectual and sensible, the noumenal and phenomenal. Indeed, the romantics' most interesting and plausible argument for their organic concept of nature exploits a very common Kantian strategy: it attempts to provide something like a *transcendental deduction* of the idea of an organism. In other words, it seeks to show that the constitutive status of the idea of an organism is the necessary condition of the possibility of experience. Whatever the ultimate merits of such a daring and difficult argument, neo-Kantian detractors of *Naturphilosophie* have failed to recognize it, let alone assess it.

If there is any general moral involved in my reexamination of these old disputes, it is that we have to break with the two dominant models of post-Kantian idealism and romanticism—that these movements mark either a progression or a decline from Kant. The neo-Kantian model of an irresponsible relapse into metaphysical dogmatism, and the neo-Hegelian model of the inevitable march toward absolute wisdom, are both worthless in assessing the philosophical complexities of these disputes. Alas, at the end of the day philosophical commitment is as difficult as any decision in life: we have to compare incommensurables, play off one *aporia* against another, and then take a leap. In the case of Kant versus the *Naturphilosophen*, we have to trade off the difficulties of the Kantian dualisms against the dangers of romantic speculation. Which is better and which worse? I, for one, cannot find a clear answer.

2. The Neo-Kantian Stereotype

Before I begin to consider the Kantian arguments against teleology and the romantic response to them, let me first set the record straight about one basic issue: namely, Kant's relation to *Naturphilosophie*. To this day the name of Kant is still invoked as a talisman to frighten off the specter of *Naturphilosophie*. Among some prominent historians of science, Kant is still seen as the friend of natural science and as the foe of metaphysical speculation; his regulative doctrine is indeed held up as the very touchstone of scientific propriety.[2] To be sure, there is some basis for a positivistic reading of Kant. Kant did condemn the metaphysics of vital materialism—a central doctrine for most *Naturphilosophen*—and he did stress that philosophy must remain within the boundaries of possible experience. Nowhere is this proto-positivistic side of Kant more in evidence than in his caustic reviews of Herder's *Ideen zur eine Philosophie der Geschichte der Menschheit.*[3]

Still, this interpretation is a simplistic stereotype. It stresses one aspect of a much more complex picture, whose other aspects bring Kant much closer to the *Naturphilosophen*. There are at least three problems with the neo-Kantian interpretation.

First, in fundamental respects, Kant was the father of *Naturphilosophie*. His dynamic theory of matter in the *Metaphysische Anfängsgründe der Natur-wissenschaften* was a formative influence on the first generation of *Naturphilosophen*, especially Schelling, Eschenmayer, H. F. Link, and A. N. Scherer. These thinkers took Kant's dynamic theory a step further by applying it to the new chemistry and the recent discoveries in electricity and magnetism.[4] Furthermore, Kant's methodological views—especially his demand for systematic unity and his insistence on synthetic a priori principles—were also very important for some *Naturphilosophen*. It is indeed somewhat ironic to find the neo-Kantians criticizing the *Naturphilosophen* for a priori speculation and system-building when so much of their inspiration for these activities came from Kant himself! Even the method of analogy, for which *Naturphilosophie* had been so severely criticized, has its Kantian roots. It was Herder who, in the first instance, had set the example for the use of this method; but Herder was simply following in the footsteps of his teacher, the author of the *Allgemeine Naturgeschichte und Theorie des Himmels.*[5]

Second, Kant's regulative doctrine was *not* the foundation of physiological and biological research in the late eighteenth and early nineteenth century, as has sometimes been argued.[6] Rather, the very opposite was the case. It is striking that virtually all the notable German physiologists of the late eighteenth century—Albrecht von Haller, J. F. Blumenbach, K. F. Kielmeyer, C. F. Wolff, Alexander von Humboldt—conceived of vital powers as causal agents rather than regulative principles.[7] Their aim was to do for the organic world what Newton had done for the inorganic: to determine its fundamental laws of motion. Although they forswore knowledge of the causes of these laws, much as Newton had declined to speculate about the cause of gravity, they still saw these causes as vital agents behind organic growth.

Third, Kant himself was deeply ambivalent about his regulative doctrines.[8] Nowhere are his vacillations more apparent than in the Appendix to the Transcendental Dialectic of the first *Kritik*. Here Kant explicitly rejects the merely hypothetical and heuristic status of the principles of the systematicity of nature, and he expressly affirms that we must assume there *is* some systematic order in nature, so that the concept of the unity of nature is "inherent in the objects" *(den Objekten selbst anhängend)*.[9] Proceeding simply according to an *as if* assumption, Kant argues, is not sufficient to justify or motivate enquiry.[10] Kant then blurs his distinction between the regulative and the constitutive, and indeed between reason and the understanding, by suggesting that the assumption of systematicity is necessary for the application of the categories themselves. Without the idea of systematic unity, he says, there would not be "coherent employment of the understanding," and not even a "sufficient criterion of empirical truth."[11] To some extent the same equivocation extends into the *Kritik der Urteilskraft* itself, where Kant sometimes states that we could not have a coherent experience at all without the application of the maxims of reflective judgment.[12]

For all these reasons, it seems to me to be inadvisable to make a sharp and fast distinction between *Naturphilosophie* and the tradition of German physiology and biology, as if *Naturphilosophie* were a corrupt metaphysics flaunting Kant's regulative guidelines, and as if physiology and biology were hard empirical science heeding them. Ultimately, there is only a distinction in degree, and not in kind, between Schelling, Hegel, and Novalis on the one hand and Blumenbach, Kielmeyer, and Humboldt on the other. Any qualitative distinction underestimates not only Kant's profound influence on *Naturphilosophie,* but also the deep tension between Kant's regulative constraints and late-eighteenth-century physiology. Even worse, it exaggerates the speculative and a priori dimension of *Naturphilosophie,* as if it had no concern with observation and experiment, while it downplays the metaphysical interests of those engaged in observation and experiment.

It is one of the more unfortunate aspects of the neo-Kantian legacy that, for generations, it has succeeded in portraying *Naturphilosophie* as an aberration from true science, which follows the path of experiment and observation. Fortunately, in recent decades it has become clear that this picture is profoundly anachronistic. It cannot come to terms with some very basic facts: that there was no clear distinction between philosophy and science in this period, and that there was no such thing as a pure empirical science limited to only observation and experiment. In the late eighteenth and early nineteenth century, *Naturphilosophie* was not a metaphysical perversion of, or deviation from, "normal" empirical science. Rather, it was normal science itself. From our contemporary perspective it is hard to imagine a scientist who is also a poet and philosopher. But this is just what is so fascinating and challenging about *Naturphilosophie,* which has to be understood in the context of its own time as the science of its day.

3. Kant's Arguments for Regulative Constraint

Whatever Kant's doubts and hesitations about the regulative doctrine, there can be little doubt that, at least sometimes, he affirmed it. For Kant repeatedly insists in the third *Kritik* that the idea of the purposiveness of nature has only a regulative validity. It was on this very important point, of course, that he came into conflict with the *Naturphilosophen.* Although they shared a very similar concept of the purposiveness of nature, Kant denied, while the *Naturphilosophen* affirmed, its constitutive status. The question then arises: Why did the romantics make this assumption in the face of the Kantian critique of knowledge?

To assess the legitimacy of their case, it is first necessary to consider the challenge facing them: Kant's powerful arguments for the regulative status of teleology. There are at least three such arguments, which in some respects dovetail with one another. It is noteworthy that two of them appear in their most explicit form not in the *Kritik der Urteilskraft* but in two obscure works of the 1780s: the 1786 *Metaphysische Anfangsgründe der Naturwissenschaft* and the 1788 essay "Über den Gebrauch teleologischer Prinzipien in der Philosophie."[13] It is also interesting to note that some of these arguments were, at least by implication, directed against *Naturphilosophie,* given that their target was Herder's vital materialism in his *Ideen zur einer Philosophie der Geschichte der Menschheit,* a seminal work for the romantic generation.[14]

It is important to see that Kant's arguments against teleology concern one very specific concept: what Kant calls a "natural purpose" *(Naturzweck).* This concept is explicitly defined in §65 of the *Kritik der Urteilskraft,* a seminal text for the romantics' own conception of teleology. Something is a natural purpose, Kant explains, only if it satisfies two essential conditions. First, it must have *organic unity,* where each part is inseparable from the whole, and where the very idea of the whole determines the place of each part within it. Second, it must be *self*-generating and *self*-organizing, so that all its parts are reciprocally the cause and effect of one another, and so that it has no external cause. Kant argues that this second condition is also necessary, since the first condition alone (organic unity) is not sufficient to regard something as a natural purpose, given that it can also be satisfied by a machine. Only things that also meet the second condition are *natural* purposes because they produce themselves and do not have some external cause or designer.

Kant's analysis of the concept of a natural purpose was decisive for the romantics, who accepted both its main points. Their organic concept of nature began from Kant's concept of nature, and then generalized it for nature as a whole. All of nature, then, is a giant natural purpose that consists in myriad smaller natural purposes. According to this concept, there is no fundamental difference in kind between the ideal and real, the mental and physical, since they are only different degrees of organization and development of living force. Mind is very organized and developed matter, and matter is less organized and developed mind. It is important to see that such an organic concept does not abrogate the mechanical, whose laws remain in force as much as ever; but it does see the mechanical as a limiting case of the organic. While the organic explains the parts of nature with respect to the whole, the mechanical simply treats these parts in relation to one another, as if they were somehow self-sufficient. The mechanical explains a given event by prior events acting on it, and so on *ad infinitum;* the organic explains why these parts act on one another in the first place.

Of course, it is just this flight of speculative fancy whose wings Kant was so intent to clip. The conflict between Kant and the *Naturphilosophen* could not be more clear and precise: Kant denied and they affirmed the constitutive validity of the concept of a natural purpose. Kant's denial works against applying the concept on both a macro- or microcosmic scale.

Kant's first argument against giving constitutive status to the idea of a natural purpose, which appears in its most detailed form in the "Über den Gebrauch" essay, is essentially skeptical. It states that we have *no means of knowing* whether objects in nature, such as vegetables and animals, are really purposive; in other words, we have no way to prove that such objects are really organisms rather than just very complex machines. According to Kant, we understand the power to act from purposes only through our own *human* experience, and more specifically when we create something according to our will, which consists in "the power to produce something according to an idea" (VIII, 181). If, therefore, something cannot act according to ideas, we have no right to assume that it has the power to act for ends. Hence the concept of a natural purpose, of a being that acts purposively yet does not have a will, is "completely ficitious and empty" *(völlig erdichtet und leer)* (181).

In drawing such a conclusion Kant is not saying that the concept is completely *meaningless*—in that case it could hardly have even a regulative status—but only that it has no *reference*. His point is simply that we *know of* purposiveness only in the cases of beings that act with will and understanding, and that we therefore cannot make verifiable claims about the purposiveness of beings that do not have will and understanding. In a nutshell, Kant's argument is that intentionality—in the sense of conscious end or goal-directed action—is the *criterion* of purposiveness, and that such a criterion cannot be satisfied due to the intrinsic limits of human knowledge.

Kant's second argument, which appears in §68 of the third *Kritik*, might be called his anti-Frankenstein stratagem. This argument consists in a simple application of the central principle of the critical philosophy, or what he calls the principle behind its "new method of thought."[15] According to this principle, which Kant explicitly restates in §68, "we have complete insight only into that which we can make ourselves and according to our own concepts" (V, 384). This principle means that organisms are incomprehensible to us, Kant argues, because we do not have it within our means to create or produce them. We can indeed create some *material* thing, just as nature can produce one. But we have no power to produce the infinitely complex structure of an organism. Hence if we know only what we can produce, and if we cannot produce organisms, it follows that we cannot know organisms.

Kant's third argument is directed against hylozoism or vital materialism, the doctrine that matter consists in *vis viva* or living force. To ascribe natural purposes to living things, it is not necessary to be a hylozoist, because it is possible to hold that such purposes are characteristic only of *living* or *organic* matter. Hylozoism is the stronger thesis that living force is essential to *matter as such;* it therefore implies that there is no difference between the organic and inorganic. Still, hylozoism is sufficient, even if not necessary, to justify the ascription of purposes to things, for it maintains that living forces are purposive.

Kant's argument against hylozoism proceeds from his analysis of matter in the *Anfangsgründe*. According to his second law of mechanics, the law of inertia, every change in matter must have an *external* cause, that is, it persists in rest or motion, in the same direction and with the same speed, unless there is some external cause to make it change its direction and speed (IV, 543). This law implies, therefore, that changes in matter cannot be *internal*, or that matter has no *intrinsic* grounds of determination. This means for Kant that matter is essentially *lifeless;* for he defines life as the faculty of a substance to act from an *internal* principle, its power to change *itself.* Kant vehemently insists that the very possibility of natural science rests on fully recognizing these implications of the law of inertia; in his view, hylozoism is at best speculative and at worst anthropomorphic; hence he condemns it as nothing less than *"der Tod aller Naturphilosophie."*

Kant's polemic against hylozoism appears to be ambiguous, vacillating unstably between two very different contentions: (1) that ascribing life to material things is *meaningless* because it is contrary to the very idea of matter, and (2) that attributing life to material things is *problematic* because we cannot ever *know* whether they are really purposive. The first contention would mean that teleology is a *fiction,* while the second would give it a *hypothetical* status. Although Kant indeed makes both these contentions, the tension is only apparent because they are directed against two very different versions of hylozoism, which he himself distinguishes (§65, V, 374–375 and §73, V, 394–395). The first contention is directed against the doctrine that matter as such or by its very nature is living. Kant maintains that this doctrine is flatly contrary to the essence of matter, which is inertia. The second contention is targeted against the doctrine that, though matter itself is not living, *there is still some living force or substance within it* that somehow directs and organizes its activity. Against this doctrine Kant makes two points: first, we have no empirical evidence that there is such a principle in matter, because experience only validates the law of inertia; and, second, the concept of a living force inherent in matter is essentially circular, because we explain its appearances by appeal to living force and then explain living force by its appearances.

On the basis of these arguments, Kant concludes that the concept of an organism or a natural purpose has only a regulative status. To avoid some common misunderstandings, it is important to see precisely what such a conclusion means. Except for the most radical version of vital materialism, Kant is not saying that this concept is only a fiction, as if it were false that there are organisms in nature. Rather, he is saying that this concept has only a *problematic* status; in other words, we have no *evidence* or *reason* to assume the existence or nonexistence of natural purposes. While it is indeed possible that there are such purposes, it is also possible that there are none at all because they might be, for all we know, really only very complicated machines. True to his vocation as a critical philosopher, whose only goal is to determine the limits of our cognitive powers, Kant neither affirms nor denies the *sui generis* status of organisms; alternatively, he neither affirms nor denies the possibility of mechanism. Thus he states explicitly in §71 of the third *Kritik:* "We are quite unable to prove that organized natural products cannot be produced through the mechanism of nature" (V, 388). When Kant denies the possibility of a complete mechanical explanation of organisms, when he famously denies that there will never be a Newton to explain the growth of a single blade of grass, he does so not because he thinks that organisms *are* extramechanical—for that too would be a dogmatic claim to knowledge—but only because he thinks that it is a *necessary limitation of the human understanding* that we cannot fully understand an organism mechanically, and that we must resort to teleology to make them comprehensible to ourselves.

4. The First Line of Defense

How did the *Naturphilosophen* defend themselves against this array of arguments?[16] Their first strategy would be to diminish the size of their target, purging the concept of a natural purpose of all its traditional theological associations. Schelling, Hegel, Schlegel, and Novalis did not wish to retain or revive the old metaphysical notion of providence, according to which everything in nature follows a divine plan. Rather, they believed that their teleology is completely intrinsic, limited to the ends of nature itself. According to their view, nature is an end in itself, and the purpose of all of nature is not to realize any end beyond itself.

While this strategy scores an important point—that teleology need not carry the traditional baggage of physico-theology—it still does not blunt Kant's main arguments. Although Kant sometimes wrote as if the concept of the objective purposiveness of nature inevitably led to a physico-theology (§75, V, 398–399), the thrust of his arguments are directed against the concept of a *natural purpose (Naturzweck),* and therefore against the idea that nature alone is *self*-generating and *self*-organizing. Hence his target was indeed the central doctrine of the *Naturphilosophen:* an immanent teleology.

Limiting the question to the realm of nature itself, it seems that the *Naturphilosophen* could still avoid Kant's arguments. All they would have to do is point out that the concept of a natural purpose need not involve any of the shaky assumptions Kant attributed to it. More specifically, they could make two replies to Kant. First, they could maintain that the idea of a natural purpose does not necessarily imply intentionality, that is, the attribution of a *will* to a living thing. To state that an object is a natural purpose is not to assume that there is some intention behind its creation, still less that there is some kind of will within the object itself. Rather, all that it means is that the object is an organic unity, where the idea of the whole precedes its parts, and where the parts are mutually interacting, the cause and effect of one another. These are indeed the necessary and sufficient characteristics of a natural purpose on Kant's own account of that concept. So, by his own reckoning, there should be no need to demonstrate the existence of intentionality.[17] Second, the *Naturphilosophen* could also contest that the idea of living matter entails that there is some kind of *soul* or *spirit* within matter itself that somehow directs and organizes its growth. It is important to see that, like Kant, the *Naturphilosophen* were also opposed to any form of animism and vitalism that postulated some *supernatural* force or immaterial substance behind organic growth. Like almost all physiologists of the late eighteenth century, they too wanted to avoid the dilemma of materialism versus vitalism.[18] While they held that materialism is too reductivist because it cannot explain the *sui generis* structure of organisms, they also rejected vitalism because it is too obscurantist, involving an appeal to some occult force or supernatural agency.[19]

It is important to see that the teleology of the *Naturphilosophen* is first and foremost a form of holistic explanation. It involves a very different paradigm or concept of explanation from that of mechanism. It claims that to explain an object by its natural purpose is to explain it holistically, where the purpose is the idea of the whole. This whole is an organic unity, irreducible to its parts, each of which is intelligible only from its place within the whole. Such holistic explanation is the opposite of mechanical explanation, which involves an antithetical concept of the whole. According to this concept, the whole is the mere sum total of its parts, each of which is self-sufficient apart from the whole. The difference between these forms of explanation then amounts to two different whole–part conceptions. Either the whole precedes its parts or the parts precede the whole. This is the difference between what Kant calls a *totum* or *compositum*,[20] or, in the language of the third *Kritik*, a synthetic or analytic universal.

All this makes it seem as if there is really no dispute between Kant and the *Naturphilosophen* after all. Kant is denying the attribution of purposiveness to objects in nature only in a very strong sense, one that implies the existence of intentionality or spiritual powers in nature, whereas the *Naturphilosophen* are affirming it in a weaker sense, one that has no such implications. Furthermore, Kant agrees with the *Naturphilosophen* that teleological explanations are irreducible to mechanical ones.[21]

But the appearances of sweet harmony here are very deceptive. To conclude that there are no differences between Kant and the *Naturphilosophen*
would be all too hasty. It would fail to appreciate the full force of Kant's
arguments, and indeed the main point at issue between him and the *Naturphilosophen*. To see why, let us take a closer look at the *status controversiae*.

5. The Limits of Experience

Although the *Naturphilosophen* deny that the concept of a natural purpose
refers to some kind of occult substance or supernatural power, they still give
it some ontological status or objective reference. It is not that teleology is
only a distinctive form of explanation, one that is logically irreducible to
mechanism. On the contrary, teleology has a constitutive status, an objective reference, in two fundamental respects. First, it refers to a distinctive
structure, function, or form of the organic; second, it denotes a force behind
this structure, function, or form. To be sure, this force is not supernatural,
and still less is it a kind of entity; but it is a form of causal agency, a force
whose manifestations are organic structures, functions, or forms.

Of course, it is precisely these ontological assumptions that Kant contests.
He doubts not only that there is a specific kind of causal agency behind organic growth, but also that there is a distinctive structure, form, or function of an organism. The whole point behind his regulative doctrine is precisely to bracket both of these assumptions. Hence even if we drop the
ontology of vital spirits and supernatural forces, Kant is still at odds with the
Naturphilosophen.

To be more precise, Kant could concede that the idea of a natural purpose
does not involve any assumptions about an intention, soul, or spirit. Furthermore, he could acknowledge—as he indeed insists—that the idea of a
whole in a natural purpose is irreducible to its parts. Still, even if he makes
these concessions, Kant still disputes that the concept of a natural purpose
has objective validity. For even if teleological explanations are logically irreducible to mechanical ones, we still have to ask: What right do we have to
assume that these explanations refer to some unique form of structure or
causality in the natural world? After all, Kant insists that teleology is a necessary method of explaining nature *for us*, given the limitations of our human understanding; in other words, we cannot know that there really are
unique structures, functions, or forms in nature that are irreducible to mechanical causes. For all we know, organisms might be simply very complicated mechanisms. Again, Kant was quite explicit and emphatic about this

point: "We are quite unable to prove that organized natural products cannot be produced through the mechanism of nature" (§71, V, 388).[22]

The first naive and natural response to Kant's challenge is to claim that observation and experiment do confirm the existence of unique living structures or forms. At the end of the eighteenth century, this line of reasoning was indeed very prevalent among some of the leading physiologists in Germany—thinkers like J. F. Blumenbach, C. F. Wolff, and K. F. Kielmeyer—who had a profound influence on the development of *Naturphilosophie*.[23] Blumenbach, Wolff, and Kielmeyer maintained that it is possible to provide convincing empirical evidence that some living things actually generate and organize themselves. Their confidence is easily comprehensible once it is placed in historical context. During the first half of the eighteenth century there were two fundamental theories about the origin and development of life: *preformation* and *epigenesis*.[24] According to preformation, organisms are already preformed in the embryo, and their development involves little more than an increase in size. According to epigenesis, however, organisms originally exist only as inchoate "germs" or "seeds," and their development consists in the actual generation of an organism's characteristic structure and organization. Toward the close of the eighteenth century, the theory of preformation had been severely discredited, chiefly because it could not account for the many empirical facts amassing against it—for example, to take the most spectacular case, the regeneration of freshwater polyps. Hence, in his influential tract *Über den Bildungstrieb*, Blumenbach confessed that he had to abandon his previous allegiance to preformation because of the sheer weight of experimental evidence against it, which he then proceeded to describe in great detail.[25] And, in his famous dispute with Albrecht Haller, Wolff contended that his theory of epigenesis did not rest on the fallacious inference that what could not be observed (a preformed embryo) did not exist, as Haller insinuated, but on the simple observation of what did exist. After making months of painstaking observations, Wolff concluded that he saw under his microscope nothing less than the *generation* of intestinal tissue in chick embryos; there was no preformed structure observable anywhere; and all that could be seen was the formation of an inchoate mass into a differentiated structure. So, in Wolff's view, those who denied epigenesis were in the same embarrassing predicament as Galileo's critics: they simply refused to look through the microscope.[26]

These developments are striking and dramatic, and they are crucial in explaining the rise of the organic concept of nature among the *Natur-*

philosophen. Still, they need not be intimidating for a Kantian. Unperturbed, he will maintain that, even if observation and experiment show that something is self-organizing *without* a preformed structure, this still does not prove that it is a natural purpose. The problem is that, for all we know, the thing might still be acting entirely because of mechanical causes. The attribution of purposes to nature implies that there *is* some other form of causality not strictly reducible to mechanism; but no amount of experience can ever be sufficient to exclude entirely the operation of hidden mechanical causes. Of course, one of the reasons the physiologists and *Naturphilosophen* inferred the existence of natural purposiveness from their observations is that they believed they had already refuted mechanism. Because they had independent arguments against mechanism, they believed they could safely exclude the possibility that self-generation and self-organization arose from hidden mechanical causes. Usually, they made two kinds of argument against mechanism. First, they claimed that the structure of an organism is too complex to have arisen from mechanical causes alone. Second, they contended that a natural purpose is very different from a mechanism because it implies that that an object is the cause of itself, whereas mechanism implies that all causes are external to a thing.

Neither of these arguments are conclusive, however. Both make invalid inferences—and, indeed, the very kind of dogmatic inferences that Kant exposes in the third *Kritik*. The first assumes that because *we cannot conceive* the structure arising from mechanical causes it could not have done so, which is to make a dogmatic inference from the limits of our cognitive powers to what must exist. The second assumes that because the concept of a purpose involves a different form of explanation from that of mechanism, it therefore must also refer to a special kind of structure or cause; but this is just the point that Kant questions when he maintains that the concept of a purpose has a strictly problematic status. Although Kant himself argues that we cannot use mechanism to explain organism, he does so for a very different reason from the *Naturphilosoph:* it is not because of any presumed insight into the objective nature of organisms but because of the limitation of our powers of knowledge. The *Naturphilosophen* were dogmatic in their critique of mechanism, however, because they assumed that the impossibility of explaining an organism according to mechanical causes came from the *objective* nature of an organism itself. They therefore excluded the very possibility that Kant wanted to keep open: that organisms, for all we know, could still be produced by mechanism.

6. The Transcendental Deduction of the Organic

As I have explained the controversy so far, it seems as if Kant has trumped the *Naturphilosophen,* who were guilty of dogmatism after all. Although they were perhaps not as naive as the neo-Kantians portrayed them, their defense of *Naturphilosophie* still cannot justify giving constitutive status to the idea of an organism. The Kantians, it seems, can just keeping on wearing their perukes, powdering and curling them with tender care.

But this is not the end of the story, whose most interesting and important chapter remains to be told. It is now necessary to consider the romantics' fundamental rationale for *Naturphilosophie,* an argument implicit in all their writings on nature, and that would have been explicitly given by all of them if we were to only ask. To understand this argument it is necessary to go back in history and reconstruct the context behind the development of the organic view of nature in the late 1790s. Much of that context was set by the early criticism of Kant's philosophy, and especially by the reaction against his dualisms.

Many of Kant's early critics charged that his dualisms—whatever the initial rationale for them—made it impossible for him to solve his own problems.[27] According to Solomon Maimon,[28] whose reaction was typical and influential, Kant's dualisms were so severe that they undermined any attempt to answer the central question of transcendental philosophy: "How is synthetic a priori knowledge possible?" If the understanding and sensibility are such heterogeneous faculties—if the understanding is an active, purely intellectual faculty, which is beyond space and time, and if sensibility is a passive, purely empirical faculty, which is within space and time—then how do they interact with one another to produce knowledge? Kant had stressed that there must be the most intimate interchange between these faculties if knowledge is to be possible—"Concepts without intuitions are empty, intuitions without concepts are blind," as he put it in a famous slogan—yet he had so radically divided them that any interchange between them seemed impossible. The problem here, Maimon maintained, was analogous to, and indeed just as severe as, Descartes's classic difficulty regarding his mind–body dualism.

It was in this context that the *Naturphilosophen* first developed their own organic concept of nature. One of the main motivations behind this concept was to surmount Kant's problematic dualisms, and so to resolve the outstanding problem of transcendental philosophy. The young romantics held that it is possible to bridge these dualisms only by giving *constitutive status* to the concept of an organism. Of course, Kant himself had already set the stage for such an argument in the third *Kritik* by proposing that the concept of an organism mediate between the noumenal and the phenomenal. The only sticking point between him and the *Naturphilosophen* then concerned the regulative versus constitutive status of this concept. But here the *Naturphilosophen* would insist that transcendental philosophy itself demanded giving this concept constitutive status; for only under the assumption that *there is* an organism is it possible to explain the *actual interaction* between the subjective and objective, the ideal and the real, the noumenal and phenomenal. To leave the concept with a purely regulative status simply left the mystery of their actual interaction. Hence, for these reasons, the *Naturphilosophen* believed that the concept of an organism had its own transcendental deduction: it was nothing less than a necessary condition of possible experience. Here we witness once again a phenomenon often seen in the history of post-Kantian thought: that it was necessary to transcend Kant's limits to solve his own problems.[29]

It is important to add that this transcendental argument in behalf of an organism was not simply a *possible* strategy; it is not merely a historical reconstruction of an implicit line of reasoning. Rather, it can be found more or less explicitly in the early writings of Schelling and Hegel. It was Schelling who first suggested this argument in the introduction to his 1797 *Ideen zur eine Philosophie der Natur.* Hegel later developed it, in his characteristically dense and obscure prose, in his *Differenzschrift.* Since Schelling's arguments are clearer and the prototype for Hegel's, I will focus upon them here.

It is striking that, in the introduction to his *Ideen,* Schelling raises the question "What problems must a philosophy of nature resolve?" and answers it by referring to the basic problem of transcendental philosophy: "How a world outside us, how a nature and with it experience, is possible?"[30] Schelling makes it perfectly explicit, therefore, that *Naturphilosophie* has a *transcendental* task: its basic objective is to solve the problem of knowledge. The solution to this problem is especially difficult, Schelling explains, because all knowledge requires some form of correspondence or connection between the subjective and objective, the ideal and the real, or the transcendental and empirical. Such a connection or correspondence seems impossible, however, because these realms appear to be completely heterogeneous from one another. To explain the possibility of knowledge, then, it is necessary to unite these realms, to forge a bridge between them.

Schelling then argues at length that this problem cannot be resolved from conventional Kantian premises.[31] He contends that the orthodox Kantian distinction between the form and matter of experience simply reinstates the dualism that gave rise to the problem of knowledge in the first place. The Kantians cannot bridge the gulf between these realms, he explains, because they so sharply distinguish between the form and matter of experience that they cannot explain how the intellectual, ideal, and subjective forms interact with the empirical, real, and objective matter. They simply state that the forms are imposed on this matter, though they offer no explanation of how that is possible.

In the *Ideen* Schelling only offers some suggestions about how the Kantian dualisms could be overcome; and while he is critical of the Kantian regulative constraints, he also does not dare to abolish them.[32] However, in some later works, especially his 1798 *Entwurf eines Systems der Naturphilosophie* and his 1800 *System des transcendental Idealismus,* he puts forward a solution to the problem of the Kantian dualisms that clearly goes beyond Kant's regulative limits. Schelling's solution is nothing less than his organic concept of nature. If nature is an organism, then it follows that there no distinction in kind but only one of degree between the mental and the physical, the subjective and objective, the ideal and the real. They are then simply different degrees of organization and development of a single living force, which is found everywhere within nature. These apparent opposites can then be viewed as interdependent. The mental is simply the highest degree of organization and development of the living powers of the body; and the body is only the lowest degree of organization and development of the living powers of the mind.

Whatever the merits or flaws of Schelling's organic concept, it should be clear by now that it simply begs the question against him to dismiss the concept as transcendent metaphysics. This famous complaint of the neo-Kantians ignores the transcendental strategy of *Naturphilosophie;* even worse, it also begs important questions about how to solve the problems posed by the Kantian dualisms. Alas, those who demand that we go back to Kant often seem to forget why philosophers were compelled to go beyond him in the first place.

7. A Final Settling of Accounts

Now that we have seen the dialectical struggle between Kant and the *Naturphilosophen,* how should we assess its outcome? What was at stake?

For all the difficulties of Kant's dualisms, it would be wrong to think that he had been superseded by his romantic successors. Perhaps the constitutive status of the organic is the only means to overcome the difficulties of his dualisms, just as Schelling and Hegel argue. Yet Kant himself was perfectly aware of these difficulties; and he believed that it was necessary to live with them all the same. Unlike the romantics, he was content to leave the connection between understanding and sensibility, the intellectual and empirical, a mystery.[33] To be sure, he sometimes wrote about a single source of these faculties; but he regarded any theory about this source as very speculative, and in any case not strictly necessary to explain the possibility of empirical knowledge. If a transcendental deduction presupposes the *fact* of some interaction between these heterogeneous faculties, it does not follow that it has to explain that fact. After all, it is not as if the skeptic can dispute the fact of interconnection; he gains a foothold only in disputing the extravagent theories about it.

It is precisely here that we seem to come to the last crossroads, the final parting of the ways. The diverging paths are Kantian modesty versus post-Kantian curiosity, Kantian skepticism versus post-Kantian speculation. But, once again, this proves to be too simplistic. For if in one respect Schelling's organic concept goes beyond Kant, flying in the face of his regulative limits, in another respect it is entirely warranted by him, entirely in keeping with his spirit, if not his letter. This concept was the inevitable result of joining together two very Kantian lines of thought. First, the dynamic theory of matter, which claims that matter is not inert extension but active force. The fundamental premise behind this theory is that mechanism is insufficient to explain matter, which consists in forces of attraction and repulsion. Second, the idea that nature is a unity, a systematic whole, where the idea of the whole precedes all its parts. On the basis of these Kantian themes Schelling already had sufficient rationale for his organic concept of nature. For if mechanism cannot explain matter itself, let alone life and mind, then it fails as the paradigm to explain all of nature. The only other plausible candidate is organicism. The great advantage of organicism is that it does justice to the unity and systematicity of nature. It exlains matter and mind according to a single principle, seeing both as different degrees of organization and development of living force. There is no need to distinguish between the realms of the mechanical–material and the organic–immaterial since the mechanical is only a limiting case of the organic. We can now see clearly why Schelling wanted to go that extra step beyond Kant in demanding not only a *dynamic* but also a *vital* conception of matter. For if we insist on the principle of the unity of nature, only a vital concept unites the organic and inorganic, the mental and the physical, into one natural world.

Of course, Kant himself would never take this step, and indeed he fought against it with all the passion and energy at his command. The reason is not hard to fathom. For him, organicism came only at an enormous price: the loss of moral freedom. If we accept organicism, then we must abandon that dualism between the noumenal and phenomenal that Kant saw as the precondition of moral action and responsibility. Indeed, the organic concept does mean extending the realm of natural explanation not only to the domain of life and mind but also to the realm of the noumenal or rational. From its antidualistic perspective, there can be only an artificial and arbitrary borderline between reason and the mental, the noumenal and the living. There is a continuum throughout all of nature extending from the most primitive matter to the most subtle and sophisticated forms of consciousness; the rational in all its forms is nothing less than the highest organization and development of the living forces inherent in all of nature. Although it gives pride of place to human rationality in the hierarchy of nature, the organic concept still sees rationality as one more manifestation of the forces within nature. Inevitably, the dominion of natural necessity then intrudes into the realm of the moral.

Of course, Schelling and the romantics gave a different assessment of the whole problematic. For them, dualism was not the solution but the problem. It was dualism that came with such a heavy price. Dualism meant the end of the unity of nature, the sancrosanct *lex continui*; it made a mystery out of moral decision and action; and it left unintelligible the interaction between the intellectual and sensible involved in all knowledge. But abandoning dualism made it necessary for the romantics to explain the very issue for which Kant had defended it in the first place: the possibility of freedom.

What the romantics have to say about freedom is another issue, which is far beyond the scope of this chapter to investigate. Suffice to say for now that the issues involved in legitimating their organic concept of nature are much more complicated than they first appear. They raise all kinds of questions about the limits of knowledge, the meaning of the organic, the relationship between the mental and physical, and even the possibility of freedom itself. If I have shown that the organic concept is more than naive speculation—and if I have also shown that the Kantian critique is more than positivist dogmatism—I will have achieved my purposes here.

CHAPTER 10

Religion and Politics
in *Frühromantik*

1. Some Troubling Stereotypes

In 1835, in his brilliant *Die romantische Schule,* Heinrich Heine related some amusing stories about his encounters with August Wilhelm Schlegel, who was then at the height of his fame as the leading spokesman for the romantic school in Germany.[1] When he first attended Schlegel's lectures at Bonn University in 1819, Heine tells us, he was deeply impressed. Schlegel was heavily perfumed, and dressed according to the latest Parisian fashion. "He was elegance and decorum itself, and whenever he spoke of the prime minister of England he would always add 'my friend.'" Schlegel was so thin, so wasted, and so brilliant that he seemed to be pure spirit. But when Heine encountered Schlegel again, some ten years later on the streets of Paris, his impression was very different. The pure spirit was dead, and only the body lived on. No longer the brilliant literary historian, Schlegel had grown old and fat. He gloated in the honors showered upon him, wearing all his badges and medals around his neck. Whenever he would laugh, Heine wrote, it was like "an old lady who had just put a sugar cube in her mouth."

Heine's portrait was, of course, deliberately slanted, designed to poke fun at a figure whose politics he could not abide. In *Die romantische Schule* we are left in no doubt about the reasons for his contempt. Here Heine interpreted German romanticism as an essentially reactionary movement whose main goal was to revive the religion and arts of the Middle Ages.[2] He could never forgive or forget that some of the romantics had converted to Catholicism and worked for Metternich. In Heine's view, the romantics' literary endeavors were inspired by their reactionary political values. The Schlegel brothers conspired against Racine, he wrote, with the same zeal as Minister Stein against Napoleon.[3] Heine then made a simple but striking and seductive contrast between classicism and romanticism.[4] While the classicist is a humanist who thinks that the end of humanity is realized here on earth, the romantic is a Christian who believes that the highest good is achieved only in heaven. If the political ideals of the humanist are liberty and equality, those of the romantic are faith in church and state. For Heine, then, romanticism was little more than the literary form of the Restoration, and the ultimate source of its inspiration came from Christianity itself.

Heine's portrait of romanticism has been—and still remains—profoundly influential. It was espoused by other German radicals of the 1840s, such as Karl Marx and Arnold Ruge, who saw romanticism as the enemy ideology, or what they called "the Christian-Germanic Restoration principle."[5] Until very recently, this has been the official Marxist view of romanticism.[6] Yet, even in his own day, Heine's portrait did not lack critics. In 1850, Hermann Hettner, one of the most eminent literary historians of the nineteenth century, pointed out its chief difficulty: that Heine's interpretation of *Romantik* was anachronistic, judging the entire romantic movement from the views of some of its last representatives.[7] Of course, in their later years some of the romantics (Friedrich Schlegel, Adam Müller, Archim von Arnim) were reactionaries who supported Metternich and the Roman Catholic Church; but in their earlier years, in the 1790s, they were champions of the French Revolution.

For Hettner, the problem with romanticism was not that it was reactionary but that it was apolitical.[8] Romanticism was fundamentally an aesthetic movement, which made art an end in itself, never to be compromised by social or political reality. Because of his impotence in the political world, the romantic would retreat into the world of the literary imagination, the only place where he could enjoy complete freedom. Hettner's views too became very influential. They have found their main modern champion in the work of Carl Schmitt, whose notorious *Politische Romantik* simply revived Hettner's thesis.[9]

Now, with the benefit of much hindsight, it seems to me that we can finally say that both Heine and Hettner are wrong. Hettner's criticisms of Heine are indeed telling. Although Heine's portrait does hold for some figures of late romanticism—so called *Spätromantik*—it is completely false for almost all the leading thinkers of early romanticism—so called *Frühromantik*—whose politics were very liberal and progressive. But Hettner's interpretation, and by implication that of Schmitt, is flawed too. It is simply false that politics was not essential to the early romantics, as if it were nothing more than an instrument or occasion for their literary imagination. If we consider the early philosophical fragments of the romantics, most of which were published only after 1960, and so unavailable to Hettner and Schmitt, it becomes overwhelmingly clear that politics was an integral element of romantic philosophy. The main problem with the apolitical interpretation, however, is that it cannot do justice to some of the romantics explicit and emphatic statements about their fundamental beliefs.

If we wish to know someone's fundamental values it is only necessary to know their answer to one classical question—namely, the question Aristotle raised in Book I of the *Nicomachean Ethics:* What is the highest good?[10] The romantics had a clear answer to this question, which was still very much alive in late-eighteenth-century Germany. They maintained firmly and passionately that the highest good was *Bildung,* human excellence or perfection, the self-realization and development of all human powers as a whole.[11] Like Aristotle, they also held that such excellence or perfection can be realized only in the community or state. They reaffirmed the classical Aristotelian doctrine that the state is prior to the individual, that man is a political animal, a mere beast or god apart from the *polis.* Hence, for the romantics as for Aristotle, politics became the first art or science. In his early *Ueber das Studium der griechischen Poesie* Schlegel echoes Aristotle: "Political judgment is the highest of all viewpoints."[12]

If, then, we are to understand *Frühromantik,* we have to turn Hettner and Schmitt upside down. For the early romantics, art is subordinate to politics, not politics to art. Far from making art an end in itself, the romantics subordinated it to the ethical and political. For they held that the purpose of art is *Bildung,* the education of humanity, which is achieved only in the state. Hence the young Friedrich Schlegel wrote to his brother: "The soul of my doctrine is that humanity is the highest end, and art exists only for its sake."[13]

For similar reasons, it seems that we should also stand Heine on his head. For the romantics tell us that the highest good is *Bildung,* human excellence and perfection, which is the *credo* of humanism, the very doctrine that Heine saw as the antithesis of romanticism. But it is just here that matters begin to get complicated. If the early romantics were *not* reactionaries who defended Roman Catholic dogma, neither were they radicals who proclaimed an atheistic humanism. Rather, they saw the closest connection between their humanism and religion. Although they claimed the highest good was *Bildung,* they also insisted that this could not be achieved without religion. Religion was not only a means to, but an essential part of, *Bildung;* indeed, it was nothing less than the guiding force behind it.[14]

So the romantics wanted a humanistic religion or a religious humanism. But, for Heine, Ruge, and Marx, this was an impossibility, an oxymoron, a *contradicto en adjecto*. Recall that on their view humanism is atheistic, progressive, and liberal, and that religion is reactionary, the chief pillar of the state of the *ancien régime*. This raises a very tricky question: How did the romantics think they could synthesize humanism and religion? Why, unlike Heine, Ruge, and Marx, did they see no contradiction in combining them?

2. Radical Chic in the 1790s

Prima facie it might seem that there is not that much of a problem here. It appears that Heine, Ruge, and Marx have a very limited conception of religion, one which limits it to the theism of Christian tradition. Surely, one might say, that should not pass for our understanding of religion in general. There were many other forms of Christianity, some of which were allied with the most progressive social causes. We only need to think of the radical spiritualist sects during the Reformation that were the source of so many modern liberal values.

We shall soon see that romantic religion was indeed very progressive and liberal, and that it had very little to do with the traditional theism Heine ascribed to it. But it is important to see now that the problem of consistency runs much deeper than this. We cannot simply point to the other more liberal and progressive form of religion held by the romantics and so have done with it.

The root of the problem is that the more we examine the sources of romantic humanism and religion, the more we find that they each stem from two philosophers completely at odds with one another. Romantic humanism has its source in Fichte; and romantic religion has its origins in Spinoza. But there are few philosophers more antithetical, more at odds about all the fundamental issues, than these two.

To give a better idea of the problem at hand here, let me explain in a little more detail why the romantics were attracted to Fichte and Spinoza in the first place. Once we see that they were attracted to conflicting aspects of Fichte and Spinoza, we will have a much better feeling for the tension they had to resolve. This tension derives from two completely antithetical views about religion and politics. Specifically, the problem is how to reconcile a *Fichtean* humanism with a *Spinozist* religion.

There can be no doubt that Fichte and Spinoza were the most influential philosophers on the young romantics. Hölderlin, Friedrich Schlegel, and

Novalis attended Fichte's early lectures in Jena, which left an indelible impression on them; and, until 1798, Schelling was virtually a disciple of Fichte. Such was the power that Fichte held over these young minds that they had to struggle mightily to gain their independence from him. Ironically, though, the years of Fichte's greatest influence in Germany—roughly from 1794 to 1799—were also the heyday of the Spinoza revival, which began in 1786 with the publication of Jacobi's *Briefe über die Lehre von Spinoza*. In that remarkable work Jacobi made the sensational revelation that Lessing confessed to him in the summer of 1780 that he was a Spinozist. In revealing Lessing's confession, Jacobi's aim was to warn the public against the dangers of Spinozism, which, in his view, was tantamount to atheism and fatalism. Yet Jacobi's warning backfired, leading to one public declaration of Spinozism after another. If Lessing could confess his Spinozism, many reasoned, then so could they too. Among the most prominent to make such a confession were Goethe and Herder.

Growing up in the 1790s, the young romantics were inevitably drawn into the vortex of the pantheism controversy. Their notebooks give more than ample evidence of their study of, and sympathy for, Spinozism. For them, Spinoza was *"der Gott betrunkene Mensch."*[15] To write *"Hen kai pan"*—*"Eins und Alles"*—in *Stammbücher* became something of a fashion. Famously, in his *Reden über die Religion* Schleiermacher asks us to make an offering to "the holy rejected Spinoza."[16] Yet, by the time he made this request, the offerings were already piled rather high.

It is not difficult to understand how anyone growing up in the 1790s would be seduced by Fichte and Spinoza. From completely opposing perspectives, they were the most radical and progressive philosophers of the 1790s. To be in the vanguard, to be on the cutting edge of the *Zeitgeist,* meant following in their footsteps.

What the romantics saw in Spinoza was first and foremost his attempt to rationalize religion. Spinoza's famous dictum *deus sive natura,* his identification of God with the infinitude of nature, seemed to resolve the conflict between reason and faith, which had preoccupied philosophers and theologians throughout the Enlightenment. Spinoza's dictum divinized nature as much as it naturalized the divine, and so it seemed to make a religion out of science, a science out of religion. If God were the same as "the one and all"—if the divine were nothing more than the unity of nature, the systematic unity of all its laws—then there is no warrant for opposing reason and faith. Instead, the objects of religion and science are one and the same. The conflict between reason and faith arose in the first place only because the divine was conceived as something supernatural. If God were an entity beyond the natural world, then we could prove his existence either through the Bible (with theism) or through rational inferences (with deism). But, by the end of the eighteenth century, both theism and deism were on their last legs. Theism not only rested its case on miracles, which were hard to square with science, but it also suffered greatly from the new biblical criticism; and deism had collapsed under the relentless barrage of skeptical arguments. Only Spinoza's pantheism did not seem in danger of such obsolescence. The reality of Spinoza's God was as palpable as that of nature itself. Rather than being a mysterious spirit, like the God of traditional theism, or an irrelevant abstraction, like the God of deism, Spinoza's God was present equally within everyone alike. Since we are all modes of the single infinite substance, we only have to reflect on ourselves to find the divine within us.

It is important to see that the romantic attraction to Spinoza was not only epistemological; for here again political factors played a decisive role. To understand these factors, it is worthwhile to keep in mind another remark of Heine: that pantheism had always been the secret religion of Germany, the faith of its cultural underground.[17] Heine knew whereof he spoke. Since the end of the seventeenth century in Germany, Spinoza had become the patron saint of radical Protestants, of all those discontented reformers who accused Luther of selling out to the princes and betraying his two grand ideals: religious liberty and the priesthood of all believers. These radicals embraced Spinoza for a variety of reasons, all of them perfectly Protestant. They saw Spinoza's separation of church and state as a guarantee of religious liberty; they embraced his critique of the Bible because it freed Lutheranism from its biblicism, its deadening emphasis on the letter as a rule of faith; and they loved his pantheism because it seemed to justify the equality and priesthood of all believers. After all, if God is infinitely present within everyone alike, we are all equal; and then there is no need for a priest or spiritual authority to mediate our relationship with God. Of course, Spinoza was a Jew, at least by background; but for these radical Protestants, who were ecumenical to the bone, that was all the more reason to embrace him. What could better show their universalist credentials? And, in any case, did Spinoza not live with the brethren at Rijnsberg? Was the affinity in doctrine that accidental after all?

Despite constant persecution, the flames of religious radicalism in Germany never died out; and clandestine editions of the *Ethica* and *Tractatus* never ceased to circulate. The radical ideals lived on well into the eighteenth century, when they found their foremost exponents in writers like Gottfried

Arnold, Conrad Dippel, Johann Edelmann, and finally Lessing and Herder themselves. When the romantics embraced Spinozism in the late 1790s they were—somewhat unwittingly—carrying on the tradition of the radical reformers. The Spinoza revival of the 1790s was nothing less than the last great manifestation of the radical reformation. Its finest literary and philosophical expression was Schleiermacher's *Reden.*

What chiefly attracted the romantics to Fichte was his radical concept of freedom, specifically his claim that the self is only what it *posits* itself to be. This concept was radical in two respects. First, it means that the self has no eternal essence, which it somehow realizes or develops of necessity; rather, its essence is created by itself. For Fichte, whose position anticipates Sartre, the self is only what it makes of itself.[18] Second, the self can create not only itself but also its world, which also ought to be the product of its reason. By this second claim Fichte did not mean that the self *has* created its world—as if it were somehow divine—but only that it has the *power* to do so; it can approach the ideal of a completely rational world through infinite striving.[19]

Read in the context of the 1790s Fichte's radical concept had a clear political message, one his young listeners would not have missed for a moment. What Fichte was saying is that the social and political world is not an eternal order to which we must submit; rather it too is something that we can create according to the demands of our own reason. Fichte was preaching not resignation but action; he was indeed insisting that we have not only the right but the duty to transform the social and political world according to reason. Hence his popular 1794 *Vorlesungen über die Bestimmung des Gelehrten* closes on a rousing note: *"Handeln! Handeln!, das ist es, wozu wir da sind."*[20]

3. Fichte versus Spinoza

Now that we have seen why the romantics were so attracted to Fichte and Spinoza it is easy to understand why they wanted to join both philosophers into a single system. We can find the romantic project for such a synthesis expressed, more or less explicitly, in their early notebooks and fragments.[21] This project is crucial, I believe, for understanding early German romanticism. All too often the romantic worldview is interpreted as a poetic version of Fichte's *Wissenschaftslehre* or Spinoza's *Ethica;* it is seen as one or the other, never both. Yet these interpretations miss what is most central to and characteristic of the philosophy of *Frühromantik:* the attempt *to wed* Fichte and Spinoza.

Of course, though, it is just this project that is the great paradox. The very idea of a synthesis of Fichte and Spinoza seems utterly absurd as soon as we consider the deep conflicts between them. These conflicts are especially apparent in those aspects of Fichte and Spinoza that most attracted the romantics—namely, Fichte's political radicalism and Spinoza's pantheistic religion.

Prima facie there does not seem to be that much of a conflict. For was not Spinoza's pantheism also progressive and radical? Did he not defend the same political values as Fichte? Indeed, Fichte had no quarrel with Spinoza's republicanism, egalitarianism, and defense of toleration. It would seem, then, that he should embrace Spinoza as a fellow radical, as even a martyr in the struggle for the same political causes. Yet, rather than doing so, Fichte spurned Spinoza, declaring him his archenemy. Notoriously, he declared that there were only two possible philosophies: his and that of his archenemy, Spinoza.[22] The choice between his philosophy and Spinoza's was for him *the* crucial test of philosophical loyalty and committment.

Why did Fichte see such a conflict between himself and Spinoza? In his *Erste Einleitung in die Wissenschaftslehre* Fichte himself gave a vivid and simple account of the main issue dividing them.[23] The two possible philosophies were either his idealism or Spinoza's realism, or as he sometimes put it in Kantian terms, "criticism" or "dogmatism." If we are idealists, we make the self absolute and explain nature as its product; if we are realists, we make nature the absolute and explain the self as its product. In other words, either we place the absolute *inside* us with criticism, so that it is immanent to experience, or we place it *outside us* with dogmatism, so that it transcends experience. There is no way of reconciling idealism and realism, Fichte insisted, because they are incompatible concepts of the absolute, the single infinite reality. If both were true, we would have to divide the infinite; but, obviously, there can be only one infinite reality, only one thing answering to the definition of the infinite: that of which nothing greater can be conceived.

Fichte often wrote as if the choice between his philosophy and Spinoza's was an essentially personal one, a matter of individual choice. In some famous lines,[24] he declared that the philosophy one chose depended on the kind of person one was; but he might well have said the converse: which philosophy one chose determined the kind of person one was, and indeed one's basic attitude toward the world. Because he was an idealist, the Fichtean was an activist, committed to infinite striving, a ceaseless struggle to make the world a better place; because he was a realist, the Spinozian was a quietist, acquiescing to the divine power moving through him, which acted from the necessity of its own nature alone.

Although Fichte sometimes said that the choice between his philosophy and Spinoza's was essentially personal, he also accused Spinoza of a basic logical fallacy,[25] one that Kant had called "the fallacy of pure reason": hypostasis, reification, projecting the ideas of reason outside us, as if they were an alien power to which we must submit, when they are in fact only the product of our own activity.[26] This fallacy was the arch-sin of all metaphysical dogmatism, Kant taught, and its removal required nothing less than a critique of reason. The critique supplied an effective remedy for this malady: reformulating a *constitutive* principle, which pretends to describe something that exists, into a *regulative* principle, which prescribes tasks for our reason. In other words, what seemed to be an object of belief had to become a goal for action. Spinoza committed this very fallacy, Fichte argued, when he made the infinite something outside us—the single infinite substance—when it is in truth nothing more than something within us: our infinite power to change the world according to reason. It is indeed for just this reason that Fichte called Spinoza "a dogmatist," for hypostasis was the characteristic fallacy of dogmatism.

Fichte's critique of Spinoza is really the basis for his own humanism. The immediate result of his critique is that the idea of the infinite is really only a goal for action, not an object of belief. In other words, we should strive to make the kingdom of God a reality on the earth rather than believe in its existence in heaven. Like Kant, Fichte understood the traditional idea of the kingdom of God in *ethical* terms; this kingdom symbolized the moral ideal of the highest good—namely, the perfect correspondence of virtue and happiness, the total harmony of duty and reward. Yet he went a step further than Kant in also interpreting this traditional ideal in political terms. The highest good did not exist in some supernatural realm after life; rather, it was a goal for us to achieve in this life: the perfect republican constitution where there is complete justice, where those who labor receive rewards in proportion to their efforts. Hence Fichte's humanism was ultimately atheistic.[27] To believe in the existence of God and the highest good was to hypostatize the ideals of reason.

We can now see why there was such a conflict between Fichte's radicalism and Spinoza's pantheism. Very simply, Fichte's radicalism is a form of atheistic humanism, denying the existence of the God that Spinoza sees as the single reality. In more Kantian terms, we could say this: Spinoza maintains the *constitutive* status of the infinite, while Fichte insists on its *regulative* status.

We might admit this difference but still ask: Why can we not affirm the existence of God *and* remain committed to Fichte's radical ideals? Why can we not be both Fichtean activists *and* Spinozian pantheists? Here again Fichte would resist any attempt at conflation. And for good reasons. Spinoza's pantheism undermines Fichte's activism in two fundamental ways. First, it erases radical freedom. If God acts from the necessity of his own nature, and if all human actions are modes of the divine nature, then they too will be necessary. What I think or do will be simply what God thinks or does through me; someone cannot act otherwise anymore than the eternal divine nature can change. Second, Spinoza seems to undermine any motivation to change the world. For him, the essence of God is rational; and since everything expresses or manifests the essence of God, everything is completely and perfectly rational. Why bother to change the world, then, if everything is already an embodiment of divine reason?

It is important to see that, for Fichte, there was always the closest connection between his atheism and belief in freedom. If we believe that the infinite already exists, if we make it an object of belief, then we alienate our freedom. We surrender our autonomy, our power to change the world according to our own reason, because we project outside ourselves some alien realm of being to which we must conform. Rather than making the real world conform to our demands, we make ourselves conform to the demands of some imaginary world. It was especially this element of alienation and resignation behind Spinozism, I believe, that motivated Fichte's intense animus against Spinoza. For all its progressive elements, Spinoza's pantheism ultimately undermined the motivation for social and political change. Indeed, precisely because it seemed so progressive, Spinoza's religion was more dangerous than traditional theism. Hence, paradoxically, Fichte would drop more obloquy on Spinoza's head than even the most conservative theist.

Whatever the source of the conflict between Fichte and Spinoza, and however reconcilable it ultimately might be, it is important to see that the tensions were not merely implicit. They are not artificial reconstructions of the philosophical historian; rather, they were direct experiences of the romantics themselves. The tension was perfectly explicit, a conflict over which the romantic soul spent many a sleepless night. Time and again we find the romantics torn between Fichte's radicalism and Spinoza's pantheism. There are moments when they seem to be saying, with Fichte, that we live in a world of our own creation, that we have the power to create the Kingdom of God on earth through our own efforts. "The starting point of modern culture," Friedrich Schlegel once wrote, "is the revolutionary wish to realize the kingdom of God on earth."[28] Yet there are also moments when they seem to embrace Spinoza's single infinite substance and to surrender themselves into the arms of the one and all. Nowhere is this tension more apparent than in Hölderlin's *Hyperion*, where Hyperion, the hero of the novel, vacillates constantly between these two attitudes toward the world, a political activism that would change everything and a religious quietism that would surrender itself to the infinite. In an unmistakable allusion to the conflict between Fichte and Spinoza, Hölderlin wrote that sometimes we feel as if we are everything and the world nothing; and sometimes as if the world is everything and we are nothing.[29] *Hyperion* is nothing less than Hölderlin's attempt to reconcile these two attitudes toward the world. The same tension appears in another seminal text of early romanticism, Schelling's *Briefe über Dogmatismus und Kriticizismus*. This work was most probably the product of conversations between Schelling and Hölderlin regarding the conflict between Fichte and Spinoza. The first letters present us with a stark choice between two different visions of the world: a philosophy of freedom that celebrates the heroic struggle to change the world; and the philosophy of necessity, which warns us of our vanity and advises us to surrender ourselves into the arms of the infinite.[30]

Given that the conflict between Fichte and Spinoza runs so wide and deep, how did the romantics attempt to reconcile them? The young Hölderlin and Schelling sometimes despaired of a solution. It was they who first claimed—Fichte's famous lines only echo them—that the choice between them was ultimately a matter of personal decision. Yet something more came of all those sleepless nights. In the late 1790s we find the young romantics struggling to find a deeper philosophical solution. It is now time to see what form it took.

4. Revitalizing Spinoza

The heart of the romantic synthesis lay in the reinterpretation of Spinoza. To some extent it is misleading to write about the revival of Spinozism in the 1790s because the German romantics were not, strictly speaking, Spinozists. They reinterpreted Spinoza in ways utterly at odds with some of Spinoza's fundamental doctrines. If he knew of them, Benedictus would have screamed betrayal. Yet it is precisely through this *re*interpretation that the romantics made Spinoza more congenial to Fichte's idealism.

The crucial precedent for the romantic reinterpretation of Spinoza was Herder's 1787 tract *Gott, Einige Gespräche*. Whether there was a direct influence or not, some of the fundamental tenets of Herder's reinterpretation of Spinoza reappear in Schelling, Hölderlin, Novalis, Friedrich Schlegel, and the young Hegel. It seems to me that the Herder text is far more important than F. H. Jacobi's *Briefe über die Lehre von Spinoza,* which has lately received most attention as the source of the romantic understanding of Spinoza.[31]

In his 1787 tract Herder reinterprets Spinoza's philosophy as a vitalistic pantheism or a pantheistic vitalism. He makes Spinoza into a champion of an organic worldview, according to which all of nature forms one vast living organism. In remolding Spinoza in this light Herder self-consciously fuses him with his great metaphysical contemporary: Leibniz.[32] For it was Leibniz who made the essence of substance into living force, *vis viva.* What we must do, Herder believes, is combine Spinoza's monism and naturalism with Leibniz's vitalism. Ironically, Herder was reviving the two great dogmatic metaphysicians at the very same time as Kant was desperately attempting to bury them in the *Kritik der reinen Vernunft.*

Despite his sympathy for such arch-metaphysicians, Herder had scant sympathy for Spinoza's dogmatic method, his procedure *more geometrico* of beginning with axioms and definitions and then deriving theorems through rigorous deduction. A student of Kant's in the 1760s, he had little confidence in such a method, which he saw as a relic of defunct scholasticism. The proper procedure of metaphysics, Herder claimed, was that outlined by Kant in his *Prize Essay:* it should generalize the results of the empirical sciences. But it was precisely in this regard that Spinoza's philosophy had proven itself to be so antiquated. For Spinoza based his philosophy on the mechanistic paradigm of explanation of Cartesian physics. Like Descartes, Spinoza had assumed that matter is inert extension, and that one body moves only if another body directly acts on it through impact. But it was just this paradigm, Herder contended, that was no longer adequate in modern physics. All the new data from experiments in chemistry, electricity, and magnetism had shown that matter does not consist in inert extension but in active force. The research indicated that matter most probably consists in attractive and repulsive forces. If this were so, then mechanism was in very serious trouble; for one of the classic problems of mechanism was its apparent incapacity to explain attractive forces. These results seemed to imply action at a distance, which could not be accounted for on the basis of impact.

Never for a moment did Herder doubt Spinoza's naturalism, his conception of nature as infinite and everything in nature happening according to necessary laws. Like Spinoza, he too wanted to uphold the unity of nature; and he too was an implacable opponent of all forms of dualism. Yet now, with the evident breakdown of mechanism, would it be possible to sustain Spinoza's monism and naturalism? Clearly, these doctrines would have to be reinterpreted according to the latest results from the sciences. For Herder, this meant first and foremost reinterpreting Spinoza's single infinite substance so that it was now living force, the force of all forces, *"die Urkraft aller Kräfte."*[33] Such a move guaranteed the unity and continuity of nature because there was no longer any dualism between the mental and physical, the organic and inorganic. If we assume that matter is living force, then we are no longer caught in the classic dilemma of dualism versus materialism. For we can now explain both mind and matter as different degrees of organization and development of living force. While matter is the lower degree of organization and development of living force, mind is its highest degree of organization and development. This is not a form of reductivism because there is still a difference between the mental and physical; nevertheless, the difference is in degree rather than kind.

It should be clear that Herder's organic reinterpretation of Spinoza would never have pleased Benedictus himself. It introduces at least two alien elements into Spinoza's system. First, an element of teleology. If substance is living force, then it ceases to be inert and eternal, as Spinoza conceived it; rather, it now undergoes change and development, evolving from the inchoate, indeterminate, and potential into the organized, determinate, and actual. Since this development realizes the essence or nature of substance, it should be understood as purposive, flatly contrary to his Spinoza's strictures against teleology. But Herder believed that Spinoza's ban on teleology worked against only the old fashioned *external teleology,* which saw purposes as imposed on nature by God for the sake of man; he had little against an *internal teleology,* which saw purposes as the essence or inherent nature of things themselves. Second, Herder brings into Spinozism the idea of a hierarchy of nature, "a great chain of being." Insofar as nature is an organic whole, it has the structure of a pyramid, displaying stages or levels of organization and development. According to this hierarchy, the pinnacle of nature, the highest degree of organization and development of living force, is nothing less than man himself. Hence man regains his privileged position in the order of nature that he had lost in Spinoza's system. Spinoza had conceived man as simply one finite mode of nature like any other; to give him a higher position was simply crude anthropocentrism and anthropomorphism.

The romantics attempt to synthesize Fichte's idealism and Spinoza's naturalism was essentially based on this reinterpretation of Spinoza. Now that human self-consciousness was restored as the purpose and pinnacle of nature, Fichte could say that the self should be the first principle of philosophy after all. Fichte was indeed right in placing self-consciousness at the center of all things, as the basis to explain all of nature, for self-consciousness is the purpose of nature, the highest degree of organization and development of *all* its living powers. Where Fichte went astray, however, was in interpreting the *final* cause as a *first* cause. He had wrongly assumed that the ego is the first cause of nature when it really is only the final cause, the ultimate purpose for which things exist. Fichte had failed to make that fundamental distinction so crucial to the organic interpretation of the world—namely, that between what is first in the order of being and what is first in order of explanation.

The romantics' vitalism also allowed them to give a much greater role to human agency in the cosmos than anything ever imagined by Spinoza. In Spinoza's vision of things, human agency and awareness ultimately makes little difference to the divine. God has a complete, perfect, and self-sufficient nature, which remains the same whether we humans exist or not; although we depend on God, God does not depend on us. For the romantics, however, God depends on human beings as much as they depend on God. For it is only through human self-consciousness and activity that the divine nature finally realizes itself. If there were no human self-consciousness or agency, the divine nature would still exist, to be sure, yet it would remain imperfect, potential, inchoate, and indeterminate. It is only through our activity, then, that we perfect, complete, and realize the divine, so that human activity is divine itself.

By giving such a greater role to human agency, the romantics could claim to do justice to Fichte's activism. When Fichte made the divine a goal or ideal of human activity, he was not so wrong after all. Because it is only through our activity that the divine realizes itself, we have good reason to make it the goal of our activity. It indeed seems that we now have more reason to be activist than ever, for our activity now has a divine sanction behind it. We make the world a better place not only for ourselves, but for God.

5. Final Assessment

Such, in very crude outline, is the romantic synthesis of Fichte and Spinoza, idealism and realism. What are we to make of it? Whatever its ultimate truth or falsity, there is something to be said for it. Vitalistic pantheism is a remarkably imaginative and perfectly coherent worldview. It synthesized in a remarkable fashion some of the many competing ideas of its generation. It is indeed striking how much it accommodates Fichte's idealism within its general Spinozistic naturalism.

Yet it cannot be said that it is entirely successful, at least as a synthesis of Fichte and Spinoza. It is possible to hear Fichte howling in protest in the backgound, screaming with all that indignant bluster that made him such a troublesome personality. And it is not difficult to imagine the sources of his discontent. For the reasons behind Fichte's fierce opposition to Spinozism still remain in place.

The first problem is that vitalistic pantheism still has no room for his concept of radical freedom. Since the romantics gave a constitutive status to the idea of the infinite, and since the infinite realizes itself of necessity throughout nature, there is no place for radical freedom, which claims not only that we have the power to create ourselves, but also that we have the power to act otherwise. The romantics' naturalism undermines both these assumptions. According to it, God acts from the necessity of his nature; and everything is simply a mode of God. Hence it is not we who act, but God who acts through us. The only sense of freedom permitted in Spinoza's universe is that of definition VII of the *Ethica:* that which is *causi sui*, acting from the necessity of one's own nature alone. Notoriously, that definition applies to God alone.

Of course, once we abandon radical freedom, Fichte's activism soon goes with it. If history, no less than nature, is a manifestation of the divine reason, what point is there in changing society and the state according to our reason? Whatever we do will realize the divine reason and cannot be otherwise; it seems that we have no choice but to wait for the divine reason to act through us; in other words, just as Fichte warned, we end forfeiting our autonomy. To be sure, the romantic synthesis still saw God as the *purpose* of history; but the problem was that God was also the *cause* of history too, so that all of history seemed to be little more than an exercise in divine self-realization. Admitting this poses anew, however, the dangers of antinomianism and fatalism.

It is indeed striking how the romantics themselves began to draw some of these consequences. In his *Reden über die Religion* Schleiermacher preached that religion should not attempt to accelerate the progress of humanity; rather, its only task is to contemplate the divine as it works its way through history.[34] We should not become disgruntled with society as it stands, Schleiermacher wrote, because all places within the social division of labor are the product of divine necessity.[35] In his *Transcendentalphilosophie* Friedrich Schlegel did not hesitate to draw deterministic consequences from his organic concept of nature: he completely banished the Kantian–Fichtean conception of freedom on the grounds that it was a false abstraction from nature and history.[36] And finally Schelling, in his *System der gesamten Philosophie*, virtually debunked the notion of responsibility on the grounds that whatever I did was the divine acting through me.[37]

So, despite its alliance with progressive values, romantic pantheism still has troubling quietistic consequences. It is in this quietism, I would suggest, that we can find one source of the romantics' later conservatism. The more the romantics saw the divine order everywhere, even in present social and political institutions, and the more they regarded that order as the product of necessity, the less motivation they had to change things, they more resigned they became. Schleiermacher's shift from activity to contemplation marks the beginning of the end of the early progressive period of *Frühromantik*.

In the end, then, it appears that we have come full circle, that Heine has been vindicated after all. For it seems as if the romantics' religion *was* a source of their conservatism. Even if their religion was not a conservative form of theism, and even if it was a liberal and progressive form of pantheism, it still posed the danger of quietism. Yet the irony is even richer than this. For no one believed more deeply in the benign political consequences of pantheism than Heine himself, who defended it passionately against the charges of fatalism and quietism.[38] This suggests that no one was a better romantic than Heinrich Heine himself.

So, ultimately, the romantic synthesis of Fichte and Spinoza, of humanism and religion, remains problematic. In a synthesis of such antithetical philosophers something had to give: the radicalism and activism of Fichte's philosophy, the very features that once had so attracted the romantics. Still, despite the collapse of the synthesis, the romantics' vital pantheism seems to me (for all the reasons stated in the last section) to have been one of the most creative and interesting attempts in the history of philosophy to surmount the classical dilemma between humanism and religion. The problems that so troubled the romantics—the sources of torment behind all their sleepless nights—are still with us.

ABBREVIATIONS

NOTES

BIBLIOGRAPHY

INDEX

ABBREVIATIONS

AA   Kant, Immanuel. *Gesammelte Schriften*, Akademie Ausgabe, ed. Wilhelm Dilthey et al. Berlin: de Gruyter, 1902–. All references to the *Kritik der reinen Vernunft* (KrV) are to the first and second editions, cited as "A" and "B" respectively.

EPW   *Early Political Writings of the German Romantics*, ed. and trans. Frederick C. Beiser. Cambridge: Cambridge University Press, 1992.

HKA   Hardenberg, Friedrich von. *Novalis Schriften, Kritische Ausgabe*, ed. Richard Samuel, Hans Joachim Mähl, and Gerhard Schulz. Suttgart: Kohlhammer, 1960–1988.

GSA   Hölderlin, Friedrich. *Sämtliche Werke, Grosse Stuttgarter Ausgabe*, ed. Friedrich Beissner. Stuttgart: Kohlhammer, 1961.

GW   Hegel, Georg Wilhelm Friedrich. *Gesammelte Werke*, ed. Nordrhein-Westfälischen Akademie der Wissenschaften. Hamburg: Meiner, 1989–.

KA   Schlegel, Friedrich. *Kritische Friedrich Schlegel Ausgabe*, ed. Ernst Behler, Jean Jacques Anstett, and Hans Eichner. Munich: Schöningh, 1958–.

KGA   Schleiermacher, Friedrich Daniel. *Kritische Gesamtausgabe*, ed. Günter Meckenstock, et al. Berlin: de Gruyter, 1984–.

NA   Schiller, Friedrich. *Werke, Nationalausgabe*, ed. L. Blumenthal and Benno von Wiese. Weimar: Böhlaus Nachfolger, 1943–1967.

SKA   Schelling, Friedrich Wilhelm Joseph. *Schelling Historische-Kritische Ausgabe*, eds. H. M. Baumgartner, W. G. Jacobs, H. Krings, and H. Zeltner. Stuttgart-Bad Cannstatt: Fromann, 1976–.

NOTES

Introduction

1. One of the very few philosophers to take the romantics seriously in the anglophone world was Josiah Royce, who devoted a chapter to it in his influential book *The Spirit of Modern Philosophy* (Boston: Houghton and Mifflin, 1882), pp. 164–189. This was not passing lip-service on Royce's part, for he had a long-standing interest in Schiller. See his neglected early article "Schillers Ethical Studies," *Journal of Speculative Philosophy* 12 (1878), 373–392.

2. See Theodore Ziolkowski, *German Romanticism and Its Institutions* (Princeton: Princeton University Press, 1990); Andrew Bowie, *Aesthetics and Subjectivity* (Manchester: Manchester University Press, 1990); Gerald Izenberg, *Impossible Individuality: Romanticism, Revolution, and the Origins of Modern Selfhood, 1787–1802* (Princeton: Princeton University Press, 1992), the first two parts of which discuss Schlegel and Scheiermacher; Richard Eldridge, *The Persistence of Romanticism* (Cambridge: Cambridge University Press, 2001), the first half of which treats "post-Kantian Romanticism"; Azade Seyhan, *Representation and Its Discontents: The Critical Legacy of German Romanticism* (Berkeley: University of California Press, 1992); Julia Lamm, *The Living God: Schleiermacher's Appropriation of Spinoza* (University Park: Pennsylvania State University Press, 1996); and Charles Larmore, *The Romantic Legacy* (New York: Columbia University Press, 1996). Another sign of growing interest is Henry Hardy's publication of Isaiah Berlin's *Roots of Romanticism* (Princeton: Princeton University Press, 1999). It is noteworthy, however, that the lectures on which this book were based were originally given in 1965. Berlin deserves credit for being one of the very few to champion the intellectual and philosophical importance of romanticism in the sterile post–World War II intellectual landscape. In this regard, as in many others, he was a *Stimme in der Wüste*.

3. See Phillipe Lacoue-Labarthe's and Jena-Luc Nancy's *L'Absolu Litteraire*, translated by Phillip Bernard and Cheryl Lester as *The Literary Absolute* (Albany: SUNY Press, 1988). Elizabeth Millán Zaibert has translated parts of Manfred Frank's *Unendliche Annäherung*. See *The Philosophical Foundations of Early German Romanticism* (Albany: SUNY Press, 2003).

4. See Margaret Stoljar's translation of Novalis, *Philosophical Writings* (Albany: SUNY Press, 1997); the translations in Jochen Schulte-Sasse et al., *Theory as Practice* (Minneapolis: University of Minnesota Press, 1997); Thomas Pfau's translation of Hölderlin, *Essays and Letters on Theory* (Albany: SUNY Press, 1988), and three essays of Schelling in *Idealism and the Endgame of Theory* (Albany: SUNY Press, 1994); Andrew Bowie's translation of Schleiermacher, *Hermeneutics and Criticism* (Cambridge: Cambridge University Press, 1998); and my book *The Early Political Writings of the German Romantics* (Cambridge: Cambridge University Press, 1996).

5. The Institute, organized by Karl Ameriks and Jane Kneller, was held from June 26 to July 30, 2001, at Fort Collins, Colorado.

6. See Chapter 4.

7. This is especially the case with Schleiermacher, who was, even more than Friedrich Schlegel, the champion of individualism in ethics. In his 1802 *Grundlinien einer Kritik der bisherigen Sittenlehre*, his chief and only published work on ethics, Schleiermacher defends both individualism and the universality of reason. He continues to insist that ethics should become a systematic and rigorous science. See *Werke in Vier Bänden* (Leipzig: Meiner, 1928), I, 247–252.

8. All the way from the banks of the Neckar to Lake Onondaga I can hear a howl of protest from Manfred Frank for being placed among such company. No one has contested aspects of postmodernist philosophy with more passion, culture, and intelligence than Frank. See especially his *Die Unhintergehbarkeit von Individualität: Reflexionen über Subjekt, Person und Individiuum aus Anlaß ihrer «postmodernen» Toterklärung* (Frankfurt: Suhrkamp, 1986), where he defends romantic hermeneutics and individuality as antidotes to the excesses of deconstruction (pp. 116–131). Despite this, I remain partially deaf to his protest. For, on the whole, Frank sees the early romantics as proto-postmodernists, placing them in the tradition of the critique of reason that ends in postmodernism. See his "Zwei Jahrunderte Rationalitätskritik und ihre postmoderne Überbietung," in *Die Unvollendete Vernunft: Moderne versus Postmoderne*, ed. Dietmar Kamper and Willem van Reijen (Frankfurt: Suhrkamp, 1987), pp. 99–121, esp. 106. More importantly, the hallmark of his interpretations of Novalis, Hölderlin, and Schelling has been his tireless insistence that these thinkers affirm the thesis that the ground of rationality presupposes something that transcends rationality. Such a thesis is flatly contrary to the Platonic tradition, to which the early romantics belong. In attributing such a view to the early romantics Frank has firmly placed them in the camp of the postmodernists; they might as well be the mouthpieces of Heidegger and Derrida, who have made their careers in espousing just such a thesis. And so Frank has betrayed his allies to his enemy. On my critique of Frank's interpretation of *Frühromantik*, see Chapters 4 and 5.

9. See Berlin, *Roots of Romanticism;* Seyhan, *Representation and Its Discontents;* Paul de Man, *Blindness and Insight: Essays in the Rhetoric of Contemporary Criticism* (Minneapolis: University of Minnesota Press, 1983), and *The Rhetoric of Romanticism* (New York: Columbia University Press, 1984); Alice Kuzniar, *Delayed Endings:*

Nonclosure in Novalis and Hölderlin (Athens: University of Georgia Press, 1987); Phillipe Lacoue-Labarthe and Jean-Luc Nancy, *The Literary Absolute;* and Manfred Frank, *Einführung in frühromantische Ästhetik* (Frankfurt: Suhrkamp, 1989).

10. In his *Irony and the Discourse of Modernity* (Seattle: University of Washington Press, 1990), pp. 37–73, Behler sees Friedrich Schlegel's concept of irony as essentially modern. However, Behler has also stressed the affinity of Schlegel's hermeneutics with postmodernism. See his "Friedrich Schlegels Theorie des Verstehens: Hermeneutik oder Dekonstruktion?" in *Die Aktualität der Frühromantik*, ed. Ernst Behler and Jochen Hörisch (Paderborn: Schöningh, 1987), pp. 141–160, esp. 157, 159.

11. *Athenäumsfragment* no. 53, KA II, 173.

12. Nowhere is this more apparent than in Paul de Man's "The Rhetoric of Temporality," in *Blindness and Insight*, pp. 187–229. De Man insists that Schlegel regards irony as "an endless process that leads to no synthesis," and he criticizes Peter Szondi for thinking that irony is a movement toward a recovered unity (pp. 219–229). De Man is correct that irony allows for no final synthesis or organic wholeness; but that does not mean, as he implies, that irony is antisystematic. The lack of an end does not entail the lack of a goal. Wholeness and systematicity remain a regulative ideal, an ideal that we should strive to approach even if we cannot attain it. That the early romantics adopt systematicity as a regulative ideal is a central lesson of Manfred Frank's brilliant *Unendliche Annäherung* (Frankfurt: Suhrkamp, 1997), pp. 502, 617, 715. On de Man, see also Chapter 1, note 7 and Chapter 2, note 21.

13. See, for example, Schlegel's 1800 *Vorlesungen über die Transcendentalphilosophie*, KA XII, 1–105; Schelling's 1799 *Erster Entwurf eines Systems der Naturphilosophie*, *Sämtliche Werke*, ed. K. F. A. Schelling (Stuttgart: Cotta, 1856–1861), III, 269–326; Novalis's 1798–1799 *Das Allgemeine Brouillon*, HKA III, 242–478, which was material for his *Enzyklopädie;* and Schleiermacher's 1812–1813 *Ethik, Werke*, ed. Otto Braun and Johannes Brauer (Leipzig: Meiner, 1928), II, 245–420.

14. In his admirable study of the aphorisms of *Frühromantik*, Gerhard Neumann has argued that the aphorisms of the young romantics should not be understood as antisystematic in intention. See his *Ideenparadiese: Untersuchungen zur Aphoristik von Lichtenberg, Novalis, Friedrich Schlegel und Goethe* (Munich: Fink, 1976), pp. 17, 281–288.

15. In his *Der philosophische Diskurs der Moderne* (Frankfurt: Suhrkamp, 1985), pp. 110–115, Jürgen Habermas has argued that the romantics, especially Friedrich Schlegel, were the forefathers of Nietzsche's Dionysus. Some recent scholarship has stressed how many of Nietzsche's ideas have their roots in *Frühromantik*. See, for example, Seyhan, *Representation and Its Discontents*, pp. 136–151; and Ernst Behler, "Nietzsche und die Frühromantische Schule," in *Nietzsche-Studien* 7 (1978), 59–96. Behler rightly points out, however, that Schlegel and Nietzsche had very different conceptions of tragedy and that Schlegel would not have shared Nietzsche's understanding of the Dionysian

(pp. 72–77). To be sure, Dionysus was an important figure for the romantics; they did not, however, interpret him in Nietzche's sense. On the role of Dionysian symbolism in *Frühromantik*, see Manfred Frank's *Der Kommende Gott* (Frankfurt: Suhrkamp, 1982), pp. 12–19, 245–360.

16. *Pace* Ernst Behler, *Confrontations: Derrida, Heidegger, Nietzsche* (Stanford: Stanford University Press, 1991), p. 148.

17. On the need for a Platonic interpretation of Schlegel's philosophy, see Chapter 4 and my *German Idealism* (Cambridge: Harvard University Press, 2002), pp. 435–437, 454–461.

1. The Meaning of "Romantic Poetry"

1. Arthur Lovejoy, "On the Discrimination of Romanticisms," *Proceedings of the Modern Language Association* 39 (1924), 229–253; reprinted in Lovejoy, *Essays in the History of Ideas* (New York: Capricorn, 1960), pp. 228–253.

2. See, for example, Isaiah Berlin, *The Roots of Romanticism* (Princeton: Princeton University Press, 1999), pp. 18–20, 134.

3. Most notable in this regard is the work of René Wellek, "The Concept of Romanticism in Literary History," in *Concepts of Criticism* (New Haven: Yale University Press, 1963), pp. 129–221.

4. For the periodization of German romanticism, see Paul Kluckhohn, *Das Ideengut der deutschen Romantik,* 3rd ed. (Tübingen: Niemeyer, 1953), pp. 8–9; and Ernst Behler, *Frühromantik* (Berlin: de Gruyter, 1992), pp. 9–29.

5. See Friedrich to August Wilhelm Schlegel, December 1, 1797, KA XXIV, 53.

6. Behler, *Frühromantik*, pp. 22–23.

7. This interpretation ultimately goes back to Heinrich Heine, who maintained in his 1835 *Die romantische Schule* that *Romantik* is *"nichts anders als die Wiedererweckung der Poesie des Mittelalters."* See *Sämtliche Schriften*, ed. Klaus Briegleb (Frankfurt: Ullstein, 1981), V, 361. Heine's interpretation was reinforced by Hermann Hettner and G. G. Gervinus, two of the most prominent nineteenth-century literary historians. See Hettner, *Die romantische Schule in ihren inneren Zusammenhange mit Göthe und Schiller* (Braunschweig: Friedrich Vieweg, 1850), p. 37; and Gervinus, *Geschichte der poetischen Nationalliteratur der Deutschen* (Leipzig: Engelmann, 1844), V, 589–599. Despite Haym's *Die romantische Schule* (Berlin: Gaertner, 1870), which stressed a more holistic approach and the importance of romantic philosophy, science, and history, the literary interpretation persists. Indeed, it has been recently reinstated by Phillipe Lacoue-Labarthe and Jena-Luc Nancy in their popular and influential book *The Literary Absolute*, translated by Phillip Barnard and Cheryl Lester (Albany: SUNY Press, 1988), pp. 3, 5, 12, 13. They virtually define romanticism in terms of its absolutization of literature. The object of their study, they explicitly insist, is "the question of literature." Although they also insist that romanticism is not just literature but also theory of literature (p. 12), they still see it essentially as "this absolute literary operation" (whatever that is). This is a step backward in the study of *Frühromantik*.

More surprisingly, the literary interpretation has also been more recently revived by Ernst Behler in his *German Romantic Literary Theory* (Cambridge: Cambridge University Press, 1993). Despite his valuable work on the philosophy of the early romantics, Behler never really grew out of the literary interpretation. Thus he maintains that the main concerns of the early romantics were in poetry and literature (p. 8), and that they had only an amateur interest in philosophy (p. 5). The Schlegel brothers were mainly interested in the theory of poetry, and philosophy was for them only of marginal significance (p. 73). Behler's literary approach has been reaffirmed by one of his students, Azade Seyhan, who maintains that the mission of the young romantics was "establishing literature's critical foundation." See *Representation and Its Discontents: The Critical Legacy of German Romanticism* (Berkeley: University of California Press, 1992), p. 2.

Nowhere are the limitations and narrowness of the literary approach more evident than in the work of Paul de Man, who takes features of romantic literary style as evidence for its general worldview. Rather than taking Schlegel's metaphysics, epistemology, ethics, and politics as the basis for understanding his style, he does just the opposite. For example, he argues that "the dialectical relationship between subject and object is no longer the central statement of romantic thought" because "this dialectic is located entirely in the temporal relationships that exist within a system of allegorical signs." See his "The Rhetoric of Temporality," in *Blindness and Insight* (Minneapolis: University of Minnesota Press, 1983), p. 208. I will not comment here on what de Man means by "the dialectical relationship between subject and object"; most of his statements on romantic epistemology and metaphysics are far too vague and decontextualized to be of any value. De Man's criticisms of the organic and holistic approach toward romanticism come only at the expense of neglecting its *Naturphilosophie* and social and political theory.

8. It might be objected that there is really nothing new in such an interpretation, since it has been generally recognized that the romantics used *romantische Poesie* in such a broad sense. I readily admit the point. I do not claim, however, any originality for my interpretation. My only purpose in reasserting it is that, *despite the general recognition of the broad meaning of the term,* literary scholars still persist in ignoring it and understanding it in a more narrow literary sense. This will become especially clear in the next section, where I show that all parties to the classical dispute about the meaning of *romantische Poesie* presuppose that the term has a strictly literary meaning.

9. KA XVI, 89 (no. 4): "Alle Prosa is poetisch.—Sezt man Prosa der π [*Poesie*] durchaus entgegen, so ist nur die logische eigentlich Prosa."

10. See Schlegel's *Ueber das Studium der Griechischen Poesie,* KA I, 206. Cf. "Von der Schönheit in der Dichtkunst," KA XVI, 7 (no. 7).

11. "Von der Schönheit in der Dichtkunst III," KA XVI, 13 (no. 54).

12. Rudolf Haym, *Die romantische Schule* (Berlin: Gaertner, 1970), pp. 248–260.

13. Arthur Lovejoy, "The Meaning of 'Romantic' in Early German Romanticism," *Modern Language Notes* 21 (1916), 385–396. Reprinted in Lovejoy, *Essays in the History of Ideas* (New York: Putnam, 1955), pp. 183–206.

14. Hans Eichner, "Friedrich Schlegel's Theory of Romantic Poetry," *Publications of the Modern Language Association* 71 (1956), 1018–1041.

15. See *Ueber das Studium der griechischen Poesie*, KA I, 219–222.

16. See especially Schlegel's early essay "Vom Wert des Studiums der Griechen und Römer," KA I, 621–642, and *Ueber das Studium der griechische Poesie*, KA I, 232–233.

17. See nos. 38, XVI, 102; 55, XVI, 90; 781, XVI, 152. Cf. no. 65, XVIII, 24.

18. See nos. 699, XVI, 144; 754–755, XVI, 150.

19. See, for example, no. 739 XVI, 148. Cf. Schlegel's later account of the romantic in the *Gespräch über Poesie*, KA II, 333–334.

20. See nos. 42, XVI, 118; 500–501, XVI, 126.

21. See the fragment "Von der Schönheit in der Dichtkunst III," KA XVI, 13 (no. 54).

22. See nos. 120, XVI, 213; 43, XVI, 258.

23. This is Caroline and A. W. Schlegel's essay "Die Gemählde," which appeared in *Athenäum* II (1799), 39–151.

24. By 1798 Schlegel had abandoned his belief that philology could be a rigorous science and conceived of it as an art instead. See the fragments "Zur Philologie I" and "Zur Philologie II" (nos. 2, XVI, 35; 48, XVI, 39).

25. See nos. 313, XVI, 110; 586, XVI, 134. Cf. *Kritische Fragmente* no. 115, KA II, 161, and *Philosophische Lehrjahre* no. 632, KA XVIII, 82.

26. See nos. 423, XVI, 120; 330, XVI, 112.

27. See no. 606, XVI, 136.

28. See nos. 106, XVI, 590; 590, XVI, 134; 982, XVI, 167. Cf. *Philosophische Lehrjahre* no. 740, KA XVIII, 91.

29. See KA II, 335.

30. See ibid., 284–285. Schlegel states that *Poesie* is within everyone, and that it is their *"eigenstes Wesen"* and *"innerstes Kraft,"* and indeed *"die unsichtbaren Urkraft der Menschheit."*

31. Ibid., 304.

32. J. Hoffmeister, *Wörterbuch der philosophische Begriffe* (Hamburg: Meiner, 1955), p. 476.

33. Diogenes Laertius, *Lives of the Philosophers* III, 83–85. The same classification appears in Aristotle, *Metaphysics* VI, 1, 1025b 25.

34. A. W. Schlegel, *Vorlesungen über dramatische Kunst und Litteratur*, in *Sämmtliche Werke*, ed. Eduard Böcking (Leipzig: Weidmann, 1846), V, 5. Cf. *Vorlesungen über schöne Literatur und Kunst*, where *Poesie* is defined as *"eine freye schaffende Wirksamkeit der Fantasie."* See *Vorlesungen über Ästhetik* I, 186.

35. Schelling, *Philosophie der Kunst* §§63–64, *Sämtliche Werke*, ed. K. F. A. Schelling (Stuttgart: Cotta, 1856–1861), V, 460–461.

36. Novalis, *Fragmente und Studien* (1799–1800), HKA III, 563 (no. 56). Cf. II, 534 (no. 36): "Dichten ist zeugen."

37. Ibid., III, 560 (no. 35). See also HKA II, 390 (no. 45): "Sollte *practisch* und poetisch eins seyn—und letzeres nur absolut practisch in specie bedeuten?"

38. Ibid., III, 558 (no. 21); III, 639 (no. 507).

39. See Ernst Behler, "Friedrich Schlegels Theorie der Universalpoesie," *Jahrbuch der deutschen Schiller Gesellschaft* 1 (1957), 211–252. Behler maintains that in *Athenäumsfragment* no. 116 Schlegel limited his project to *Poesie* in a narrow sense but later extended it to all arts and sciences (p. 211). However, he also scores against himself by presenting evidence from the notebooks that Schlegel had developed the project in the broader sense as early as 1798, the beginning of the *Athenäumsjahre* (pp. 223–225).

40. Schlegel writes about *Transcendentalpoesie,* which is the creative power within everyone, of which literature is only one manifestation. See nos. 560, XVI, 131; 704, XVI, 144, 1050, XVI, 172.

41. See especially nos. 108, II, 160; 37, II, 151; and 42, II, 152.

42. This ambiguity was first noted by Eichner, "Schlegel's Theory of Romantic Poetry," pp. 1037–1038.

43. See "Ueber die Grenzen des Schönen," KA I, 36–37.

44. See no. 586, XVI, 134.

45. See nos. 617–618, XVI, 137.

46. See no. 27, XVI, 206.

47. See no. 79, XVI, 91–92.

48. KA II, 156. Cf. no. 89, II, 158. An earlier version appears in the literary notebooks, no. 576, XVI, 133.

49. KA II, 182.

50. Ibid., p. 192.

51. Novalis, *Vorarbeiten* II, 545 (no. 105).

52. Novalis, *Vermischte Bemerkungen* II, 436–438 (no. 65). Cf. *Fragmente und Studien* III, 558 (no. 513).

53. Novalis, *Glauben und Liebe* II, 497–498 (no. 39).

54. Schelling, *System des transcendentalen Idealismus, Sämtliche Werke* III, 613–629.

55. See *Athenäum* III (1800), 236. Cf. "Vorerrinerung," I (1798), iii–iv.

56. Schlegel, *Ideen* no. 37; cf. no. 65, KA II, 259, 262; and Novalis, *Blütenstaub* no. 32, HKA II, 427.

57. I again take issue here with Ernst Behler, "Die Poesie in der frühromantischen Theorie der Brüder Schlegel," *Athenäum* 1 (1991), 13–40. Behler's claim that philosophy was only one of the *Randgebiete* of the Schlegels' interests in *Poesie* (p. 14) underplays the extent to which the meaning of the concept is unintelligible apart from their philosophy.

2. Early German Romanticism

1. See Rudolf Haym, *Die romantische Schule* (Berlin: Gaertner, 1870); Paul Kluckhohn, *Das Ideengut der deutschen Romantik,* 3d ed. (Tübingen: Niemeyer, 1966); Fritz Strich, *Deutsche Klassik und Romantik,* 4th ed. (Bern: Francke Verlag, 1949); Benno von Wiese, "Zur Wesensbestimmung der frühromantischen Situation," *Zeitschrift für Deutschkunde* 42 (1928), 722–729; H. A. Korff, "Das Wesen

der Romantik," *Zeitschrift für Deutschkunde* 43 (1929), 545–561. For a useful anthology, containing these and other articles, see *Begriffbestimmung der Romantik,* ed. H. Prang (Darmstadt: Wissenschaftliche Buchgesellschaft, 1968); Ernst Behler, "Kritische Gedanken zum Begriff der europaischen Romantik," in *Die europäische Romantik,* ed. E. Behler (Frankfurt: Athenäum, 1972), pp. 7–43.

2. See Chapter 1, note 7.

3. See Haym, *Die romantische Schule,* pp. 7, 13, whose philosophical and interdisciplinary approach remains his lasting contribution to the study of *Frühromantik.* Unfortunately, Haym's approach has not been followed by literary historians. Regarding their persistent failure to study and understand the philosophical dimension of *Frühromantik,* I can only reaffirm what Oskar Walzel said long ago: "Solange die philosophischen Gedankengänge deutscher Literatur nur eine Aschenbrödelrolle in literaturhistorischer Betrachtung spielten (und ganz überwunden ist diese Phase noch nicht), blieben die Winke, die Dilthey und Haym gegeben hatten, so gut wie unbeachtet." See his *Deutsche Romantik* (Leipzig: Teubner, 1908), pp. 2–3.

4. The thesis that *Romantik* is apolitical is very old. One of its very first exponents was Hermann Hettner, *Die romantische Schule in ihren inneren Zusammenhange mit Göthe und Schiller* (Braunschweig: Friedrich Vieweg, 1850), pp. 13–15, 28–29, 41–42. It has been a common interpretation ever since. See, for example, Georg Brandes, *Die Literatur des neunzehnten Jahrunderts in ihren Hauptströmungen* (Leipzig: Veit, 1887), pp. 351, 356; Ricarda Huch, *Ausbreitung und Verfall der Romantik* (Leipzig: Haessel, 1902), pp. 306–307; and Oskar Walzel, *Deutsche Romantik* (Leipzig: Teubner, 1908), p. 113. Though both Walzel and Hettner note the later political interests of the romantics, they claim that they are absent in *Frühromantik.* Carl Schmitt's *Politische Romantik* (2nd ed. [Munich: Duncker and Humblot, 1925]) simply carried on this earlier tradition. The same conception of *Frühromantik* is common in Anglo-Saxon interpretations. See, for example, Ralph Tymms, *German Romantic Literature* (London: Metheun, 1955), pp. 1–9, 24–25, 37, 39; and Lascelles Abercrombie, *Romanticism* (London: Martin, Secker and Warburg, 1926), pp. 48–50.

5. Aristotle, *Nicomachean Ethics* I, chaps. 1 and 5, 1094a and 1997b.

6. See Schleiermacher, *Über das höchste Gut,* and *Über den Wert des Lebens,* in KGA I/1, 81–125 and I/1, 391–471; and Schlegel, *Transcendentalphilosophie,* "Theil II: Theorie des Menschen," KA XII, 44–90. "Theil II" is devoted to characterizing *"die Bestimmung des Menschen"* (p. 45; cf. p. 47).

7. See his 1827 essay "Über den Begriff des höchsten Gutes. Erste Abhandlung," and his 1830 essay "Über den Begriff des höchsten Gutes. Zweite Abhandlung," in Schleiermachers *Werke,* ed. Otto Braun and Johannes Bauer (Leipzig: Meiner, 1928), I, 445–494. In his *Ethik (1812–1813)* Schleiermacher argues that the concept of the highest good is the central concept of ethics, which the concepts of duty and virtue presuppose. See his *Ethik (1812–1813),* ed. Hans-Joachim Birkner (Hamburg: Meiner, 1981), §§87–90, p. 16.

8. *Ideen* no. 37, KA II, 259. Cf. no. 65, KA II, 262.

9. *Blütenstaub* no. 32, HKA II, 427.

10. See Hölderlin to his brother, September 1793, GSA VI, 92.

11. *Athenäum* III (1800), 236. Cf. "Vorerinnerung," I (1798), iii–iv.

12. The *locus classicus* for this criticism is Schleiermacher's *Vertraute Briefe über Friedrich Schlegels Lucinde*, KGA I/3, 157–158. See also his *Grundlinien einer Kritik der bisherigen Sittenlehre*, in *Werke* I, 271–272.

13. Friedrich Schlegel, *Athenäumsfragmente* nos. 262, 406 and *Ideen* nos. 29, 60, in KA II, 210, 242, 258, 262.

14. Most notably, in his 1794 *Vorlesungen über die Bestimmung des Gelehrten, Sämtliche Werke*, ed. I. H. Fichte (Berlin: Veit, 1845–1846), VI, 297, 310.

15. On the development of this tradition in the eighteenth century, see Robert Norton, *The Beautiful Soul* (Ithaca: Cornell University Press, 1995).

16. On the use of "reflection," see Schelling's introduction to *Ideen zu einer Philosophie der Natur, Sämtliche Werke*, ed. K. F. A. Schelling (Stuttgart: Cotta, 1856–1861), II, 13, 14; on the use of "opposition," see Hegel's *Differenzschrift, Werkausgabe* II, 20, 22. On the use of "estrangement," see Hegel's Jena lectures (1805–1806), *Jenaer Realphilosophie II*, ed. Johannes Hoffmeister, (Hamburg: Meiner, 1967), pp. 218, 232, 237–238, 257.

17. On the antimodernist or reactionary interpretation, see Heine, *Die romantische Schule, Sämtliche Werke*, ed. Klaus Briegleb (Frankfurt: Ullstein, 1981), V, 379–82; Ruge, *Unsere Klassiker und Romantiker seit Lessing*, in *Sämmtliche Werke* (Mannheim: Grohe, 1847), I, 8–11; Haym, *Die romantische Schule*, p. 3. On the modernist or progressivist interpretation, see, for example, Werner Krauss, "Franzöische Aufklärung und deutsche Romantik," in *Romantikforschung seit 1945*, ed. Klaus Peter (Meisenheim: Anton Hain, 1980), pp. 168–179, esp. 177–178.

18. The *locus classicus* for this critique of Rousseau is the final lecture of Fichte's 1794 lectures *Bestimmung des Gelehrten*, in *Sämtliche Werke* VI, 335–346. These lectures were seminal for Hölderlin, Novalis, and Friedrich Schlegel.

19. See Shlomo Avineri, *Hegel's Theory of the Modern State* (Cambridge: Cambridge University Press, 1972), pp. 16n, 21–22, 33. Avineri's influential assessment of the originality and importance of Hegel's political philosophy rests on an anachronistic conception of romanticism, which essentially equates it with the final stages of the movement or *Spätromantik*. This has been the stumbling block of all left-wing interpretations of romanticism.

20. See, for example, Alois Stockman, *Die deutsche Romantik* (Freiburg: Herder and Co., 1921), pp. 13–17; Oskar Walzel, "Wesenfragen deutscher Romantik," *Jahrbuch des Freien deutschen Hochstifts* 29 (1929), 253–276; Adolf Grimme, *Vom Wesen der Romantik* (Braunschweig: Westermann, 1947), p. 13; René Wellek, "The Concept of Romanticism in Literary History" and "Romanticism Re-examined," in *Concepts of Criticism*, ed. Stephen G. Nichols (New Haven: Yale University Press, 1963), pp. 165, 220; Morse Peckham, "Toward a Theory of Romanticism," in *Proceedings of the Modern Language Association* 66 (1951), 5–23; and Lawrence Ryan, "Romanticism," in *Periods of German Literature*, ed. J. M. Ritchie (London: Oswald Wolff, 1966), pp. 123–143.

21. See, for example, Paul de Man, "The Rhetoric of Temporality," in *Blindness and*

Insight, 2nd ed. (Minneapolis: University of Minnesota Press, 1983), pp. 187–228, esp. 220–228; and Alice Kuzniar, *Delayed Endings: Nonclosure in Novalis and Hölderlin* (Athens: University of Georgia Press, 1987), pp. 1–71. On de Man, see the Introduction, note 12 and Chapter 1, note 7.

22. This distinction, which was first made by Condillac, was affirmed by Friedrich Schlegel, who stressed its importance in his letters to his brother dated August 28, 1793, and October 1793. See KA XXIII, 130, 143–144.

23. The *loci classici* of the Marxist interpretation are Georg Lukács, "Die Romantik als Wendung in der deutschen Literatur," in *Fortschritt und Reaktion in der deutschen Literatur* (Berlin: Aufbau, 1947), pp. 51–73; and Claus Träger, "Ursprünge und Stellung der Romantik," *Weimarer Beiträge* 21 (1975), 37–57. Both have been reprinted in *Romantikforschung seit 1945,* pp. 40–52, 304–334. Noting the romantics' opposition to modern civil society and their extension of some aspects of *Aufklärung,* Träger argues that *Frühromantik* cannot be regarded as simply reactionary, and he duly criticizes other Marxist scholars (pp. 312–313, 328–329). Nevertheless, Träger still develops his own more qualified version of the reactionary interpretation, which sees *Frühromantik* as a form of reactionary utopianism (pp. 307–308, 323). His own more nuanced account still fails to discriminate between *Frühromantik* and other political currents of the 1790s.

24. Two notable exceptions are Hans Mayer and Werner Krauss, who, in a conference held in Leipzig in 1962, criticized Lukács's simplistic assessment of *Romantik.* Mayer and Krauss stressed some of the progressive aspects of *Romantik* and its continuity with the Enlightenment. See Mayer, "Fragen der Romantikforschung," in *Zur deutschen Klassik und Romantik* (Pfülligen: Günter Neske, 1963), pp. 263–305; and Werner Krauss, "Französische Aufklärung und deutsche Romantik," in *Perspektiven und Probleme: Zur französischen Aufklärung und deutschen Aufklärung und andere Aufsätze* (Neuwied: Leuchterhand, 1965), pp. 266–284 (reprinted in *Romantikforschung seit 1945,* pp. 168–179). Mayer and Krauss were those proverbial exceptions that prove the rule, however. Their papers were denounced by the party faithful (Klaus Hammer, Henri Poschmann, Hans-Ulrich Schnuchel) in a report on the conference. See "Fragen der Romantikforschung," *Weimarer Beiträge* 9 (1963), 173–182. Mayer was accused *inter alia* of failing to appreciate the role of *Romantik* in the development of German facism. The faithful argued that there was little need to move beyond Marx's conception of *Romantik* as a reactionary movement (p. 175).

25. Nowhere is this failure more apparent than in Lukács's claim that the romantics wanted to revive absolutism. See "Romantik als Wendung," in *Romantikforschung,* p. 41.

26. On some of the differences between *Frühromantik* and the reactionary currents of the 1790s, see my *Enlightenment, Revolution, and Romanticism: The Genesis of Modern German Political Thought, 1790–1800* (Cambridge, Mass.: Harvard University Press, 1992), pp. 223, 281–288.

27. On the politics of the Berlin *Aufklärer,* see ibid., pp. 309–317. On the romantic reaction to enlightened absolutism, see Novalis, *Glauben und Liebe* no. 36, HKA II, 494–495; and Schleiermacher, "Gedanken I," KGA I/2, 1–49, which is a cri-

tique of J. A. Eberhard's defense of absolutism, *Ueber Staatsverfassungen und ihre Verbesserungen* (Berlin: Voß, 1792–1793).

28. This mistake was pointed out long ago, by Hettner in 1850. See his *Die romantische Schule*, pp. 2–3.

29. Haym, *Die romantische Schule*, pp. 4–5. It cannot be said, however, that Haym strictly followed his own methodology. His account of Novalis, for example, still shows heavy traces of the standard liberal reaction against later romanticism.

30. Aristotle, *Nicomachean Ethics* I, chap. 2, 1094a–b.

31. See *Ueber das Studium der griechischen Poesie*, KA I, 324–325.

32. Aristotle, *Politics* VII, chap. 8, 1328a; cf. ibid., III, chap. 9, 1280a–b.

33. This is evident in the case of Schlegel, Schleiermacher, and Hegel. See, for example, Schlegel's early essay "Über die Grenzen des Schönens," KA I, 42; and Schleiermacher's *Monologen*, KGA I/3, 32–33. On the source of Hegel's communitarianism, see note 35.

34. The best translation of the Schiller text is by Elizabeth Wilkinson and L. A. Willoughby, *On the Aesthetic Education of Man* (Oxford: Clarendon Press, 1967). For a translation of parts of the Novalis, Schleiermacher, and Schlegel texts, see my *The Early Political Writings of the German Romantics* (Cambridge: Cambridge University Press, 1996). For a translation of the Hegel text, see *G. W. F. Hegel, System of Ethical Life (1802–1803)*, ed. and trans. H. S. Harris and T. M. Knox (Albany: SUNY Press, 1979).

35. In his 1802 *Über die wissenschaftliche Behandlungsarten des Naturrechts, Werkausgabe* II, 505, Hegel explicitly appealed to Aristotle's famous dictum.

36. Novalis, *Glauben und Liebe* no. 36, HKA II, 494–495; and Schleiermacher, "Gedanken I," KGA I/1, 28 (no. 102).

37. The preference for a mixed constitution is apparent in Schlegel, *Athenäumsfragmente* nos. 81, 214, 369, KA II, 176, 198, 232–233; Novalis, *Politische Aphorismen* nos. #66–68, HKA II, 504–503; and Hegel, *System der Sittlichkeit*, GW VI, 361.

38. In this respect romantic medievalism had its origins in the Enlightenment, and so cannot be understood as a reaction against it. On the continuity of *Aufklärung* and *Romantik* regarding medievalism, see Werner Krauss, "Französische Aufklärung und deutsche Romantik," in *Romantikforschung seit 1945*, pp. 168–179.

39. See Hegel, *Werkausgabe* I, 533, 536.

40. Thus Schmitt, *Politische Romantik*, pp. 20–26.

41. See, for example, Schiller's "Über den Grund des Vergnügens an tragische Gegenstände," NA XX, 133–147. Here Schiller insists on the *sui generis* quality of aesthetic pleasure, and criticizes those who subordinate art to moral or political ends. Yet he also stresses that aesthetic pleasure does not diminish but enhances the higher calling of art. Aesthetic pleasure consists in the free play of our faculties, and such freedom arises from and represents deeper moral ends. It is precisely by virtue of such pleasure that we discover the real meaning of freedom and that humanity is an end in itself.

42. See Schiller to Körner, February 8, 1793, NA XXVI, 182.

43. A. W. Schlegel, *Sämtliche Schriften,* ed. Edvard Böcking (Leipzig: Weidmann, 1846), XI, 65. On Schiller's influence on A. W. Schlegel, see Josef Körner, *Romantiker und Klassiker: Die Brüder Schlege in ihre Beziehungen zu Schiller und Goethe* (Berlin: Askanischer Verlag, 1924), p. 64.
44. Friedrich to August Wilhelm Schlegel, October 16, 1793, KA XXIII, 143.

3. Early Romanticism and the *Aufklärung*

1. This interpretation became entrenched through some of the standard literary histories of the nineteenth century. See, for example, G. G. Gervinus, *Geschichte der poetischen Nationalliteratur der Deutschen* (Leipzig: Engelmann, 1844), V, 589–599, esp. 594; and Hermann Hettner, *Geschichte der deutschen Literatur im Achtzehnjahrhundert,* 8th ed. (Berlin: Aufbau, 1979), II, 641–642 (first published: Braunschweig: Vieweg, 1862–1870). See also Gervinus, *Aus der Geschichte des neunzehnten Jahrhunderts seit den Wiener Vorträgen* (Leipzig, 1855), I, 346–349; and Hettner's *Die romantische Schule in ihrem inneren Zusammenhange mit Göthe und Schiller* (Braunschweig: Vieweg, 1850), pp. 139–188. For other sources opposing *Romantik* and *Aufklärung,* see notes 2 and 3.
2. See Heinrich Heine, *Die romantische Schule,* in *Sämtliche Schriften,* ed. Klaus Briegleb (Frankfurt: Ullstein, 1981), V, 379–382; Arnold Ruge, *Unsere Klassiker und Romantiker seit Lessing,* in *Sämmtliche Werke* (Mannheim: Grohe, 1847), I, 8–11; and Rudolf Haym, *Die romantische Schule* (Berlin: Gaertner, 1870), p. 3.
3. The nationalist appropriation of romanticism began with Wilhelm Scherer, *Geschichte der deutschen Literatur,* 7th ed. (Berlin: Weidmann, 1894), p. 633; and "Die deutsche Literaturrevolution," in *Vorträge und Aufsätze zur Geschichte des geistigen Lebens in Deutschland und Österreich* (Berlin: Weidmann, 1874), p. 340. It was also encouraged by Wilhelm Dilthey, "Goethe und die dichterische Phantasie," *Erlebnis und die Dichtung,* 15th ed. (Göttingen: Vandenhoeck and Ruprecht, 1970), pp. 124–125. In the 1920s the equation of *Romantik* with German identity and opposition to the *Aufklärung* solidified. See, for example, Alois Stockmann, *Die deutsche Romantik* (Freiburg: Herder and Co., 1921), pp. 27–28, 34, 36; Georg Mehlis, *Die deutsche Romantik* (Munich: Rösl and Cie, 1922), pp. 26–28; H. A. Korff, "Das Wesen der Romantik," *Zeitschrift für Deutschkunde* 43 (1929), 545–561; and Paul Kluckhohn, *Die deutsche Romantik* (Bielefeld: Velhagen and Klassing, 1924), p. 3. The national-socialist interpretation took the nationalist interpretation to extremes, opposing the "French–Jewish Enlightenment" to the German spirit. In this vein, see especially Walther Linden, "Umwertung der deutschen Romantik," *Zeitschrift für Deutschkunde* 47 (1933), 65–91. Linden was an important spokesman for the national-socialist cause.
4. On the liberal reaction, see, for example, A. O. Lovejoy, "The Meaning of Romanticism for the Historian of Ideas," *Journal of the History of Ideas* 2 (1941), 257–278, esp. 270–278. On the Marxist reaction, see Georg Lukács, "Die Romantik als Wendung in der deutschen Literatur," in *Fortschritt und Reaktion in der deutschen Literatur* (Berlin: Aufbau, 1947), pp. 51–73.

5. On the misconceptions surrounding the romantics' relationship to Roman Catholicism, see A. W. Porterfield's still useful article "Some Popular Misconceptions concerning German Romanticism," *Journal of English and Germanic Philology* 15 (1916), 470–511, esp. 497–501. After surveying the entire romantic
movement, Porterfield concludes (p. 499): "In short, with regard to *Seelenkultur*
and affiliation with the visible Church, Roman Catholicism played no great role
in German Romanticism while German Catholicism played a very negligible
role."

6. On the periodization of German romanticism, see Paul Kluckhohn, *Das Ideengut
der deutschen Romantik,* 3rd ed. (Tübingen: Niemeyer, 1953), pp. 8–9; and Ernst
Behler, *Frühromantik* (Berlin: de Gruyter, 1992), pp. 30–51. For a somewhat different periodization, see Harro Segeberg, "Phasen der Romantik," in *Romantik-
Handbuch,* ed. Helmut Schanze (Stuttgart: Kröner, 1994), pp. 31–78.

7. See, for example, Helmut Schanze, *Romantik und Aufklärung: Untersuchungen zu
Friedrich Schlegel und Novalis,* 2nd ed. (Nuremberg: Hans Carl, 1976); Werner
Krauss, "Französische Aufklärung und deutsche Romantik," in *Romantikforschung
seit 1945,* ed. Klaus Peter (Meisenheim: Anton Hain, 1980), pp. 168–179;
Wolfdietrich Rasch, "Zum Verhältnis der Romantik zur Aufklärung," in
Romantik: Ein literaturwissenschaftsliches Studienbuch (Königstein: Athenäum,
1979), pp. 7–21; and Ludwig Stockinger, "Das Auseinandersetzung der
Romantiker mit der Aufklärung," in *Romantik-Handbuch,* pp. 79–105.

8. On this direction in scholarship, see Gerhart Hoffmeister,
"Forschungsgeschichte," in *Romantik-Handbuch,* pp. 177–206, esp. 178.

9. See, for example, A. W. Schlegel, *Vorlesungen über schöne Kunst und Literatur,* ed. J.
Minor (Heilbronn, 1884), II, 65–70; Novalis, "Christenheit oder Europa," HKA
II, 515–516; and Schleiermacher, *Monologen,* KGA I/3, 30–31.

10. On the central role of the ideal of *Bildung* for the *Aufklärung,* see Moses Mendelssohn's classic essay "Ueber die Frage: was heisst aufklären?" *Berlinische
Monatsschrift* 4 (1784), 193–200.

11. Compare *Apology* 38a–b and 33b.

12. Novalis, *Glauben und Liebe* no. 39, HKA II, 498.

13. The traditional view that the romantics became disillusioned with the Revolution after the execution of the king and the onset of the Terror is untenable. On
the reaction of the romantics to the Revolution, see my *Enlightenment, Revolution, and Romanticism: The Genesis of Modern German Political Thought, 1790–1800*
(Cambridge, Mass.: Harvard University Press, 1992), pp. 228–229, 241–244,
250–253, 266–267.

14. See, for example, Schlegel's *Ideen* no. 41, KA II, 259; Novalis, *Glauben und Liebe*
no. 36, HKA II, 495; and Schleiermacher's *Reden,* KGA II/1, 196.

15. See Schlegel, *Athenäumsfragmente* nos. 81, 212–214, 369–370; and Novalis,
Glauben und Liebe nos. 22, 37, HKA II, 490, 496.

16. See, for example, Novalis, HKA II, 518, 522; and Schlegel, *Vorlesungen über
Transcendentalphilosophie,* KA XII, 44, 47, 56–57, 88.

17. Thus in the 1790s *Aufklärer* like Christian Garve, Ernst Ferdinand Klein, J. A.

Eberhard, and C. G. Svarez continued to defend absolute monarchy against the ideas of the Revolution. On the reaction of the *Aufklärer* toward the Revolution, see *Enlightenment, Revolution, and Romanticism*, pp. 309–317; and Zwi Batscha, *Despotismus von jeder Art reizt zur Widersetzlichkeit: Die Französische Revolution in der deutschen Popularphilosophie* (Frankfurt: Suhrkamp, 1989).

18. In his *Hölderlin und die franzöische Revolution* (Frankfurt: Suhrkamp, 1969), pp. 85–113, Pierre Bertaux has assembled evidence that Hölderlin was involved in a plot to establish a Swabian republic. On the whole, however, Hölderlin insisted on the value of gradual evolutionary change and the need for *Bildung*. See, for example, his January 10, 1797 letter to J. G Ebel, and his January 1, 1799 letter to his brother, GSA, VI/1, 229–230, 303–305.

19. Hence those scholars who insist that *Romantik* be classified as either radical or reactionary, progressive or regressive, present us with a false choice. In his "Fragen der Romantikforschung," in *Zur deutschen Klassik und Romantik* (Pfulligen: Neske, 1963), p. 302, Hans Mayer criticizes Lukács for imposing such a schema on the study of *Romantik*. Mayer does not explain, however, why this schema is problematic. Its problematic status becomes apparent, however, as soon as we locate the romantics in the context of the 1790s, where their position emerges as belonging to the moderate center.

20. See Hölderlin, GSA IV/1, pp. 297–299. For a translation, see my *The Early Political Writings of the German Romantics* (Cambridge: Cambridge University Press, 1996), pp. 3–5. The authorship of this manuscript has been a much disputed question, which we need not decide here. The author was either Schelling, Hegel, or Hölderlin. For the controversy surrounding the autorship, see the essays collected by Rüdiger Bubner, *Hegel-Tage Villigst 1969. Das älteste Systemprogramm, Studien zur Frühgeschichte des deutschen Idealismus, Hegel Studien Beiheft* 9 (1973); and by Christoph Jamme, *Mythologie der Vernunft: Hegels «ältestes Systemprogramm» des deutschen Idealismus* (Frankfurt: Suhrkamp, 1984).

21. Kant, KrV, A xii.

22. See, for example, Novalis, *Heinrich von Ofterdingen*, HKA I, 280–283; Hölderlin, *Hyperion*, GSA III, 93, and his June 2, 1795 letter to his brother, GSA VI/1, 208–209; Schlegel, *Athenäumsfragmente* nos. 1, 47, 48, 56, 89, 96, KA II, 165, 172, 173, 178, 179.

23. Schlegel, *Athenäumsfragment* no. 281, KA II, 213.

24. See Schlegel's "Ueber Lessing," KA II, 100–125, and *Lessings Gedanken und Meinungen*, KA XIII, 46–102. On Schlegel's admiration for Lessing, see Johanna Kruger, *Friedrich Schlegels Bekehrung zu Lessing* (Weimar: Duncker, 1913); and Klaus Peter, "Friedrich Schlegels Lessing: Zur Wirkungsgeschichte der Aufklärung," in *Humanität und Dialog: Lessing und Mendelssohn in neuer Sicht* (Detroit: Wayne State University Press, 1979), pp. 341–352.

25. On the romantic ethic of individualism, see Schlegel, *Athenäumsfragmente* no. 16, KA II, 167, and *Ideen* no. 60, KA II, 262. See also Schleiermacher's *Reden*, KGA II/1, 229–230; and *Monologen*, KGA III/1, 17–18.

26. See Schlegel, *Athenäumsfragmente* nos. 1, 47, 48, 56, 89, 96, 281, KA II, 165, 172, 173, 178, 179, 213.
27. See Novalis, *Lehrling zu Sais*, HKA I, 84, 89–90, and "Christenheit oder Europa," HKA III, 515–516; see also Hölderlin, *Hyperions Jugend*, GSA III, 199.
28. See Novalis, *Glauben und Liebe* no. 36, HKA II, 495. This sense of loss also appears in some of Schlegel's early classical essays, especially "Ueber die Grenzen des Schönen," KA I, 23. See also Schlegel's *Lucinde*, KA V, 25–29.
29. On the romantic program for a new mythology, see Schlegel, *Gespräch über die Poesie*, KA II, 311–328; Novalis, *Fragmente und Studien III* nos. 391, 395, 434, and *Freiburger Studien* no. 47; and the anonymous "Systemprogramm des deutschen Idealismus," in Manfred Frank, ed., *Materialien zu Schellings philosophischen Anfänge* (Frankfurt: Suhrkamp, 1975), pp. 110–113.
30. See Novalis, HKA II, 545 (no. 105).
31. See Schlegel, *Brief über den Roman*, KA II, 333–334. This essay should be compared with Schlegel's earlier essay "Ueber die Grenzen des Schönen," KA I, 34–44, esp. 42, where he argues that the highest form of aesthetic enjoyment is love.
32. Both Schelling and Schlegel formed their political principles along Fichte's lines. See Schelling, *Neue Deduktion des Naturrechts, Sämtliche Werke*, ed. K. F. A. Schelling (Stuttgart: Cotta, 1856–1861), I, 247–280; and Schlegel, "Versuch über den Begriff des Republikanismus," KA VII, 11–25. Novalis had a high opinion of Fichte's *Grundlage des Naturrechts*. See his *Tagebücher* no. 70, May 27, 1797.

4. *Frühromantik* and the Platonic Tradition

1. See, for example, Nicolai Hartmann, *Die Philosophie des deutschen Idealismus* (Berlin: de Gruyter, 1923), I, 188; Georg Lukács, *Fortschritt und Reaktion in der deutschen Literatur* (Berlin: Aufbau Verlag, 1947), p. 54; and Paul Kluckhohn, *Das Ideengut der deutschen Romantik*, 3rd ed, (Tübingen: Niemeyer, 1953), pp. 12, 107, 186. See also the sources listed in Chapter 3, notes 1–4.
2. This second distinction has been made, or at least implied, by Isaiah Berlin. See his *The Roots of Romanticism* (Princeton: Princeton University Press, 1999), pp. 21–26, 30–31, and "The Romantic Revolution: A Crisis in the History of Modern Thought," in *The Sense of Reality* (New York: Farrar, Straus and Giroux, 1996), pp. 168–193.
3. See the sources listed in Chapter 3, note 7.
4. See Wolfgang Mederer, *Romantik als Aufklärung der Aufklärung* (Frankfurt: Lang, 1987) (Salzburger Schriften zur Rechts-, Staats- und Sozialphilosophie, vol. 4).
5. See, for example, Friedrich Schlegel, *Athenäumsfragmente* nos. 47, 48, 56, 89, 96, 281, KA II, 172, 173, 178, 179, 213; Hölderlin, *Hyperion*, GSA III, 93, and his June 2, 1796 letter to his brother, GSA VI/1, 208–209; Novalis, *Henrich von Ofterdingen*, HKA I, 280–283.
6. See especially Werner Krauss, "Franzöische Aufklärung und deutsche

Romantik," in *Romantikforschung seit 1945*, ed. Klaus Peter (Meisenheim: Anton Hain, 1980), pp. 168–179.

7. See Schlegel, *Philosophische Lehrjahre* no. 13, KA XVIII, 518, and his review of the *Philosophisches Journal*, KA VIII, 30–31; and Novalis, *Allgemeine Brouillon* no. 460, HKA III, 333.

8. See, for example, Hölderlin, *Fragment von Hyperion*, GSA III/1, 163; and Schleiermacher, review of *De Platonis Phaedro*, KGA I/3, 471–472.

9. See Dieter Henrich, *Konstellationen: Probleme und Debatten am Ursprung der idealistischen Philosophie (1789–1795)* (Stuttgart: Klett-Cotta, 1991), pp. 7–46; and Manfred Frank, *Unendliche Annäherung: Die Anfänge der philosophischen Frühromantik* (Frankfurt: Suhrkamp, 1998).

10. See Frank, *Unendliche Annäherung*, pp. 27, 65–66, 662, and *Einführung in die frühromantische Ästhetik* (Frankfurt: Suhrkamp, 1989), pp. 127–129, 235.

11. See Oskar Walzel, *German Romanticism* (New York: Putnam, 1932), pp. 5, 8. The Platonic heritage is also stressed by Erwin Kircher, *Philosophie der Romantik* (Jena: Diederichs, 1906), pp. 8–34.

12. See, for example, *Republic* VI, 508, 510; and *Enneads* I, vi, 9.

13. On this distinction, see Schelling, *Fernere Darstellung, Sämtliche Werke*, ed. K. F. A. Schelling (Stuttgart: Cotta, 1856–1861), IV, 342–344, 362, 390; Novalis, *Vorarbeiten* nos. 99, 233, HKA II, 544, 576; Friedrich to A. W. Schlegel, August 28, 1793, KA XXIII, 158–159; October 16, 1793, KA XXIII, 142–144; and November 17, 1793, KA XXIII, 158–159.

14. The distinction can be found in the Cambridge Platonists. See, for example, John Smith, "Of the Existence and Nature of God," in *Select Discourses* (London, 1660), pp. 127, 131; and Henry More, *Conjectura Cabbalistica*, pp. 2–3, Preface, §3.

15. See "Von einem neuerdings erhobenen vornehmen Ton in der Philosophie," AA VIII, 387–406.

16. *Timaeus* 32d–33a; 34c–35a; 68e–69a.

17. See Hölderlin, *Hyperion*, GSA III, 81–84; Schlegel, *Gespräch über Poesie*, KA II, 324–325; Schelling, *System des transcendentalen Idealismus, Sämtliche Werke* III, 612–629; and Novalis, *Vorarbeiten* no. 31, HKA II, 533.

18. It has been objected that step 3 is false because there is no reason to assume that *only* aesthetic experience can grasp the unity of something that is an aesthetic whole; there might be, so the objection goes, other forms of access. The reply to such an objection is twofold: (1) that any grasp of an aesthetic whole must be intuitive rather than conceptual, because conceptual thinking divides its object, and (2) that such an intuition must be aesthetic (in a nontrivial sense) if its object is beautiful (according to step 2).

19. This shift is most visible in the preface to Schelling's tract *Über die Weltseele, Sämtliche Werke* II, 415–419.

20. Luther's and Calvin's nominalist heritage has been the subject of much investigation. For some good recent accounts, see Heiko Oberman, *Luther: Man between God and the Devil* (New York: Doubleday, 1992), pp. 116–123, and his "Initia

Lutheri—Initia Reformationis," in *The Dawn of the Reformation* (Edinburgh: T and T Clark, 1986), pp. 39–83. Concerning Calvin's nominalist heritage, see Alister McGrath, "John Calvin and Late Medieval Thought: A Study in Late Medieval Influences upon Calvin's Theological Development," *Archiv für Reformationsgeschichte* 77 (1986), 58–78. I have explored the nominalist background to early Protestant theology in *The Sovereignty of Reason: The Defense of Rationality in the Early English Enlightenment* (Princeton: Princeton University Press, 1996), pp. 33–41.

21. See, for example, Frank, *Einführung in die frühromantische Ästhetik,* pp. 9, 41–42, 123.

22. I take issue here with John Rawls, "Kantian Constructivism in Moral Theory," *Journal of Philosophy* 77 (1980), 515–572; and Onora O'Neill, *Constructions of Reason* (Cambridge: Cambridge University Press, 1989), pp. 3–50. For a critique of their interpretations, see Patrick Riley, *Kant's Political Philosophy* (Totawa, N.J.: Rowman and Allanheld, 1983), pp. 1–37.

23. Hence the Cambridge Platonists were very critical of the empiricist tradition for seeing the mind as a blank tablet. See Ralph Cudworth, *Treatise on True and Immutable Morality* IV, chap. 1, §2: "Knowledge is an Inward and Active Energy of the Mind it self, and the displaying of its own Innate Vigour from within, whereby it doth Conquer, Master and Command its Objects, and so begets a Clear, Serene, Victorius, and Satisfactory Sense within it self."

24. See Frank, *Einführung in die frühromantische Ästhetik,* pp. 140–141.

25. Ibid., pp. 22–24, 25–29.

26. See ibid., pp. 231–247, and *Unendliche Annäherung,* pp. 27, 65–66, 662. For a more detailed critique of Frank's distinction, see my *German Idealism:* The Struggle against Subjectivism, 1781–1801) (Cambridge, Mass.: Harvard University Press, 2002), pp. 354–355.

27. See Schlegel, *Philosophische Lehrjahre,* KA XVIII, 33 (no. 151), 65 (no. 449), 80 (no. 606), 85 (no. 658), 90 (no. 736), 282 (no. 1046), and 396 (no. 908). On Schelling's use of the term, see *Fernere Darstellung, Sämtliche Werke* IV, 404; *Bruno, Sämtliche Werke* IV, 257, 322; "Zusatz zur Einleitung" to the *Ideen zu einer Philosophie der Natur, Sämtliche Werke* II, 67, 68; and "Über das Verhältniß der Naturphilosophie zur Philosophie überhaupt," *Sämtliche Werke* V, 112.

28. See Theodor Haering, *Novalis als Philosoph* (Stuttgart: Kohlhammer, 1954).

29. A similar portrait could be painted of Hölderlin; but in his case the Platonic legacy is so deep and complex that I cannot do justice to it here. For a good account, see Michael Franz, "Platos frommer Garten: Hölderlins Platonlektüre von Tübingen bis Jena," *Hölderlin Jahrbuch* 28 (1992–1993), 111–127. See also my *German Idealism,* pp. 382–384.

30. On the history of Platonism in eighteenth-century Germany, see Max Wundt, "Die Wiederentdeckung Platons im 18. Jahrhundert," *Blätter für deutsche Philosophie* 15 (1941), 149–158; and Michael Franz, *Schellings Tübinger Platon-Studien* (Göttingen: Vandenhoeck and Ruprecht, 1996), pp. 13–152.

31. The most important edition of his writings was *Vermischten philosophischen*

    Schriften des Herrn Hemsterhuis (Leipzig, 1797). The translator is unknown. This edition was revised by Julius Hilß and reissued as *Philosophische Schriften* (Karlsruhe: Dreililien Verlag, 1912).

32. See Friedrich Schlegel's urgent request to his brother to send him Hemsterhuis's writings, in his letters of August 21 and September 29, 1793, KA XXIII, 122, 133. The importance of Hemsterhuis for August Wilhelm is apparent from his "Urtheile, Gedanken und Einfälle über Literatur und Kunst," no. 39, *Sämtliche Werke,* ed. Edvard Böcking (Leipzig: Weidmann, 1846), VIII, 12. The influence of Hemsterhuis on Novalis can be gathered from his early Hemsterhuis Studien, HKA II, 360–378.

33. KA X, 179–180.

34. See Friedrich to August Wilhelm, August 28, 1793, KA XXIII, 129–130; October 16, 1793, KA XXIII, 142–144; and November 17, 1793, KA XXIII, 158–159.

35. See, in addition to the letters cited in the preceding note, Schlegel's early fragments "Von der Schönheit in der Dichtkunst," KA XVI, 3–14, 15–31. See especially nos. 13, 15, 17, KA XVI, 8–9.

36. See KA XVIII, 252 (no. 701); XVIII, 332 (no. 108).

37. See KA XVIII, 208 (nos. 137, 146); XVIII, 303, (no. 1314). Schlegel earlier read the concept of intellectual intuition in a purely regulative sense, as the imperative for complete unity. See KA XVIII, 66 (no. 462). He later took it in a more constitutive sense, corresponding to a more positive conception of mysticism.

38. See KA XVIII, xxxvi.

39. See KA XVIII, 417 (no. 1149).

40. To Brinkmann, June 9, 1800, KGA V/4, 82.

41. To Brinkmann, April 24, 1800, KGA V/3, 486.

42. On Schleiermacher's Plato scholarship, see Julia Lamm, "Schleiermacher as Plato Scholar," *Journal of Religion* 80 (2000), 206–239.

43. KGA I/2, 221–222.

44. Ibid., 225.

45. Ibid., 227.

46. On these manuscripts see the editorial reports by Jorg Jantzen, SKA I/2, 195–196, and Manfred Durner, SKA I/5, 37. The *Timaeus* commentary has been published by Hartmut Buchner, *Timaeus (1794). Ein Manuskript zu Platon* (Stuttgart-Bad Cannstatt: Fromann Holzboog, 1994). For a very useful introduction to the significance of Schelling's early Plato manuscript, see Manfred Baum, "The Beginnings of Schelling's Philosophy of Nature," in *The Reception of Kant's Critical Philosophy,* ed. Sally Sedgwick (Cambridge: Cambridge University Press, 2000), pp. 199–215. For a detailed account of Schelling's early writings on Plato, see Franz, *Schellings Tübinger Platon-Studien,* pp. 153–282.

47. See *Ideen zu einer Philosophie der Natur, Sämtliche Werke* II, 20, 44–45.

48. Cf. *Sämtliche Werke* I, 19–20, 318.

49. See *Philosophie der Kunst* §§25–27, *Sämtliche Werke* V, 370, 388–390. Cf. *Bruno, Sämtliche Werke* IV, 229.

50. *Bruno, Sämtliche Werke* IV, 243.

51. Ibid., 299–300.
52. Ibid., 225–226.
53. Friedrich to August Wilhelm, January 15, 1792, KA XXIII, 40.
54. Cf. *Fichte-Studien* no. 143, HKA II, 133; *Das Allgemeine Brouillon* no. 934, HKA III, 448.
55. *Vorarbeiten* nos. 31, 233, HKA III, 533, 576.
56. On Novalis's discovery of Plotinus, see Hans Joachim Mähl, "Novalis und Plotin," *Jahrbuch des freien deutschen Hochstifts,* 1963, pp. 139–250.
57. Novalis to Caroline Schlegel, January 20, 1799, HKA IV, 276. Cf. Novalis to Friedrich Schlegel, December 10, 1798, HKA IV, 269.
58. *Allgemeine Brouillon* no. 896, HKA III, 440.
59. Ibid., nos. 908, 1098, HKA III, 443, 469.

5. The Sovereignty of Art

1. Thus Hölderlin writes in his *Hyperion:* "Poetry . . . is the beginning and end of this science [philosophy]. Like Minerva from the head of Jupiter, she springs from the poetry of an infinite divine being." GSA III, 81. Novalis states in his *Vorarbeiten* no. 31, HKA II, 533: "poetry is as it were the key to philosophy, its purpose and meaning." Cf. no. 280, HKA II, 590–591. Schlegel maintains in his *Gespräch über Poesie:* "The innermost mysteries of all the arts and sciences is the possession of poetry. Everything flows from there and everything returns to it" (KA II, 324). Schelling declares in the *System des transcendentalen Idealismus:* "art is the model of science, and where there is art there science should follow"; and in a similar vein: "art is the single true and eternal organon and document of philosophy." See *Sämtliche Werke,* ed. K. F. A. Schelling (Stuttgart: Cotta, 1856–1861), III, 623, 627. See too Wilhelm Wackenroder, *Herzensergießungen, Werke* (1910), I, 64–69.
2. Insofar as eighteenth-century aestheticians granted any cognitive status to art at all, it was usually of an inferior kind. Wolff had made aesthetic experience into the sense perception of perfection, which is indeed an *objective* property of things, their unity in multiplicity; but he also saw sense perception as an inferior or confused form of intellection. See his 1743 *Psychologia empirica* §§54–55. Although Baumgarten argued for the autonomous status of sensibility, so that it had its own rules and criteria of perfection, he too assigned it to the inferior faculty of knowledge. See his *Metaphysica* §§521, 533. The great exception to the subjectivist trend of eighteenth-century aesthetics is, of course, Hamann, whose remarkable 1762 work *Aesthetica in nuce* anticipates romantic doctrine in many respects, and not least in seeing art as the sole medium of metaphysical knowledge. Yet Hamann remained, as he liked to describe himself, "eine Stimme in der Wüste." His influence on the romantics would have been considerable— Jacobi, Goethe and Herder were his admirers—yet it would also have been very indirect and remote.
3. *Einführung in die frühromantische Ästhetik* (Frankfurt: Suhrkamp, 1989).

4. Ibid., pp. 9–14.

5. In describing it as a theory of truth as productivity I somewhat simplify, since Frank writes of an *"aktiven sich ins Werken setzen des Absoluten"* (p. 124; cf. p. 29). The justification for my simplification is that Frank is describing the Kantian paradigm of truth that stresses the activity of the knowing subject. The obscurity comes from Heidegger.

6. Ibid., pp. 9, 41.

7. Ibid., pp. 41–42, 123.

8. See Rudolf Haym, *Die romantische Schule* (Berlin: Gaertner, 1870), pp. 332, 354–365. In the tradition of Haym, see H. A. Korff, *Geist der Goethe Zeit* (Leipzig: Koehler and Amelang, 1964), III, 246–252; and Nicolai Hartmann, *Die Philosophie des deutschen Idealismus* (Berlin: de Gruyter, 1954), I, 220–233. Gadamer's understanding of romantic aesthetics falls in the same tradition. See his *Wahrheit und Methode*, in volume I of his *Gesammelte Werke* (Tübingen: Mohr, 1990), pp. 61–106.

9. See Schelling, *System des transcendentalen Idealismus, Sämtliche Werke* III, 622, and Schlegel, "Ueber das Verhältniß der schönen Kunst zur Natur," *Sämtliche Werke,* ed. Edvard Böcking (Leipzig: Weidmann, 1846), IX, 303–306.

10. I refer, of course, to M. H. Abrams' classic study *The Mirror and the Lamp* (New York: Oxford University Press, 1953). Whatever the merits of Abrams's distinction for English romanticism, it is false for *Frühromantik*, whose aim was to overcome just such a distinction.

11. This is plain from *Athenäumsfragment* no. 116 alone, where Schlegel insists that the romantic artist should lose himself in his object to such an extent that its characterization is his one and only task. KA II, 182. He intends romantic art to be a synthesis of the naive and sentimental, the imitative and expressive.

12. The romantics often stressed this point. To cite just three examples, Schelling argues in his *System des transcendentalen Idealismus* that the artist's conscious productivity was identical with the unconscious productivity inherent within nature itself (*Sämtliche Werke* III, 612–619); A. W. Schlegel states in his *Vorlesungen über schöne Literatur und Kunst* that art is "nature penetrating through the medium of a perfect spirit" (*Sämtliche Werke* IX, 308); and Friedrich Schlegel declares in his *Gespräch über Poesie* that all our poetry has its source within "the one poem of divinity, of which we are the part and blossom." (KA II, 285)

13. For the defense of Spinoza, see *Athenäumsfragmente* nos. 270, 274, II, 211; 301, II, 216; 450, II, 255. For the insistence on a mystical feeling for the universe, see ibid., no. 121, II, 184.

14. KA II, 317.

15. See Schelling, *Fernere Darstellung aus dem System der Philosophie, Sämtliche Werke* IV, 353–361; and Schlegel, *Philosophische Lehrjahre,* KA XVIII, 31 (no. 134); and 38 (no. 209).

16. Frank, *Einführung,* p. 127.

17. Ibid., pp. 127, 128.

18. Ibid., pp. 122–123.

19. The significant exception here is A. W. Schlegel, who is more critical of Kant than most romantics. See his *Vorlesungen über schöne Literatur und Kunst*, in *Vorlesungen über Ästhetik*, ed. Ernst Behler (Paderborn: Schöningh, 1989), I, 228–251.

20. I cannot concur, therefore, with Ernst Behler, who, in a review of Frank's work, criticizes the central place it gives to the *Kritik der Urteilskraft*. See *Athenäum* 1 (1991), 248–249. While Behler is right that Kant's work had increasingly less importance for the romantics, he tends to underestimate its earlier significance. While that significance was partly negative, it was also in no small measure positive. The early criticism of the Schlegel brothers is incomprehensible apart from Kant's argument for aesthetic autonomy.

21. See Hölderlin to Neuffer, January 16, 1794, GSA VI, 137; Hölderlin to Schiller, September 4, 1795, GSA VI, 181; and Hölderlin to Niethammer, February 24, 1796, GSA VI, 203. See also Friedrich Schlegel's early critique of Kant in "Von der Schönheit in der Dichtkunst [I]," KA XVI, 5–6, 11.

22. Frank, *Einführung*, pp. 38–39, 50–51, 93–94.

23. Ibid., pp. 122–123, 129.

24. See Hölderlin's early poem "Hymne an der Schönheit," GSA I, 132. Here Hölderlin cites §42 of the *Kritik der Urteilskraft*. See also Schlegel's "Von der Schönheit in der Dichtung," KA XVI, 24, where he defines beauty as the appearance of the good.

25. In §59 Kant states that beauty is a symbol of morality only in an analogical sense, and that analogies do not provide any cognition of an object (AA V, 531).

26. See Hölderlin, GSA III, 81–84; Schlegel, KA II, 324–325; Schelling, *Sämtliche Werke* III, 612–629; and Novalis, *Vorarbeiten* no. 31, HKA II, 533, and *Hemsterhuis Studien* no. 32, HKA II, 372–373.

27. See KrV, B 679, 681–682, 685, 688, and *Kritik der Urteilskraft* §V, AA V, 185.

28. This is most clear in the first introduction with its concept of a *technic* of nature. See AA XX, 204–205, 214, 216–217.

29. *Kritik der Urteilskraft* §65, AA V, 375; §68, AA V, 384; §73, AA V, 394–395.

30. I am not alone, of course, in stressing the importance of the organic theory, which has a long and venerable tradition. See, for example, Paul Kluckhohn, *Das Ideengut der deutschen Romantik* (Tübingen: Niemeyer, 1953), pp. 24–35; Oskar Walzel, "Wesensfragen deutscher Romantik," in *Jahrbuch des Freien deutschen Hochstiftes* 29 (1929), 253–276; Alois Stockmann, *Die deutsche Romantik* (Freiburg: Herder and Co., 1921), pp. 13–17; and Morse Peckham, "Toward a Theory of Romanticism," *Proceedings of the Modern Language Association* 66 (1951), 5–23.

31. For more details on the methodology of *Naturphilosophie*, see my *German Idealism: The Struggle against Subjectivism, 1781–1801* (Cambridge, Mass.: Harvard University Press, 2002), pp. 523–528.

32. On the influence of Herder and Kielmeyer, see Manfred Durner, "Die Naturphilosophie im 18. Jahrhundert und der naturwissenschaftliche Unterricht in Tübingen," *Archiv für Geschichte der Philosophie* 73 (1991), 71–103.

33. The resurrection of Leibniz is especially apparent from Schelling's "Einleitung" to his *Ideen zu einer Philosophie der Natur, Sämtliche Werke* II, 20. Writing of Leibniz's legacy, Schelling declares: "Die Zeit ist gekommen, da man seine Philosophie wiederherstellen kann." See also Hölderlin to Neuffer, November 8, 1780, GSA VI/1, 56.

34. See the "Einleitung" to his *Ideen zu einer Philosophie der Natur, Sämtliche Werke* II, 56.

6. The Concept of *Bildung*

1. Friedrich Schlegel, *Ideen* no. 37. Cf. no. 65 and the statement in his *Vorlesungen über die Transcendentalphilosophie*, KA XII, 57: "According to the highest view of man, the concept to which everything must be related is that of education *(Bildung)*." Cf. EPW, pp. 127, 131.

2. See the "Vorerinnerung" to the *Athenäum* I (1798), iii–iv. Cf. *Athenäum* III (1800), 296. The contributors to the journal swore to devote themselves to the realm of *Bildung* according to the following lines: *"Der Bildung Strahlen All in Eins zu fassen, Vom Kranken ganz zu scheiden das Gesunde, Bestreben wir uns true im freien Bunde."*

3. Montesquieu had an influence in Germany as great as Rousseau. On the history of his reception in Germany, see Rudolf Vierhaus, "Montesquieu in Deutschland: Zur Geschichte seiner Wirkung als politischer Schriftsteller im 18. Jahrhundert," in *Deutschland im 18. Jahrhundert* (Göttigen: Vandenhoeck and Ruprecht, 1988), pp. 9–32.

4. This argument is explicit in Novalis's *Glauben und Liebe* no. 36, HKA II, 300–301. Cf. EPW, pp. 45–46.

5. See Aristotle, *Nicomachean Ethics* I, chaps. 1 and 5, 1094a and 1997b; and Kant, *Kritik der praktischen Vernunft*, AA V, 110–111.

6. The most explicit treatments are Schleiermacher's early essays "Über das höchste Gut," KGA I/1, 81–125, and "Über den Wert des Lebens," KGA I/1, 391–471; and Friedrich Schlegel's lectures on transcendental philosophy. See KA XII, 47–49, 85–86. Cf. EPW, pp. 146–147.

7. Friedrich Schlegel explicitly rejected hedonism on such grounds in his early essay "Ueber die Grenzen des Schönen," KA I, 37. The most sustained romantic critique of hedonism appears in Schleiermacher's *Grundlinien einer Kritik der bisherigen Sittenlehre, Werke*, ed. Otto Braun and Johannes Bauer (Leipzig: Meiner, 1928), I, 81–92.

8. On the romantic critique of philistinism, see Friedrich Schlegel's novel *Lucinde*, KA VIII, 41–50; and Novalis, *Blütenstaub* no. 77, HKA II, 261–263. Cf. EPW, pp. 24–25.

9. For the romantic critique of Kant's ethics, see Schleiermacher's *Monologen*, KGA I/3, 17–18 (EPW, pp. 174–175); and Friedrich Schlegel's *Ideen*, §39 and lectures on transcendental philosophy, KA XII, 48, 72. Cf. EPW, p. 128. The source for the first criticism of Kant ultimately goes back to Schiller, and especially his treatise *Über Anmut und Würde*, which is discussed below.

10. Schiller, NA XX, 336–341.

11. Schiller, NA XX, 251–289. The entire first part is relevant to the argument reconstructed above.

12. Schiller, NA XXI, 410–412.

13. Novalis, *Glauben und Liebe* no. 39, HKA II, 303–304. Cf. EPW, p. 48.

14. Schleiermacher, KGA I/2, 169–172.

15. See A. G. Baumgarten, *Aesthetica* §§1, 14, in *Theoretische Ästhetik: Die Grundlegenden Abschnitte aus der Äesthetica,* trans. and ed. Hans Rudolf Schweizer (Hamburg: Meiner, 1983).

16. On the history of the concept of the beautiful soul, see Robert Norton, *The Beautiful Soul* (Ithaca: Cornell University Press, 1995).

17. See *Kritik der Urteilskraft* §§4–7, 15, AA V, 207–212, 226–229.

18. Schiller, NA XXVI, 174–229.

19. On the definition of *Bildung,* see Schlegel's *Vorlesungen über Transcendentalphilosophie,* KA XII, 48. On the account of modern *Bildung,* see the early essays "Vom Wert des Studiums der Griechen und Römer," KA I, 636–637, and "Ueber das Studium der Griechischen Poesie," in *Die Griechen und Römer: Historische und Kritische Versuche über das klassische Alterthum,* KA I, 232–233.

20. Such was Schlegel's remarkable formulation in the section entitled "Eine Reflexion" in his novel *Lucinde,* KA V, 72–73.

21. Thus spake Novalis's hero in *Heinrich von Ofterdingen,* HKA I, 380.

22. See "Vorarbeiten 1798" no. 105, HKA II, 334. Cf. EPW, p. 85.

23. See *Blütenstaub* no. 16, HKA II, 419. Cf. EPW, p. 11.

24. See *Ideen* no. 39, KA II, 259.

25. See Schlegel's *Brief über den Roman,* KA II, 333–334.

26. *Ideen* no. 83, KA II, 264. Cf. EPW, p. 132.

27. The main exception to this generalization is Schleiermacher's *Gelegentliche Gedanken über Universitäten in deutschem Sinn* (1808), in *Werke* IV, 533–642, which was written for the foundation of the new University of Berlin.

28. *Ueber die Philosophie,* KA VIII, 44–45.

7. Friedrich Schlegel

1. For an illuminating account of the use of the concept of the romantic in eighteenth-century Germany, see Raymond Immerwahr, "Romantic and its Cognates in England, Germany and France before 1790," in *Romantic and Its Cognates,* ed. Hans Eichner (Tornoto: University of Toronto Press, 1972), pp. 53–84.

2. The *Studiumaufsatz* was completed in draft form in early October 1795; but due to publishing delays it did not appear until January 1797. By that time Schlegel had already abandoned his neoclassicism.

3. The *locus classicus* for this argument is Arthur Lovejoy's "Schiller and the Genesis of German Romanticism," in *Essays in the History of Ideas* (New York: Putnam, 1963), pp. 207–227, esp. 216.

4. The chief examples of this view are Richard Brinkmann, "Romantische Dichtungstheorie in Friedrich Schlegels Frühschriften und Schillers Begriff der

Naiven und Sentimentalischen," *Deutsche Vierteljahrschrift für Literaturwissenschaft und Geistesgeschichte* 32 (1958), 344–371; and Raimund Belgardt, "'Romantische Poesie' in Friedrich Schlegel's Aufsatz *Über das Studium der griechischen Poesie,*" *German Quarterly* 40 (1967), 165–181.

5. The literary notebooks are in volume 16 (1981), and the philosophical note-books are in volume 18 (1963), of the *Kritische Friedrich Schlegel Ausgabe,* ed. Ernst Behler et al., (Paderborn: Schöningh, 1958–).

6. See Dieter Henrich, *Konstellationen: Probleme und Debatten am Ursprung der idealistischen Philosophie (1789–1795)* (Stuttgart: Klett-Cotta, 1991), pp. 7–46; Wilhelm Baum, "Der Klagenfurter Herbert-Kreis zwischen Aufklärung und Romantik," *Revue Internationale de Philosophie* 50 (1996), 483–514; Marcello Stamm, *Systemkrise: Die Elementarphilosophie in der Debatte* (Stuttgart: Klett-Cotta, forthcoming); and Manfred Frank, *Unendliche Annäherung: Die Anfänge der philosophischen Frühromantik* (Frankfurt: Suhrkamp, 1998).

7. This is the formulation of H. A. Korff in his influential *Geist der Goethezeit* (Leipzig: Koehler and Amelang, 1964), III, 246–249. Korff was simply following in the footsteps of Rudolf Haym, *Die romantische Schule* (Berlin: Gaertner, 1870), pp. 257–262.

8. See, for example, Lovejoy, "The Meaning of 'Romantic' in Early German Romanticism," in *Essays,* pp. 196–198.

9. The terms *romantisch* or *romantische Poesie* appear frequently in the *Studiumaufsatz,* KA I, 226, 233, 257, 280, 319, 334.

10. As Ernst Behler has argued. See his "Kritische Gedanken zum Begriff der Europäischen Romantik," *Die Europäische Romantik* (Frankfurt: Athenäum Verlag, 1972), pp. 8–22.

11. The crucial fragments are nos. 7, KA II, 147–148; 66, KA II, 155; 44, KA II, 152; 91, KA II, 158; and 60, II, 154.

12. KA II, 183. The same conclusion can be found in the literary notebooks. See, for example, nos. 606, KA XVI, 136; 106, KA XVI, 590; 590, KA XVI, 134; 982, KA XVI, 167. Cf. *Philosophische Lehrjahre* no. 740, KA XVIII, 91.

13. See too Schlegel's May 1793 letter to his brother: "*Shakespeare ist unter allen Dichtern der Wahrste.*" KA XXIII, 97.

14. Schlegel develops this philosophy mainly in two works: the *Studiumaufsatz,* KA I, 230–233, and "Vom Wert des Studiums," KA I, 629–632. I have combined the accounts given in both these works. While there are some variations between them, they are not important for our present purposes.

15. "Vom Wert des Studiums der Griechen und Römer," KA I, 621–642.

16. See "Über die Grenzen des Schönen," KA I, 35.

17. See Winckelmann, "Gedanken über die Nachahmung der griechischen Werke in Malerei und Bildhauerkunst," and "Erinnerung über die Betrachtung der Werke der Kunst," in *Werke in Einem Band,* ed. Helmut Holtzhauer (Berlin: Aufbau, 1986), pp. 11–13, 37.

18. See "Ueber die Grenzen des Schönen," KA I, 37; *Studiumaufsatz,* KA I, 211, 213, 214, 220. Schlegel's position is also more complicated and confused, however,

because he joins beauty with morality by defining beauty as the pleasing appearance of the good. See *Studiumaufsatz*, KA I, 288; and "Von der Schönheit in der Dichtkunst," KA XVI, 22 (no. 11).

19. See *Studiumaufsatz*, KA I, 217; and "Von der Schönheit in der Dichtkunst," KA XVI, 22 (no. 11).

20. Two of these fragments survive: "Von der Schönheit in der Dichtkunst III," KA XVI, 3–14; and the similarly titled "Von der Schönheit in der Dichtkunst," KA XVI, 15–31.

21. Haym, *Die romantische Schule*, pp. 251–254.

22. See his "Die Wirkung Goethes und Schillers auf die Brüder Schlegel," in *Studien zur Romantik und zur idealistischen Philosophie* (Paderborn: Schöningh, 1988), pp. 264–282, esp. 273–274.

23. See Friedrich to August Wilhelm Schlegel, June 15, 1796, KA XXIII, 312.

24. See Josef Körner, *Romantiker und Klassiker* (Berlin: Askanischer Verlag, 1924), pp. 90–95; Hans Eichner, "Friedrich Schlegel's Theory of Romantic Poetry," *Publications of the Modern Language Association* 71 (1956), 1019–1041, esp. 1028–1029, and his introduction to the *Kritische Ausgabe*, II, lxxi–lxxix.

25. Nos. 1102, KA XVI, 176; 115, KA XVI, 94; and 342, KA XVI, 113.

26. Nos. 289, KA XVI, 108; 575, KA XVI, 133; and 1110, KA XVI, 176.

27. It is in this light that one must read Schlegel's famous statement in *Athenäumsfragment* no. 216 that Goethe's *Wilhelm Meister*, along with the French Revolution and Fichte's *Wissenschaftslehre*, is one of the great tendencies of the age. Cf. Schlegel's statement in the notebooks, no. 1110, KA XVI, 176. That this is the proper interpretation of Schlegel's statement has been made evident by Körner, *Romantiker und Klassiker*, pp. 92–93; and Eichner, KA II, lxxvi.

28. See note 3 above. See also Körner, *Romantiker und Klassiker*, p. 34 n. 4, who claims that Lovejoy's essay is no advance on that of Carl Enders. See Enders, *Friedrich Schlegel: Die Quellen seines Wesens und Werdens* (Leipzig: H. Haessel, 1913), p. 380.

29. See Hans Eichner, "The Supposed Influence of Schiller's *Über naive und sentimentalische Dichtung* on F. Schlegel's *Über das Studium der griechischen Poesie*," *Germanic Review* 30 (1955), 261–264. While Eichner criticizes Haym's hypothesis that the second half of the *Studiumaufsatz* was written under Schiller's influence, he still accepts "by common consent" Lovejoy's thesis that Schiller made Schlegel abandon his neoclassical verdict against modern literature (p. 262).

30. See Schiller, *Über naive und sentimentalische Dichtung*, NA XX, 414. Of course, the coincidence in Schlegel's and Schiller's views is not accidental, given that Schlegel's theory of history followed in the footsteps of Schiller's *Ästhetische Briefe*, which had been published between 1793 and 1794.

31. Schiller, NA XX, 432, 436–437.

32. Ibid., p. 438.

33. Ibid., p. 439.

34. Thus Lovejoy, "Schiller and the Genesis of Romanticism," p. 220.

35. Friedrich to August Wilhelm, January 16, 1796, KA XXIII, 271.

36. Lovejoy, "Schiller and the Genesis of Romanticism," p. 218.

37. Schlegel was somewhat exaggerating Schiller's influence on him, since he was eager for personal and economic reasons to become a participant in the *Horen*. On the background to Schlegel's letter, see Körner, *Romantiker und Klassiker*, pp. 36–38.

38. See his letter to August Wilhelm, December 23, 1795, KA XXIII, 263.

39. See Schlegel, *Ueber das Studium der griechischen Poesie*, I, 358. Cf. Schlegel's 1804–1805 *Die Entwicklung der Philosophie in Zwölf Büchern*, KA XII, 291.

40. *Athenäumsfragment* no. 216, II, 198.

41. See Schlegel's "Literatur," in his *Europa*, I (1803), 41–63, KA III, 3–16.

42. See Schlegel's May 27, 1796 letter to his brother, where he confesses that republicanism is now closer to his heart than criticism. KA XXIII, 304–305.

43. The first edition was published in *Deutschland*, III (1796), 10–41, KA VII, 11–25.

44. For a more detailed account of Schlegel's Fichtean phase, see Frank, *Unendliche Annäherung*, pp. 578–589; and Ernst Behler, "Friedrich Schlegel's Theory of an Alternating Principle Prior to his Arrival in Jena (6 August 1796), *Revue Internationale de Philosophie* 50 (1996), 383–402.

45. Schlegel's positive review of Niethammer's *Philosophisches Journal*, of which Fichte was an editor and contributor, has been interpreted as the work of a mere disciple; see Haym, *Die romantische Schule*, pp. 225–226. But this is implausible. Not only is Schlegel very guarded in stating his opinion of Fichte's articles, but he also closed his review by expressing his doubts about all standards of judgment in philosophy, a position flatly contrary to his earlier foundationalism (VIII, 30). In any case, he wrote his review in January 1797, *after* he had disavowed any adherence to Fichte.

46. The evidence for Novalis's influence on Schlegel is very circumstantial. Schlegel visited Novalis for a week in the summer of 1796, before arriving in Jena and while he was still an ardent *Fichteaner*. Schlegel would later write about their discussions over "Fichtes Ich" (KA XXIII, 326, 328, 340). By the summer of 1796 Novalis had already become skeptical of Fichte; and by the autumn of 1796 Schlegel too shows signs of extreme skepticism. However, Novalis credits Schlegel with freeing him from Fichte's influence. See Novalis to Schlegel, June 14, 1797, KA XXIII, 372. Of course, it is possible that they freed one another from Fichte's influence, which would have been the expected result of their *Symphilosophie*.

47. On Schlegel's early ties with the Niethammer circle, see Frank, *Unendliche Annäherung*, pp. 569–593, 862–886.

48. As Frank has observed, ibid., p. 578.

49. See Schlegel to Körner, September 21 and 30, 1796, KA XXIII, 333.

50. See Schlegel's letter to J. F. Cotta, April 7, 1897, KA XVIII, 356, and his March 10, 1797 letter to Novalis, KA XXIII, 350. Though Schlegel implies that the essay is complete, he had only sketched some of his ideas. These are in the *Philosophische Lehrjahre*, KA XVIII, 31–39 (nos. 126–227).

51. The first number designates the fragment, the second number the page of the

Kritische Ausgabe. Because there are three collections of fragments, which are not consecutively numbered, it is necessary to cite both fragment and page number here.

52. See the collection entitled "Zur Wissenschaftslehre 1796," nos. 1–121, KA XVIII, 3–15; "Philosophische Fragmente 1796," Beilage I, KA XVIII, 505–516; and "Zur Logik und Philosophie," Beilage II, KA XVIII, 517–521. The more finished form of the second collection suggests that Schlegel had publication in mind; whether as part of "Geist der Wissenschaftslehre" is uncertain.

53. Both of these points follow from Schlegel's claim that every proposition and proof is infinitely perfectible. See *Philosophische Lehrjahre* nos. 12, 15, KA XVIII, 506, 507.

54. Schlegel makes this point most clearly in his later lectures on *Transcendental-philosophie*, KA XII, 96.

55. On Schlegel's complex attitude toward systematicity, see also his August 28, 1793 letter to his brother, KA XXIII, 125–126.

56. On the context of Schlegel's coherence theory, see Manfred Frank, "'Alle Wahrheit ist Relativ, Alles Wissen Symbolisch,'" in *Revue Internationale de Philosophie* 50 (1996), 403–436.

57. It has sometimes been argued that Schlegel's concept of romantic poetry was a synthesis of the modern and the classical, and that it is one-sided to consider his concept as exclusively modern, as the antithesis of his earlier classicism. See Behler, "Kritische Gedanken," pp. 10–21. While it is indeed the case that Schlegel does not oppose classicism, he does *subordinate* it to the ideal of romantic poetry. The classical becomes one element within the romantic striving for totality; or that striving is seen as an "infinitely elastic classicism."

58. See Schlegel's letter to J. F. Cotta, dated April 7, 1797, where he states that he plans to write an essay provisionally entitled "Charakteristik der sokratische Ironie" (KA XXIII, 356).

59. As Schlegel put this point in his notebooks: "*Knowing* means conditioned cognition. The unknowability of the absolute is therefore a tautologous triviality" (no. 62, KA II, 511).

60. Cf. *Athenäumsfragment* no. 51, KA II, 172–173.

8. The Paradox of Romantic Metaphysics

1. That the romantics had such a project is evident from their notebooks and fragments. On Schelling, see his *Briefe über Dogmatismus und Kriticizismus, Sämtliche Werke,* ed. K. F. A. Schelling (Stuttgart: Cotta, 1856–1861), I, 326–335. Schelling's later absolute idealism, as expressed in the *System des transcendentalen Idealismus* and *Darstellung meines Systems,* can be regarded as attempts to synthesize Fichte's idealism and Spinoza's realism. On Novalis, see, for example, *Allgemeine Brouillon* nos. 75, 634, 820, HKA III, 252, 382, 429; and *Fragmente und Studien* no. 611, HKA III, 671. On Friedrich Schlegel, see, for example, *Philosophische Lehrjahre,* KA XVIII, 31, 38, 43, 80. On Hölderlin, see the preface

to the penultimate version of *Hyperion*, GSA III/1, 236; the preface to *Fragment von Hyperion*, III/1, 163; and the final version of *Hyperion*, III/1, 38. The attempt to join Fichte and Spinoza was one of the fundamental aims of Hölderlin's early novel. This project was probably a subject of discussion between Hölderlin and Schelling around 1796–1797. See Schelling's *Briefe über Dogmatismus und Kriticizismus*, *Sämtliche Werke* I, 284–290. In the penultimate letter of the *Briefe* Schelling sketches his own idea of a synthesis of idealism and realism, which later came to fruition in his *Identitätssystem*. See ibid., pp. 326–330. It is impossible to determine who among the romantics was the original creator of this project, since they conceived it partly independently, partly jointly through conversation, around the same time, especially in the formative years 1796–1798.

2. See Fichte, *Grundlage der gesammten Wissenschaftslehre*, *Sämtliche Werke*, ed. I. H. Fichte (Berlin: Veit, 1845–1846), I, 101; and Kant, *Kritik der praktischen Vernunft*, *AA* V, 101–102.

3. See, for example, Alois Stockman, *Die deutsche Romantik* (Freiburg: Herder and Co., 1921), pp. 13–17; Oskar Walzel, "Wesenfragen deutscher Romantik," *Jahrbuch des Freien deutschen Hochstifts* 29 (1929), 253–276; Adolf Grimme, *Vom Wesen der Romantik* (Braunschweig: Westermann, 1947), p. 13; René Wellek, "The Concept of Romanticism in Literary History" and "Romanticism Re-examined" in *Concepts of Criticism*, ed. Stephen G. Nichols (New Haven: Yale University Press, 1963), pp. 165, 220; Morse Peckham, "Toward a Theory of Romanticism," *Proceedings of the Modern Language Association* 66 (1951), 5–23; and Lawrence Ryan, "Romanticism," in *Periods of German Literature*, ed. J. M. Ritchie (London: Oswald Wolff, 1966), pp. 123–143.

4. See, for example, Paul de Man, "The Rhetoric of Temporality," in *Blindness and Insight*, 2nd ed. (Minneapolis: University of Minnesota Press, 1983), pp. 187–228, esp. 220–228; and Alice Kuzniar, *Delayed Endings: Nonclosure in Novalis and Hölderlin* (Athens: University of Georgia Press, 1987), pp. 1–71.

5. This was the formulation of Hölderlin in the preface to the penultimate version of *Hyperion*, GSA III/1, 236.

6. This was Schelling's reasoning in his early Fichtean work *Abhandlungen zur Erläuterung des Idealismus der Wissenschaftslehre*, *Sämtliche Werke* I, 365–366.

7. See Kant, *KrV*, Vorrede, B xviii.

8. Ibid., B xiii, A xx, A xiv.

9. Fichte, *Grundlage der gesamten Wissenschaftslehre*, *Sämtliche Werke* I, 101.

10. This criticism is most explicit in Hölderlin's famous fragment "Urtheil und Seyn," GSA IV/1, 216–217. Hölderlin was not alone in making it, however. The same point was made by Schelling, *Briefe über Dogmatismus und Kriticismus*, *Werke* I, 329, and *Vom Ich als Princip der Philosophie*, ibid., 180–181. See too Novalis, *Fichte-Studien*, HKA II, 107 (nos. 5–7).

11. This second criticism is most apparent in early Hegel and Schelling. See their *Fernere Darstellung aus dem System der Philosophie*, in Schelling, *Sämtliche Werke* IV, 356–361, and their "Ueber das Verhältniß der Naturphilosophie zur Philosophie überhaupt," in Schelling, *Sämtliche Werke* V, 108–115.

12. For Schlegel, see, for example, *Philosophische Lehrjahr*, KA XVIII, 31 (no. 134), 38 (no. 209), 80 (no. 606). On Novalis, see *Allgemeine Brouillon*, HKA III, 382–384 (no. 634), 252 (no. 69), 382 (no. 633), 429 (no. 820), and *Fragmente und Studien*, HKA III, 671 (no. 611).

13. See Schelling, *Von der Weltseele, Sämtliche Werke* II, 496–505, and his *Erster Entwurf eines Systems der Naturphilosophie, Sämtliche Werke* III, 74–78.

14. On these experiments, see Thomas Hankins, *Science and Enlightenment* (Cambridge: Cambridge University Press, 1992), pp. 46–80.

15. See Herder, *Gott, Einige Gespräche, Sämtliche Werke*, ed. B. Suphan (Berlin: Weidmann, 1881–1913), XVI, 458–464; and Schelling, *Ideen zu einer Philosophie der Natur, Sämtliche Werke* II, 20.

16. Hegel, *Geschichte der Philosophie, Werkausgabe* XX, 165.

17. See Spinoza, *Ethica, opera*, ed. C. Gebhardt (Heidelberg: Winter 1924), II, 77, par. I, prop. xxxiv.

18. On this reasoning, see Schelling, *System der gesammten Philosophie, Sämtliche Werke* VI, §1, 138–140.

19. See ibid., §4, 141–145; Schelling and Hegel, *Fernere Darstellungen aus dem System der Philosophie, Sämtliche Werke* VI, 356–361; and Novalis, *Allgemeine Broullion*, HKA III, 382–384 (no. 634), 252 (no. 69), 382 (no. 633), 429 (no. 820).

20. See Schelling, *System der gesammten Philosophie, Sämtliche Werke* VI, §§302–317, 538–570; Schlegel, *Transcendentalphilosophie*, KA XII, 50, 52, 57, 72, 74, 86; and Novalis, *Die Lehrling zu Sais*, HKA I, 77, *Fichte-Studien*, HKA II, 154, 202, 270, and *Allgemeine Broullion*, HKA III, 271 (no. 172), 381–382 (nos. 633–634), 404 (no. 713).

21. Schlegel, *Transcendentalphilosophie*, KA XII, 57, 72, 74; and Schelling, *System der gesammten Philosophie, Sämtliche Werke* VI, §305, 541–548.

22. Schlegel, *Transcendentalphilosophie*, KA XII, 72.

23. See Schleiermacher, *Über die Religion*, KGA II/1, 232.

9. Kant and the *Naturphilosophen*

1. The crucial texts for the romantic defense of the organic view of nature are the introduction to Schelling's *Ideen zur einer Philosophie der Natur, Sämtliche Werke*, ed. K. F. A. Schelling (Stuttgart: Cotta, 1856–1861), II, 10–73, and the preface to *Von der Weltseele, Sämtliche Werke* II, 347–351; Schlegel's *Vorlesungen über Transcendentalphilosophie*, KA XII, 3–43, 91–105; Novalis's, *Allgemeine Brouillon* nos. 69, 338, 820, 460, 477, 820, and *Vorarbeiten* nos. 118, 125; and the sections on Fichte's and Schelling's systems in Hegel's *Differenz zwischen des Fichte'schen und Schelling'schen Systems der Philosophie*, and the section on "Kantische Philosophie" in Hegel's *Glauben und Wissen, Werkausgabe*, II, 52–115, 301–333. Though Hegel himself later broke with the romantics, his Jena writings prior to 1804 are some of the most important defenses of the romantic position.

2. For example, this assumption is operative in the work of Timothy Lenoir. See his "Kant, Blumenbach, and Vital Materialism in German Biology," *Isis* 71 (1980),

77–108; "The Göttingen School and the Development of Transcendental Naturphilosophie in the Romantic Era," *Studies in the History of Biology* 5 (1981), 111–205; and *The Strategy of Life: Teleology and Mechanics in Nineteenth-Century German Biology* (Chicago: University of Chicago Press, 1989). Lenoir's strategy is to free late-eighteenth- and early-nineteenth-century German physiology from the associations of *Naturphilosophie* by showing the impact of Kant on such physiologists as Blumenbach, Kielmeyer, Treviranus, and Humboldt, whom he thinks were responsive to Kant's criticisms of teleology and vitalism. For an assessment of Lenoir's views, see K. L. Caneva, "Teleology with Regrets," *Annals of Science* 47 (1990), 291–300; and Robert Richards, *The Romantic Conception of Life* (Chicago: University of Chicago Press, 2002), pp. 210, 227–228, 235.

3. See Kant, AA VIII, 45–60.
4. On these writers and their works, see Manfred Durner, "Theorie der Chemie," in the supplementary volume to *Schelling, Historisch-Kritische Ausgabe, Wissenschaftliche Bericht zu Schellings Naturphilosophischen Schriften 1797–1800* (Stuttgart: Frommann, 1994), pp. 44–56.
5. On Herder's debts to this work, see Emil Adler, *Der junge Herder und die Aufklärung* (Vienna: Europa, 1968), pp. 56–59.
6. See Lenoir, *The Strategy of Life*, p. 6.
7. See James Larson, "Vital Forces: Regulative Principles or Constitutive Agents? A Strategy in German Physiology, 1786–1802," *Isis* 70 (1979), 235–249.
8. Concerning some of Kant's equivocations, see Paul Guyer, "Reason and Reflective Judgment: Kant on the Significance of Systematicity," *Nous* 24 (1990), 17–43, and "Kant's Conception of Empirical Law," *Proceedings of the Aristotelian Society* suppl. vol. 64 (1990), 221–242. On Kant's hidden proximity to the position of Hegel, see Burkhard Tuschling, "The System of Transcendental Idealism: Questions Raised and Left Open in the *Kritik der Urteilskraft, Southern Journal of Philosophy* 30 (1991), Supplement, 109–127.
9. See KrV, B 678.
10. Ibid., B 679, 681–682, 685, 688.
11. Ibid., B 679.
12. See *Kritik der Urteilskraft* §V, AA V, 185.
13. See "Über den Gebrauch teleologischer Prinzipien in der Philosophie," AA VIII, 181–182; and *Metaphysische Anfangsgründe der Naturwissenschaften,* AA IV, 543–545. The argument of the first text recurs in the *Kritik der Urteilskraft* at §65 (V, 375); the argument of the second reappears at §§65 (V, 374–375) and 73 (V, 394–395).
14. These works were written after Kant's review of Herder's *Ideen*, in Kant, AA VIII, 45–66. The polemics in the review anticipate the later arguments.
15. See the preface to the second edition of KrV, B xviii. Cf. the first preface, A xx.
16. Here one historical caveat is necessary. The romantics did not explicitly, self-consciously, and methodically reply point-for-point to Kant's arguments. It is therefore necessary for the historian to reconstruct their response, which means

drawing out some of the implications of their general position. This requires considering what they *would* or *could* have said in response to Kant. My reconstruction is based on the texts cited in note 1 above and notes 17 and 19 below.

17. This point is involved in Schelling's and Hegel's claim that the rationality of nature is the result of its intelligible structure rather than its self-consciousness alone. This point became essential to their defense of an *objective* idealism against the *subjective* idealism of Kant and Fichte. The argument is especially apparent in Hegel's *Differenzschrift* and their joint article "Ueber den wahren Begriff der Naturphilosophie und die richtige Art, ihre Probleme aufzulösen," Schelling, *Sämtliche Werke*, 81–103.

18. Here I take issue with Lenoir, who accepts the standard caricature of *Naturphilosophie* as a species of vitalism, and distinguishes the tradition of vital materialism from *Naturphilosophie*. See his "Kant, Blumenbach and Vital Materialism," p. 108.

19. On Schelling's attempt to steer a middle path between these extremes, see Schelling's *Von der Weltseele, Sämtliche Werke* II, 496–505, and his *Erster Entwurf eines Systems der Naturphilosophie,* ibid., III, 74–78.

20. See KrV, A 438; and Inaugural Dissertation §15, Corollarium (AA II, 405). In Reflexion 3789, AA XVII, 293, Kant formulates the distinction as one between a *totum analyticum* and a *totum syntheticum.* In Reflexion 6178, AA XVIII, 481, he formulates it as a distinction between intuitive and discursive universality. See also §76 of the *Kritik der Urteilskraft,* AA V, 401–404.

21. *Kritik der Urteilskraft* §§75, AA V, 398; 82, AA V, 429.

22. Cf. ibid., §§71, AA V, 388–389; 75, AA V, 400.

23. On the influence of Blumenbach, see Lenoir, "The Göttingen School and the Development of Transcendental Naturphilosophie," pp. 128–154; and on the influence of Kielmeyer, see Manfred Durner, "Die Naturphilosophie im 18. Jahrhundert und der naturwissenschaftliche Unterricht in Tübingen," *Archiv für Geschichte der Philosophie* 73 (1991), 95–99.

24. For a brief and useful survey, see Shirley Roe, *Matter, Life and Generation: 18th Century Embryology and the Haller–Wolff Debate* (Cambridge: Cambridge University Press, 1981), pp. 1–20; Thomas Hankins, *Science and the Enlightenment* (Cambridge: Cambridge University Press, 1985), pp. 113–157; and Robert Richards, *The Meaning of Evolution* (Chicago: University of Chicago Press, 1992), pp. 5–16.

25. See J. F. Blumenbach, *Über den Bildungstrieb,* 2nd ed. (Göttingen: Dietrich, 1791), pp. 44–77.

26. See Roe, *Matter, Life and Generation,* pp. 80–83, 86.

27. This point has been underestimated, I believe, by Kant's defenders. The monistic aspirations of post-Kantian philosophy arose from an *internal* critique of Kant and not from any prior metaphysical commitments. Cf. Karl Ameriks, "The Practical Foundation of Philosophy in Kant, Fichte, and After," in *The Reception of Kant's Critical Philosophy,* ed. Sally Sedgwick (Cambridge: Cambridge University Press, 2000), pp. 109–129, esp. 118–119; and Paul Guyer, "Absolute Idealism

and the Rejection of Kantian Dualism," in *The Cambridge Companion to German Idealism,* ed. Karl Ameriks (Cambridge: Cambridge University Press, 2000), pp. 37–56.

28. See Maimon, *Versuch über die Transcendentalphilosophie, Gesammelte Werke,* ed. Valerio Verra (Hildesheim: Olms, 1965), II, 62–65, 182–183, 362–364.

29. For this reason, as well as those cited above, Lenoir's distinction between transcendental and metaphysical *Naturphilosophie* becomes very shaky. See his "The Göttingen School and the Development of Transcendental Naturphilosophie," pp. 146, 149. Such a distinction ignores the extent to which those who stressed the constitutive status of an organism used transcendental methods to justify it.

30. Schelling, *Sämtliche Werke,* II, 15.

31. Ibid., pp. 16, 25–26.

32. See Schelling's vacillation on the issue at ibid., p. 54.

33. For a more detailed account of this issue, see Dieter Henrich, "On the Unity of Subjectivity," in *The Unity of Reason,* ed. Richard Velkley (Cambridge, Mass.: Harvard University Press, 1994), pp. 17–54.

10. Religion and Politics in *Frühromantik*

1. *Sämtliche Schriften,* ed. Klaus Briegleb (Frankfurt: Ullstein, 1981), V, 418–421.

2. Ibid., pp. 361–363.

3. Ibid., pp. 380–381.

4. This contrast appears in its most explicit and elaborate form in Arnold Ruge's *Unsere Klassiker und Romantiker seit Lessing,* in *Sämtliche Werke* (Mannheim: Grohe, 1847–1848), I, 7–11, 248–249.

5. See Arnold Ruge, "Plan der Deutsch-Französische Jahrbücher," in *Sämtliche Werke* IX, 145–160.

6. See, for example, Georg Lukács, "Die Romantik als Wendung in der deutschen Literatur," in *Fortschrift und Reaktion in der deutschen Literatur* (Berlin: Aufbau, 1947), pp. 51–73. That Lukács's views were official there cannot be much doubt. When, in a conference in Leipzig in 1962, Hans Meyer and Werner Krauss criticized aspects of Lukács's interpretation, their papers were duly denounced by the party faithful. See the report by Klaus Hammer, Henri Proschmann, and Hans-Ulrich Schnuchel, "Fragen der Romantikforschung," *Weimarer Beiträge* 9 (1963), 173–182.

7. Hermann Hettner, *Die romantische Schule in ihrem inneren Zusammenhange mit Göthe und Schiller* (Braunschweig: Friedrich Vieweg, 1850), pp. 2–3.

8. Ibid., pp. 26–29, 42, 48–49, 53–55.

9. See Carl Schmitt, *Politsche Romantik,* 2nd ed. (Munich: Duncker and Humblot, 1925). Schmitt did not acknowledge Hettner's precedent.

10. See Aristotle, *Nicomachean Ethics* I, chap. 7, 1097a–1097b.

11. See, for example, Schlegel, *Ideen* nos. 37, 62, KA II, 259, 262; Novalis, *Blütenstaub* no. 32, HKA II, 427; and Hölderlin to his brother, September 1793, GSA, VI, 92. Cf. *Athenäum* III (1800), 236, and "Vorerrinerung," I (1798), iii–iv.

12. KA I, 324–325.
13. Friedrich to August Wilhelm, October 16, 1793, KA XXIII, 143.
14. See, for example, Schlegel, *Ideen* nos. 7, 14, KA II, 257; Novalis, "Christenheit oder Europa," HKA III, 509, 523–524; and Schleiermacher, *Über die Religion*, II/1, 229, 238.
15. This famous aphorism occurs in Novalis, *Fragmente und Studien II* no. 562, HKA III, 651.
16. Schleiermacher, *Über die Religion*, KGA II/1, 213.
17. Heine, *Zur Geschichte der Religion und Philosophie in Deutschland, Sämtliche Schriften*, V, 571.
18. This very modern Sartrian formulation appears perfectly explicitly in Fichte himself. See his *System der Sittenlehre, Sämtliche Werke*, ed. I. H. Fichte (Berlin: Veit, 1845–1846), IV, 36, 50, 222.
19. That Fichte was describing only an ideal is evident from his *Vorlesungen über die Bestimmung des Gelehrten, Sämtliche Werke* VI, 296–301. For this reason alone, it is incorrect to think that he believed in the *existence* of the absolute ego. The absolute ego is rather the ideal of infinite striving, what we would become if we were to be purely rational, having created the entire world.
20. Fichte, *Sämtliche Werke* VI, 345.
21. See Novalis, *Allgemeine Brouillon* nos.75, 634, 820, HKA III, 252, 382, 429, and *Fragmente und Studien* no. 611, HKA III, 671. See also Friedrich Schlegel, *Philosophische Lehrjahre*, KA XVIII, 31, 38, 43, 80. On Hölderlin, see the sources cited below, note 29. On Schelling, see his *Briefe über Dogmatismus und Kriticizismus, Sämtliche Werke*, ed. K. F. A. Schelling (Stuttgart: Cotta, 1856–1861), I, 326–335. Schelling's later absolute idealism, as expressed in the *System des transcendentalen Idealismus* and *Darstellung meines Systems,* can be regarded as the attempt to synthesize Fichte's idealism and Spinoza's realism.
22. Fichte, *Grundlage der gesamten Wissenschaftslehre, Sämtliche Werke*, I, 101.
23. Ibid., 425–430.
24. Fichte, *Erste Einleitung in die Wissenschaftslehre, Sämtliche Werke* I, 434.
25. See *Grundlage der gesamten Wissenschaftslehre, Sämtliche Werke* I, 100–101.
26. Kant, KrV, B 349–366.
27. This is a controversial interpretation. When Fichte himself was charged with atheism in 1799, he indignantly rebutted the charges. See his *Appelation an das Publicum gegen die Anklage des Atheismus, Sämtliche Werke* V, 193–238, and *Gerichtliche Verantwortung gegen die Anklage des Atheismus, Sämtliche Werke* V, 241–333. It seems to me, however, that the charges were defensible. In his "Ueber den Grund unseres Glaubens an eine göttliche Weltregierung," which occasioned the charges, Fichte identifies the divine with the moral world order, which, he says explicitly, we construct through our moral action. See *Sämtliche Werke* V, 185. The whole issue is much more complicated, however, because Fichte was in the process of changing his views around the time of the atheism controversy, and changing them in a more metaphysical direction. In any case, the crucial question here is less what Fichte explicitly says than the implications

of his general principles. Fichte's critique of Spinoza makes it evident that he could not give constitutive status to the idea of the infinite; to do so would mean committing the fallacy of hypostasis.

28. Schlegel, *Athenäumsfragment* no. 222, KA II, 202. Cf. Novalis, *Allgemeine Brouillon* no. 320: "everything predicated of God contains the doctrine of the future of humanity . . . every person that now lives from and through God should become God himself." HKA III, 297.

29. See especially the preface to the penultimate version of *Hyperion*, GSA III, 236. Cf. the preface to *Fragment von Hyperion*, III, 163; and the final version, III, 38.

30. See Schelling, *Sämtliche Werke* I, 284–290.

31. See Dieter Henrich, *Der Grund im Bewusstsein* (Stuttgart: Klett-Cotta, 1992), pp. 48–92, 146–185.

32. Herder, *Sämtliche Werke*, ed. Bernard Suphan (Berlin: Weidmann, 1881–1913), XVI, 450, 458.

33. Ibid., 453.

34. Schleiermacher, KGA II/1, 232.

35. Ibid., 229. Schleiermacher argues that we should see the divine in present social arrangments: "erfreut Euch eines jeden an der Stelle wo es steht."

36. Schlegel, KA XII, 50, 52, 57, 72, 74, 86.

37. Schelling, *Sämtliche Werke* VI, §§305–311, 471–491.

38. See *Zur Geschichte der Philosophie und Religion in Deutschland, Sämtliche Schriften* V, 570.

BIBLIOGRAPHY

Primary Sources

Aristotle. *The Complete Works,* ed. Jonathan Barnes. Princeton: Princeton University Press, 1984.

Baader, Franz. *Sämtliche Werke.* Leipzig: Bethmann, 1851–1860.

Baumgarten, Alexander. *Texte zur Grundlegung der Ästhetik,* ed. Hans Rudolf Schweizer. Hamburg: Meiner, 1983.

——— *Theoretische Ästhetik: Die grundlegenden Abschnitte aus der "Aesthetica" (1750/58),* ed. Hans Rudolf Schweizer. Hamburg: Meiner, 1983.

Blumenbach, J. F. *Über den Bildungstrieb.* 2nd ed. Göttingen: Dietrich, 1791.

Cudworth, Ralph. *Treatise on True and Immutable Morality,* ed. Edward Chandler. London: Knapton, 1731.

Eberhard, J. A. *Über Staatsverfassungen und ihre Verbesserungen.* Berlin: Voß, 1792–1793.

Fichte, Johann Gottlieb. *Sämtliche Werke,* ed. I. H. Fichte. Berlin: Veit, 1845–1846.

Goethe, J. W., *Werke, Hamburger Ausgabe,* ed. D. Kühn and R. Wankmüller. 14 vols. Hamburg: Wegner, 1955.

Hamann, J. G. *Sämtliche Werke, Historisch-Kritische Ausgabe,* ed. J. Nadler. Vienna: Herder, 1949–1957.

Hegel, G. W. F. *Werke in Zwanzig Bänden,* eds. E. Moldenhauer and K. Michel. Frankfurt: Suhrkamp, 1971.

Heine, Heinrich. *Sämtliche Schriften,* ed. Klaus Briegleb 12 vols. Frankfurt: Ullstein, 1981.

Hemsterhuis, Franz. *Philosophischen Schriften,* ed. Julius Hilß. 4 vols. Karlsruhe: Dreililien Verlag, 1912.

Herder, Johann Gottfried. *Sämtliche Werke,* ed. Bernard Suphan. 33 vols. Berlin: Weidmann, 1881–1913.

Herz, Henriette. *Berliner Salon: Erinnerungen und Portraits.* Frankfurt: Ullstein, 1986.

Hölderlin, Friedrich. *Sämtliche Werke, Grosse Stuttgarter Ausgabe,* ed. Friedrich Beissner. Stuttgart: Kohlhammer, 1961.

——— *Essays and Letters on Theory,* ed. and trans. Thomas Pfau. New York: SUNY Press, 1988.

Kant, Immanuel. *Gesammelte Schriften,* Akademie Ausgabe, ed. Wilhelm Dilthey et al. Berlin: de Gruyter, 1902–.

Maimon, Solomon. *Gesammelte Werke,* ed. Valerio Verra. Hildesheim: Olms, 1965.

Mendelssohn, Moses. "Ueber die Frage: Was heisst aufklären?" *Berlinische Monatsschrift* 4 (1784): 193–200.

More, Henry. *A Collection of Several Philosophical Writings.* 2 vols. London: Morden, 1667.

Müller, Adam. *Die Elemente der Staatskunst.* Berlin: Sander, 1809.

Plato. *The Collected Dialogues,* eds. Edith Hamilton and Huntington Cairns. Princeton: Princeton University Press, 1961.

Schelling, Friedrich Wilhelm Joseph. *Sämtliche Werke,* ed. K. F. A. Schelling. 14 vols. Stuttgart: Cotta, 1856–1861.

——— *Briefe und Dokumente,* ed. Horst Furhmanns. 2 vols. Bonn: Bouvier, 1962–1975.

——— *Historische-Kritische Ausgabe,* eds. H. M. Baumgartner, W. G. Jacobs, H. Krings, and H. Zeltner. Stuttgart-Bad Cannstatt: Fromann, 1976–.

——— *The Unconditional in Human Knowledge: Four Early Essays (1794–1796),* trans. Fritz Marti. Cranbury: Associated University Presses, 1980.

——— *Ideas for a Philosophy of Nature,* trans. Peter Heath and Errol Harris. Cambridge: Cambridge University Press, 1988.

——— *System of Transcendental Idealism,* trans. Peter Heath. Charlottesville: University of Virginia Press, 1993.

——— *Timaeus (1794): Ein Manuskrip zu Platon,* ed. Hartmut Buchner. Stuttgart-Bad Cannstatt: Fromann Holzboog, 1994.

Schiller, Friedrich. *Werke, Nationalausgabe,* ed. L. Blumenthal and Benno von Wiese. Weimar: Böhlaus Nachfolger, 1943–1967.

Schlegel, August Wilhelm. *Sämtliche Werke,* ed. Eduard Böcking. Leipzig: Weidmann, 1846.

——— *Vorlesungen über Ästhetik,* ed. Ernst Behler. Paderborn: Schöningh, 1989.

Schlegel, Friedrich. *Kritische Friedrich Schlegel Ausgabe,* ed. Ernst Behler, Jean Jacques Anstett, and Hans Eichner. Munich: Schöningh, 1958–.

——— *Friedrich Schlegel: Dialogue on Poetry and Literary Aphorisms,* eds. Ernst Behler and Roman Struc. University Park: Pennsylvania State University Press, 1968.

——— *Friedrich Schlegel's Lucinde and the Fragments,* ed. Peter Firchow. Minneapolis: University of Minnesota Press, 1971.

——— *Athenaeum: Eine Zeitschrift.* 3 vols. Berlin: Vieweg, 1798–1800. Reprint: Darmstadt: Wissenschaftliche Buchgesellschaft, 1992.

Schleiermacher, Friedrich Daniel. *Soliloquies,* trans. H. L. Friess. Chicago: Open Court, 1926.

——— *Schleiermachers Werke. Werke in Vier Bänden,* ed. Otto Braun and Johannes Brauer. Leipzig: Meiner, 1928. Reprint: Aalen: Scientia Verlag, 1981.

——— *Brouillon zur Ethik (1805–1806),* ed. Hans-Joachim Birkner. Hamburg: Meiner, 1981.

——— *Ethik (1812–1813),* ed. Hans-Joachim Birkner. Hamburg: Meiner, 1981.

────── *Kritische Gesamtausgabe,* ed. Günter Meckenstock et al. Berlin: de Gruyter, 1984–.

────── *Dialektik (1811),* ed. Andreas Arndt. Hamburg: Meiner, 1986.

────── *On Religion,* trans. Richard Crouter. Cambridge: Cambridge University Press, 1988.

────── *Hermeneutics and Criticism,* ed. Andrew Bowie. Cambridge: Cambridge University Press, 1998.

Smith, John. *Select Discourses.* London: Morden, 1660.

Spinoza, Benedictus. *Opera,* ed. C. Gebhardt. 5 vols. Heidelberg: Winter, 1924.

Steffens, Heinrich. *Was ich erlebte.* 10 vols. Breslau: Max, 1841.

Tieck, Ludwig. *Werke in vier Bänden,* ed. Marianne Thalmann. Munich: Winkler, 1963.

Wackenroder, Wilhelm. *Werke und Briefe,* ed. F. von Leyen. Jena: Diederichs, 1910.

────── *Sämtliche Werke und Briefe, Historisch-Kritische Ausgabe,* eds. Silvio Viotta and Richard Littlejohns. Heidelberg: Winter, 1991.

Secondary Sources

Abercrombie, Lascelles. *Romanticism.* London: Secker and Warbarg, 1926.

Abrams, M. H. *The Mirror and the Lamp.* New York: Oxford University Press, 1953.

────── *Natural Supernaturalism.* New York: Norton, 1971.

Adler, Emil. *Der junge Herder und die Aufklärung.* Vienna: Europa, 1968.

Ameriks, Karl, ed. *The Cambridge Companion to German Idealism.* Cambridge: Cambridge University Press, 2000.

────── "The Practical Foundation of Philosophy in Kant, Fichte and After," in *The Reception of Kant's Critical Philosophy,* ed. Sally Sedgwick, pp. 109–129. Cambridge: Cambridge University Press, 2000.

Ayrault, Roger. *La Genèse du romantisme allemand.* 3 vols. Paris: Aubier, 1961.

Batscha, Zwi. *«Despotismus von der Art reizt zur Widersetzlichkeit», Die Französische Revolution in der deutschen Popularphilosophie.* Frankfurt: Suhrkamp, 1989.

Baum, Manfred. "The Beginnings of Schelling's Philosophy of Nature," in *The Reception of Kant's Critical Philosopy,* ed. Sally Sedgwick, pp. 199–215. Cambridge: Cambridge University Press, 2000.

Baum, Wilhelm. "Der Klagenfurter Herbert Kreis zwischen Aufklärung und Romantik," *Revue Internationale de Philososophie* 50 (1996), 483–514.

Baumgardt, David. "Spinoza und der deutsche Spinozismus," *Kant-Studien* 32 (1927), 182–192.

Baxa, Jakob. *Einführung in die romantische Staatswissenschaft.* Jena: Gustav Fischer, 1923.

Beck, Lewis White. *Early German Philosophy.* Cambridge, Mass.: Harvard University Press, 1969.

Ernst Behler. "Friedrich Schlegels Vorlesungen über Transzendentalphilosophie Jena 1800–1801," in *Transzendentalphilosophie und Spekulation. Der Streit um die Gestalt einer Ersten Philosophie (1799–1807),* ed. Walter Jaeschke. Hamburg: Meiner, 1953.

——— "Friedrich Schlegels Theorie der Universalpoesie," *Jahrbuch der deutschen Schillergesellschaft* 1 (1957), 211–252.

——— "Die Kulturphilosophie Friedrich Schlegels," *Zeitschrift für philosophische Forschung* 14 (1960), 68–85.

——— "Friedrich Schlegel und Hegel," *Hegel-Studien* 2 (1963), 203–250.

——— *Friedrich Schlegel.* Hamburg: Rowohlt, 1966.

——— "The Origins of the Romantic Literary Theory," *Colloquia Germanica* (1967), 109–126.

——— "Kritische Gedanken zum Begriff der europäischen Romantik," in *Die europäische Romantik.* Frankfurt: Athenaum, 1972.

——— "Nietzsche und die früromantische Schule," in *Nietzsche-Studien* 7 (1978), 59–87.

——— *Die Zeitschriften der Brüder Schlegel.* Darmstadt: Wissenschaftliche Buchgesellschaft, 1983.

——— ed., *Die Aktualität der Frühromantik.* Paderborn: Schöningh, 1987.

——— "Friedrich Schlegels Theorie des Verstehens: Hermenutik oder Dekonstrutkion?", in *Die Aktualität der Frühromantik,* pp. 141–160.

——— *Studien zur Romantik und zur idealistischen Philosophie.* Paderborn: Schöningh, 1988.

——— "Die Wirkung Goethes und Schillers auf die Brüder Schlegel," in *Studien zur Romantik und zur idealistischen Philosophie,* pp. 264–282.

——— *Irony and the Discourse of Modernity.* Seattle: University of Washington Press, 1990.

——— *Confrontations: Derrida, Heidegger, Nietzsche.* Stanford: Stanford University Press, 1991.

——— "Manfred Frank: *Einführung in die frühromantische Ästhetik,*" *Athenäum* 1 (1991), 248–249.

——— *Frühromantik.* Berlin: de Gruyter, 1992.

——— *German Romantic Literary Theory.* Cambridge: Cambridge University Press, 1993.

——— "Friedrich Schlegel's Theory of an Alternating Principle Prior to his Arrival in Jena (6 August 1796)," *Revue Internationale de Philosophie* 50 (1996), 383–402.

——— "Schlegels Frühe Position in der Ausbildung der idealistischen Philosophie," in "Einleitung" to volume 8 of *Kritische Friedrich Schlegel Ausgabe,* pp. xxi–lxxxvii.

——— "Einleitung," *Philosophische Lehrjahre,* vol. 18 of *Kritische Friedrich Schlegel Ausgabe.*

Beiser, Frederick. *The Fate of Reason.* Cambridge, Mass.: Harvard University Press, 1986.

——— *Enlightenment, Revolution, and Romanticism: The Genesis of Modern German Political Thought, 1790–1800.* Cambridge, Mass.: Harvard University Press, 1992.

——— *The Sovereignty of Reason: The Defense of Rationality in the Early English Enlightenment.* Princeton: Princeton University Press, 1996.

——— *German Idealism: The Struggle against Subjectivism, 1781–1801.* Cambridge, Mass.: Harvard University Press, 2002.

Beiser, Frederick, ed. *The Early Political Writings of the German Romantics*. Cambridge: Cambridge University Press, 1996.

Belgardt, Raimund. "'Romantische Poesie' in Friedrich Schlegels Aufsatz *Über das Studium der griechischen Poesie*," *German Quarterly* 40 (1967), 165–185.

Bell, David. *Spinoza in Germany from 1670 to the Age of Goethe*. London: Institute of Germanic Studies, University of London, 1984.

Benjamin, Walter. *Der Begriff der Kunstkritik in der deutschen Romantik*. Bern: Francke, 1920. Vol. 1 of *Gesammelte Schriften*, eds. Rolf Tiedemann and Hermann Schweppenhäuser. Frankfurt: Suhrkamp, 1974. Pp. 7–122.

Berlin, Isaiah. "The Romantic Revolution: A Crisis in the History of Modern Thought," in *The Sense of Reality*, ed. Henry Hardy, pp. 168–193. New York: Farrar, Straus and Giroux, 1996.

——— *The Roots of Romanticism*. Princeton: Princeton University Press, 1999.

Bertaux, Pierre. *Hölderlin und die französiche Revolution*. Frankfurt: Suhrkamp, 1969.

Blackall, Eric. *The Novels of the German Romantics*. Ithaca: Cornell University Press, 1983.

Blackwell, Albert. *Schleiermacher's Early Philosophy of Life*. Cambridge: Harvard University Press, 1982. Harvard Theological Studies, No. 93.

Blankennagel, John. "The Dominant Characteristics of German Romanticism," *Publications of the Modern Language Association of America* 55 (1940), 1–10.

Böhm, Wilhelm. *Hölderlin*. 2 vols. Halle-Saale: Niemeyer, 1928.

Bowie, Andrew. *Schelling and Modern European Philosophy: An Introduction*. London: Routledge, 1993.

Brandes, Georg. *Die Literatur des neunzehnten Jahrhunderts in ihren Hauptströmungen*. Leipzig: Veit, 1887.

Brecht, Martin. "Hölderlin und das Tübinger Stift," *Hölderlin Jahrbuch* 18 (1973), 20–48.

Briefs, G. A. "The Economic Philosopy of Romanticism," *Journal of the History of Ideas* 2 (1941), 279–300.

Brinkmann, Richard. "Romantische Dichtungstheorie in Friedrich Schlegels Frühschriften und Schillers Begriffe der Naiven und Sentimentalischen," *Deutsche Vierteljahrschrift für Literaturwissenschaft und Geistesgeschichte* 32 (1958), 344–371.

——— "Frühromantik und Französische Revolution," in *Deutsche Literatur und Französische Revolution*, pp. 172–191. Göttingen: Vandenhoeck and Ruprecht, 1974.

Brunschwig, Henri. *La crise de l'état prussien à la fin du Xviiie siècle et la genèse de la mentalité romantique*. Paris: Presses Universitaires de France, 1947. Translated by Frank Jellinek as *Enlightenment and Romanticism in Eighteenth Century Prussia*. Chicago: University of Chicago Press, 1974.

Caneva, K. L. "Teleology with Regrets," *Annals of Science* 47 (99), 291–300.

Cassirer, Ernst. "Hölderlin und der deutsche Idealismus," in *Idee und Gestalt*, pp. 113–155. Berlin: Cassirer, 1924.

Cramer, Konrad, W. Jacobis, and W. Schmidt-Biggemann. *Spinozas Ethik und ihre frühe Wirkung.* Wolfenbüttel: Herzog August Bibliothek, 1981. Wolfenbütteler Forschungen 16.

Cranston, Maurice. *The Romantic Movement.* Oxford: Blackwell, 1994.

Cunningham, Andrew, and Nicholas Jardine, eds. *Romanticism and the Sciences.* Cambridge: Cambridge University Press, 1990.

Delf, H., J. Schoeps, and M. Walther. *Spinoza in der europäischen Geistesgeschichte,* Berlin: Hentrich, 1994. Studien zur Geistesgeschichte, Band 16.

De Man, Paul. *Blindness and Insight.* 2nd ed. Minneapolis: University of Minnesota Press, 1983.

———— *The Rhetoric of Romanticism.* New York: Columbia University Press, 1984.

Dick, Manfred, *Die Entwicklung des Gedankens der Poesie in den Fragmenten des Novalis.* Bonn: Bouvier, 1967. Mainzer Philosophische Forschungen, No. 7.

Dilthey, Wilhelm. *Das Erlebnis und die Dichtung.* Leipzig: Tuebner, 1907.

———— *Leben Schleiermachers,* ed. Martin Redeker. Göttingen: Vandenhoeck and Ruprecht, 1970.

Droz, Jacques. *L'Allemagne et la Révolution Francaise.* Paris: Presses-Universitaires de France, 1949.

———— *Le Romantisme Allemand et L'Etat.* Paris: Payot, 1966.

Durner, Manfred. "Schellings Begegnung mit der Naturwissenschaften in Leipzig," *Archiv für Geschichte der Philosophie* 72 (1990), 220–236.

———— "Die Naturphilosophie im 18. Jahrhundert und der naturwissenschaftliche Unterricht in Tübingen," *Archiv für Geschichte der Philosophie* 73 (1991), 71–103.

———— "Theorie der Chemie," in the supplementary volume to *Schelling, Historisch-Kritische Ausgabe. Wissenschaftliche Bericht zu Schellings Naturphilosophischen Schriften 1797–1800,* pp. 44–56. Stuttgart: Frommann, 1994.

Düsing, Klaus. "Spekulation und Reflexion: Zur Zusammenarbeit Schellings und Hegels in Jena," *Hegel-Studien* 5 (1969), 95–128.

———— "Die Entstehung des spekulativen Idealismus: Schellings und Hegels Wandlungen zwischen 1800 und 1801," in *Transzendentalphilosophie und Spekulation: Der Streit um die Gestalt einer Ersten Philosophie (1799–1807),* ed. Walter Jaeschke. Hamburg: Meiner, 1993.

Eichner, Hans. "The Supposed Influence of Schillers *Über Naive und Sentimentalische Dichtung* on F. Schlegels *Über das Studium der griechischen Poesie,*" *Germanic Review* 30 (1955), 260–264.

———— "Friedrich Schlegels Theory of Romantic Poetry," *Publications of the Modern Language Association* 71 (1956), 1018–1041.

———— "Contexts and Connotations of the Word «Romantic» at the Dawn of the Romatic Movement," *Actes du 8me Congrès de la Fédération Internationale des Langues et Littératures Modernes.* Liège, 1962.

———— *Friedrich Schlegel.* New York: Twayne, 1970.

———— "Romanticism," in *The Challenge of German Literature,* eds. Horst Daemmrich and Diether Haenicke, pp. 183–231. Detroit: Wayne State Univerity Press, 1971.

———— "German/Romantisch-Romantik-Romantiker," in *Romantic and Its Cognates,* ed. Eichner, pp. 98–156.

———— "Romantic and its Cognates in England, Germany, and France before 1790," in *Romantic and its Cognates,* ed. Eichner, pp. 17–97.

Eichner, Hans, ed., *Romantic and Its Cognates. The European History of a Word.* Toronto: University of Toronto Press, 1972.

Eldridge, Richard. *The Persistence of Romanticism.* Cambridge: Cambridge University Press, 2001.

Enders, Carl. *Friedrich Schlegel: Die Quellen seines Wesens und Werdens.* Leipzig: Haessel, 1913.

Esposito, J. *Schelling's Idealism and Philosopy of Nature.* Cranbury: Associated University Presses, 1977.

Faber, Richard. *Die Phantasie an die Macht.* Stuttgart: Metzler, 1970. Texte Metzler 12.

Fischer, Ernst. *Ursprung und Wesen der Romantik.* Frankfurt: Sender, 1986.

Fischer, Kuno. *Schellings Leben, Werke und Lehre.* Heidelberg: Winter, 1872.

Frank, Manfred. "Die Philosophie des sogenannten 'magischen Idealismus,'" *Euphorion* 63 (1969), 88–116.

———— *Materialien zu Schellings philosophischen Anfängen.* Frankfurt: Suhrkamp, 1975.

———— "Ordo inversus: Zu einer Reflexionsfigur bei Novalis, Hölderlin, Kleist und Kafka, in *Geist und Zeichen: Festschrift für Arthur Henkel,* ed. H. Anton, B. Gajek, and P. Pfaff. Heidelberg: Winter, 1977.

———— *Der Kommende Gott.* Frankfurt: Suhrkamp, 1982.

———— *Eine Einführung in Schellings Philosophie.* Frankfurt: Suhrkamp, 1985.

———— *Die Unhintergehbarkeit von Individualität: Reflexionen über Subjekt, Person und Individuum aus Anlaß ihrer «postmodernen» Toterklärung.* Frankfurt: Suhrkamp, 1986.

———— "Aufklärung als Analytische und Synthetische Vernunft. Vom Französischen Materialismus über Kant zur Frühromantik," in *Aufklärung und Gegenaufklärung in der europäischen Literatur, Philosophie und Politik von der Antike bis zur Gegenwart,* ed. Jochen Schmidt. Darmstadt: Wissenschaftliche Buchgesellschaft, 1989.

———— *Einführung in die frühromantische Ästhetik.* Frankfurt: Suhrkamp, 1989.

———— *Das Problem «Zeit» in der deutschen Romantik.* Paderborn: Schöningh, 1990.

———— "Philosophical Foundations of Early Romanticism," in *The Modern Subject,* ed. Karl Ameriks and Dieter Sturma. Albany: SUNY Press, 1995.

———— "Alle Wahrheit ist Relativ, Alles Wissen Symbolisch," *Revue Internationale de Philosophie* 50 (1996), 403–436.

———— *Unendliche Annäherung: Die Anfänge der philosophischen Frühromantik.* Frankfurt: Suhrkamp, 1997.

———— "Wie reaktionär war eigentlich die Frühromantik," *Athenäum* 7 (1997), 141–166.

———— "Intellektuale Anschauung," in *Die Aktualität der Frühromantik,* pp. 96–126.

Immerwahr, Raymond. "The First Romantic Aesthetics," *Modern Language Quarterly* 21 (1960), pp. 3–25.

———— "Zwei Jahrhunderte Rationalitätskritik und ihre postmoderne Überbietung," in *Die Unvollendete Vernunft: Moderne versus Postmoderne,* ed. Dietmar Kamper and Willem van Reijen, pp. 99–121. Frankfurt: Suhrkamp, 1987.

Franz, Michael. "'Platons frommer Garten.' Hölderlins Platonlektüre von Tübingen bis Jena," *Hölderlin Jahrbuch* 28 (1992–1993), 111–127.

———— *Schellings Tübinger Platon-Studien.* Göttingen: Vandenhoeck and Ruprecht, 1996.

Furst, Lilian. *The Contours of European Romanticism.* Lincoln: University of Nebraska Press, 1979.

Gervinus, Georg Gottfried. *Geschichte der poetischen Nationalliteratur der Deutschen.* Leipzig: Engelmann, 1844.

———— *Schriften zur Literatur.* Berlin: Aufbau Verlag, 1962.

Gleckner, Robert, and Gerald Enscoe, eds. *Romanticism: Points of View.* Engelwood Cliffs: Prentice-Hall, 1962.

Gloy, Karen, and Paul Burger, eds. *Die Naturphilosophie im deutschen Idealismus.* Stuttgart: Fromann, 1994.

Grimme, Adolf. *Vom Wesen der Romantik.* Braunschweig: Westermann, 1947.

Guyer, Paul. "Kant's Conception of Empirical Law," *Proceedings of the Aristotelian Society* suppl. vol. 64 (1990), 221–242.

———— "Reason and Reflective Judgment: Kant on the Significance of Systematicity," *Nous* 24 (1990): 17–43.

———— *Kant and the Experience of Freedom.* Cambridge: Cambridge University Press, 1996.

———— "Absolute Idealism and the Rejection of Kantian Dualism," in *The Cambridge Companion to German Idealism,* ed. Karl Ameriks, pp. 109–129. Cambridge: Cambridge University Press, 2000.

Habermas, Jürgen. *Der philosophische Diskurs der Moderne.* Suhrkamp: Frankfurt, 1985.

Haering, Theodor. *Novalis als Philosoph.* Stuttgart: Kohlhammer, 1954.

Hammacher, Werner. *Entferntes Verstehen: Studien zu Philosophie und Literatur von Kant bis Celan.* Frankfurt: Suhrkamp, 1998.

Hammer, Klaus, and Henri Poschmann. "Fragen der Romantikforschung," *Weimarer Beiträge* 9 (1963), 173–182.

Hankins, Thomas. *Science and the Enlightenment.* Cambridge: Cambridge University Press, 1985.

Hartmann, Nicolai. *Die Philosophie des deutschen Idealismus.* Berlin: de Gruyter, 1923.

Hasler, Ludwig. *Schelling, Seine Bedeutung für eine Philosophie der Natur und der Geschichte.* Stuttgart: Fromann-Holzboog, 1981.

Haym, Rudolf. *Die romantische Schule.* Berlin: Gaertner, 1870. Reprinted: Darmstadt: Wissenschaftliche Buchgesellschaft, 1977.

Heckmann, R., and H. Krings, eds. *Zur Auseinandersetzung mit der Naturphilosophie des jungen Schelling.* Stuttgart: Fromann, 1985.

Hendrix, Gerd. *Das politsiche Weltbild Friedrich Schlegels.* Bonn: Bouvier, 1962. Schriften zur Rechtslehre und Politik, Band 36.

Henrich, Dieter. *Hegel im Kontext.* Frankfurt: Suhrkamp, 1971.

——— *Konstellationen: Probleme und Debatten am Ursprung der idealistischen Philosophie (1789–1795)* Stuttgart: Klett-Cotta, 1991.

——— *Der Grund im Bewußtsein: Untersuchungen zu Hölderlins Denken (1794–1795).* Stuttgart: Klett-Cotta, 1992.

——— *The Unity of Reason,* ed. Richard Velkley. Cambridge, Mass.: Harvard University Press, 1994.

Hettner, Hermann. *Die romantische Schule in ihrem inneren Zusammenhange mit Göthe und Schiller.* Braunschweig: Vieweg und Sohn, 1850.

——— *Geschichte der deutschen Literatur im Achtzehnten Jahrhundert.* 8th ed. Berlin: Aufbau Verlag, 1979. First published Braunschweig: Vieweg, 1862–1870.

Hiebel, Friedrich. *Novalis.* Bern: Francke, 1972.

Hoffmeister, Gerhart. "Forschungsgeschichte," in *Romantik-Handbuch,* ed. H. Schanze, pp. 177–206. Tübingen: Kroner, 1994.

Hoffmeister, Johannes. *Hölderlin und die Philosophie.* Leipzig: Meiner, 1942.

——— *Wörterbuch der philosophische Begriffe.* Hamburg: Meiner, 1955.

Huch, Ricarda. *Blüthezeit der Romantik.* Leipzig: Haessel, 1899.

——— *Ausbreitung und Verfall der Romantik.* Leipzig: Haessel, 1902.

——— *Die Romantik.* Leipzig: Haessel, 1924.

Hughes, Glyn. *Romantic German Literature.* London: Edward Arnold, 1979.

Immerwahr, Raymond. *Romantisch: Genese und Tradition einer Denkform.* Frankfurt: Athenäum, 1972.

Izenberg, Gerald. *Impossible Individuality: Romanticism, Revolution, and the Origins of Modern Selfhood 1787–1802.* Princeton: Princeton University Press, 1992.

Jacob, Margaret. *The Radical Enlightenment: Pantheists, Freemasons and Republicans.* London: George, Allen and Unwin, 1981.

Jacobs, Wilhelm. *Zwischen Revolution und Orthodoxie?: Schelling und seine Freunde im Stift und an der Universität Tübingen. Texte und Untersuchungen.* Stuttgart-Bad Cannstatt: Fromann-Holzboog, 1989. Spekulation und Erfahrung: Abt. 2, Untersuchungen, Band 12.

Jamme, Christoph. *«Ein Ungelehrtes Buch» Die philosophische Gemeinschaft zwischen Hölderlin und Hegel in Frankfurt 1797.* Bonn: Bouvier, 1983.

Janz, Rolf-Peter. *Autonomie und soziale Funktion der Kunst: Studien zur Ästhetik von Schiller und Novalis.* Stuttgart: Metzler, 1973.

Kircher, Erwin. *Philosophie der Romantik.* Jena: Eugen Diederichs, 1906.

Kluckhohn, Paul. *Die deutsche Romantik.* Bielefeld: Verlag von Velhagen and Klasing, 1924.

——— *Personlichkeit und Gemeinschaft: Studien zur Staatsauffassung der deutschen Romantik.* Halle: Niemeyer, 1925.

——— *Das Ideengut der deutschen Romantik.* 3rd ed. Tübingen: Niemeyer, 1953.

——— *Die Auffassung der Liebe in der Literatur des 18. Jahrhunderts und in der deutschen Romantik.* 3rd ed. Tübingen: Niemeyer, 1966.

Knight, D. M. "The Physical Sciences and the Romantic Movement," *History of Science* 9 (1970), 54–75.

Knittermeyer, Heinrich. *Schelling und die romantische Schule.* Munich: Reinhardt, 1929.

Korff, H. A. "Das Wesen der Romantik," *Zeitschrift für Deutschkunde* 43 (1929), 545–561.

———— *Geist der Goethezeit.* 4 vols. Leipzig: Koehler and Amelang, 1966.

Körner, Josef, *Romantiker und Klassiker: Die Brüder Schlegel in ihre Beziehungen zu Schiller und Goethe.* Berlin: Askanischer Verlag, 1924. Reprint: Darmstadt: Wissenschaftliche Buchgesellschaft, 1971.

Krauss, Werner. "Franzöische Aufklärung und deutsche Romantik," in *Perspektiven und Probleme: Zur französische und deutschen Aufklarung und andere Aufsätze,* pp. 266–284. Neuwied: Luchterhand, 1965. Reprinted in Peter, *Romantischforschung seit 1945,* pp. 168–179.

Kruger, Johanna. *Friedrich Schlegels Bekehrung zu Lessing.* Weimar: Duncker, 1913.

Kuhlmann, H. *Schellings Früher Idealismus.* Stuttgart: Metzler, 1993.

Kurzke, Hermann. *Romantik und Konservatismus.* Munich: Fink, 1987.

———— *Novalis.* Munich: Beck, 1988.

Kuzniar, Alice. *Delayed Endings: Non-Closure in Novalis and Hölderlin.* Athens: University of Georgia Press, 1987.

Lacoue-Labarthe, Phillipe, and Jean-Luc Nancy. *The Literary Absolute,* trans. Phillip Barnard and Cheryl Lester. Albany: SUNY Press, 1988.

Lamm, Julia. *The Living God: Schleiermacher's Theological Appropriation of Spinoza.* University Park: Pennsylvania State University Press, 1996.

———— "Schleiermacher as Plato Scholar," *Journal of Religion* 80 (2000), 206–239.

Lange, E., and G. Biedermann, eds. *Die Philosophie des jungen Schelling.* Weimar: Böhlaus Nachfolger, 1977.

Larmore, Charles. *The Romantic Legacy.* New York: Columbia University Press, 1996.

Larson, James. "Vital Forces: Regulative Principles of Constitutive Agents? A Strategy in German Physiology, 1786–1802," *Isis* 70 (1979), 235–249.

———— *Interpreting Nature: The Science of Living Form from Linnaeus to Kant.* Baltimore: Johns Hopkins, 1994.

Lauth, Reinhard. *Die Entstehung von Schellings Identitätsphilosophie in der Auseinandersetzung mit Fichtes Wissenschaftslehre.* Freiburg: Alber, 1975.

Lenoir, Timothy. "Generational Factors in the Origin of *Romantische Naturphilosophie,*" *Journal of the History of Biology* 11 (1978), 57–100.

———— "Kant, Blumenbach, and Vital Materialism in German Biology," *Isis* 71 (1980), 77–108.

———— "The Göttingen School and the Development of Transcendental Naturphilosophie in the Romantic Era," *Studies in the History of Biology* 5 (1981), 111–125.

———— *The Strategy of Life: Teleology and Mechanics in Nineteenth-Century Biology,* pp. 1–53. Chicago: University Chicago Press, 1989.

Linden, Walter. "Umwertung der deutschen Romantik," *Zeitschrift für Deutschkunde* 47 (1933), 65–91.

Lion, Ferdinand. *Romantik als deutsches Schicksal.* Stuttgart: Rowohlt, 1947.

Lovejoy, Arthur. "The Meaning of Romantic in Early German Romanticism," *Modern Language Notes* 31 (1916). Reprinted in *Essays in the History of Ideas*, pp. 183–206. New York: Capricorn, 1960.

────── "Schiller and the Genesis of German Romanticism," *Modern Language Notes* 35 (1920). Reprinted in *Essays in the History of Ideas*, pp. 207–227.

────── "On the Discrimination of Romanticisms," *Publications of the Modern Language Association* 39 (1924), 229–253. Reprinted in *Essays in the History of Ideas*, pp. 228–253.

────── "The Meaning of Romanticism for the Historian of Ideas," *Journal of the History of Ideas* 2 (1941), 257–278.

Lukács, Georg. "Die Romantik als Wendung in der deutschen Literatur," in *Fortschritt und Reaktion in der deutschen Literatur*, pp. 51–73. Berlin: Aufbau Verlag, 1947.

────── *Die Zerstörung der Vernunft*. Berlin: Aufbau, 1955.

Mähl, Hans-Joachim. "Novalis und Platon," *Jahrbuch des freien deutschen Hochstifts* 1963: 139–250.

────── *Die Idee des goldenen Zeitalters im Werk des Novalis*. Heidelberg: Winter, 1965.

Marcuse, Ludwig. "Reaktionäre und Progressive Romantik," *Monatshefte* 44 (1952), 195–201.

Mayer, Ernst. "Fragen der Romantikforschung," in *Zur deutschen Klassik und Romantik*, pp. 263–305. Pfülligen: Günter Neske, 1963.

Mayer, Hans. *Zur deutschen Klassik und Romantik*. Pfüllingen: Günther Neske, 1963.

Mederer, Wolfgang. *Romantik als Aufklärung der Aufklärung*. Frankfurt: Lang, 1987. Salzburger Schriften zur Rechts-, Staats- und Sozialphilosophie, Band 4.

Mehlis, Georg. *Die deutsche Romantik*. Munich: Rösl and Cie, 1922.

Meinecke, Friedrich. *Weltbürgertum und Nationalstaat: Studien zur Genesis der deutschen Nationalstaats*. Munich: Oldenbourg, 1908.

Mennemeier, Franz Norbert. *Friedrich Schlegels Poesiebegriff dargestellt anhand der literaturkritischen Schriften*. Munich: Fink, 1971.

Menninghaus, Winfried. *Unendliche Verdopplung: Die frühromantische Grundlegung der Kunsttheorie im Begriff absoluter Selbstreflexion*. Frankfurt: Suhrkamp, 1987.

Metzger, Wilhelm. *Gesellschaft, Recht, und Staat in der Ethik des deutschen Idealismus*. Heidelberg: Winter, 1917.

Michel, Willy. *Ästhetische Hermeneutik und frühromantische Kritik*. Göttingen: Vandenhoeck and Ruprecht, 1982.

Molnár, G. *Novalis' "Fichte Studies."* The Hague: Mouton, 1970.

Müller, Andreas. *Die Auseinandersetzung der Romantik mit den Ideen der Revolution*. Halle: Niemeyer, 1929. *Deutsche Vierteljahrschrift für Literaturwissenschaft und Geistesgeschichte*. Buchreihe Band 16.

Nauen, Franz. *Revolution, Idealism and Human Freedom: Schelling, Hölderlin, and Hegel, and the Crisis of Early German Idealism*. The Hague: Nijhoff, 1971.

Neubauer, John. *Bifocal Vision: Novalis Philosophy of Nature and Disease*. Chapel Hill: University of North Carolina Press, 1971. Studies in Germanic Languages and Literature, No. 68.

────── *Novalis*. Boston: Twayne, 1980.

Neumann, Gerhard. *Ideenparadiese: Untersuchungen zur Aphoristik von Lichtenberg, Novalis, Friedrich Schlegel und Goethe.* Munich: Wilhelm Fink Verlag, 1976.

Nivelle, Armand. *Frühromantische Dichtungstheorie.* Berlin: de Gruyter, 1970.

Norton, Robert. *The Beautiful Soul.* Ithaca: Cornell University Press, 1995.

Nowak, Kurt. *Schleiermacher und die Frühromantik.* Göttingen: Vandenhoeck and Ruprecht, 1986.

——— *Schleiermacher.* Göttingen: Vandenhoeck and Ruprecht, 2001.

O'Brian, W. *Novalis.* Durham: Duke University Press, 1995.

Peckham, Morse. "Toward a Theory of Romanticism," *Proceedings of the Modern Language Association* 66 (1951), 5–23.

Peter, Klaus. *Idealismus als Kritik: Friedrich Schlegels Philosophie der unvollendeten Welt.* Stuttgart: Kohlhammer, 1973.

——— *Friedrich Schlegel.* Stuttgart: Metzler, 1978.

——— "Friedrich Schlegels Lessing: Zur Wirkungsgeschichte der Aufklärung," in *Humanität und Dialog: Lessing und Mendelssohn in neuer Sicht,* ed. Ehrhard Bahr, Edward Harris, and Laurence Lyon. Detroit: Wayne State University Press, 1979.

Peter, Klaus, ed. *Romantikforschung seit 1945.* Meisenheim: Anton Hain, 1980. Neue Wissenschaftliche Bibliothek 93.

Petersen, Julius. *Die Wesensbestimmung der deutschen Romantik.* Leipzig: Quelle and Meyer, 1926.

Pikulik, Lothar. *Frühromantik.* Munich: Beck, 1992.

Poetzsche, Albert. *Studien zur frühromantischen Politik und Geschichtsauffassung.* Leipzig: Voigtländer Verlag, 1907. Beiträge zur Kultur und Universalgeschichte, Heft 3.

Poggi, S., and M. Bossi, eds. *Romanticism in Science.* Dordrecht: Kluwer, 1994.

Porter, Roy, and Mukuláš Teich, eds. *Romanticism in National Context.* Cambridge: Cambridge University Press, 1988.

Porterfield, Allen Wilson. *An Outline of German Romanticism, 1766–1866.* Boston: Ginnn and Co., 1914.

——— "Some Popular Misconceptions concerning German Romanticism," *Journal of English and Germanic Philology* 15 (1916), 471–511.

Prang, Helmut, ed., *Begriffsbestimmung der Romantik.* Darmstadt: Wissenschaftliche Buchgesellschaft, 1968.

——— *Romantik-Handbuch.* Tübingen: Kröner, 1994.

Prawer, Siegbert, ed. *The Romantic Period in Germany.* New York: Schocken, 1970.

Rasch, Wolfdietrich. "Zum Verhältnis der Romantik zur Aufklärung," in *Romantik: Ein Literaturwissenschaftliches Studienbuch,* pp. 7–21. Königstein: Athenäum Verlag, 1979.

Rawls, John, "Kantian Constructivism in Moral Theory," *Journal of Philosophy* 77 (1980), 515–572.

Reiss, Hans. "Introduction" to *The Political Thought of the German Romantics 1793–1815,* pp. 1–43. Oxford: Blackwell, 1955.

Richards, Robert. *The Romantic Conception of Life.* Chicago: University of Chicago Press, 2002.

Riley, Patrick. *Kant's Political Philosophy.* Totawa: Rowman and Allanheld, 1983.

Roe, Shirley. *Matter, Life and Generation: 18th-Century Embryology and the Haller–Woff Debate.* Cambridge: Cambridge University Press, 1981.

Roger, Jacques. *The Life-Sciences in Eighteenth-Century French Thought.* Stanford: Stanford University Press, 1997. First published as *Les Sciences de la vie dans la pensée francaise au XVIIIe siécle.* Paris: Armand Colin, 1963.

Roisch, Ursula. "Analyse einiger Tendenzen der westdeutschen bürgerlichen Romantikforschung seit 1945," *Weimarer Beiträge* 16, no. 2 (1970), 53–81.

Ruge, Arnold. *Unsere Classiker und Romantik seit Lessing,* vol. 1 of *Sämtliche Werke.* Mannheim: J. P. Grohe, 1847–1848.

Ryan, Lawrence. "Romanticism," in *Periods of German Literature,* ed. J. M. Ritchie. London: Oswalf Wolff, 1966.

Samuel, Richard. *Die poetische Staats- und Geschichtsaufffassung von Friedrich von Hardenberg.* Frankfurt: Diesterweg, 1925. Deutsche Forschungen, Band 12.

——— "Zur Geschichte des Nachlasses Friedrich von Hardenbergs (Novalis)," *Jahrbuch der deutschen Schillergesellschaft* 2 (1958), 301–347.

Sandkühler, Hans Jörg. *Friedrich Wilhelm Joseph Schelling.* Stuttgart: Metzler, 1970.

Sandkühler, Hans Georg, ed. *Natur und geschichtlicher Prozeß.* Frankfurt: Suhrkamp, 1984.

Schanze, Helmut. *Romantik und Aufklärung: Untersuchungen zu Friedrich Schlegel und Novalis.* 2nd ed. Nürnberg: Hans Carl Verlag, 1976. Erlanger Beiträge zur Sprach- und Kunst Wissenschaft, Band 27.

Schanze, Helmut, ed. *Romantik-Handbuch.* Tübingen: Kröner, 1994.

Sheehan, James. *German History, 1770–1866.* Oxford: Oxford University Press, 1989.

Scherer, Wilhelm. *Vorträge und Aufsätze zur Geschichte des geistigen Lebens in Deutschland und Österreich.* Berlin, Weidmann, 1874.

——— *Geschichte der deutschen Literatur.* 7th ed. Berlin: Weidmann, 1894.

Schlagdenhauffen, Alfred. *Frederic Schlegel et son Groupe: La Doctrine de L'Athenaum.* Paris: Les Belles Lettres, 1934. Publications de la Faculté des Lettres de l'Université de Strasbourg, No. 64.

——— "Die Grundzüge des Athenäum," *Zeitschrift für deutsche Philologie* 88 (1969), 19–41.

Schmidt-Biggemann, W., and Karlfried Gründer. *Spinoza in der Frühzeit seiner religiösen Wirkung.* Heidelberg: Winter, 1994. Wolfenbütteler Studien zur Aufklärung 12.

Schmitt, Carl. "Politische Theorie und Romantik," *Historische Zeitschrift* 123 (1921), 377–397.

——— *Politische Romantik.* 2nd ed. Munich: Duncker and Humblot, 1925.

Scholz, Gunter. *Die Philosophie Schleiermachers.* Darmstadt: Wissenschaftliche Buchgesellschaft, 1984. Erträge der Forschung, Band 217.

Schröder, Winfried. *Spinoza in der deutschen Frühaufklärung.* Würzburg: Königshausen and Neumann, 1987.

Seyhan, Azade. *Representation and Its Discontents: The Critical Legacy of German Romanticism.* Berkeley: University of California Press, 1992.

Silz, Walter. *Early German Romanticism.* Cambridge, Mass.: Harvard University Press, 1929.

Simon, Heinrich. *Der magische Idealismus. Studien zur Philosophie des Novalis.* Heidelberg: Winter, 1906.

Snelders, H. A. M. "Romanticism and Naturphilosophie and the Inorganic Natural Sciences 1797–1840: An Introductory Survey," *Studies in Romanticism* 9 (1970), 193–215.

Snow, Dale. *Schelling and the End of Idealism.* Albany: SUNY Press, 1996.

Stefansky, Georg. *Das Wesen der deutschen Romantik.* Stuttgart: J. B. Metzler, 1923.

Steffens, Heinrich. *Was ich erlebte.* 10 vols. Breslau: J. Max, 1841.

Stockinger, Ludwig. "Das Auseinandersetzung der Romantiker mit der Aufklärung," in *Romantik-Handbuch,* ed. Helmut Prang, pp. 79–105. Tübingen: Kröner, 1994.

Stockman, Alois. *Die deutsche Romantik: Ihre Wesenzüge und ihre ersten Vertreter.* Freiburg: Herder and Co., 1921.

Strich, Fritz. *Deutsche Klassik und Romantik, oder Vollendung und Unendlichkeit.* 4th ed. Bern: Francke Verlag, 1949.

Tekiner, Deniz. *Modern Art and the Romantic Vision.* Lanham: University Press of America, 2000.

Träger, Claus. "Ideen der französichen Aufklärung in der deutschen Aufklärung," *Weimarer Beiträge* 14, no. 1 (1968), 175–186.

––––––– "Novalis und die ideologische Restauration: Über den romantischen Ursprung einer methodoschen Apologetik," *Sinn und Form* 13 (1968), 618–660.

––––––– "Ursprünge und Stellung der Romantik," *Weimarer Beiträge* 21 (1975), 206–234.

Tilliette, Xavier. *Schellung: Une Philosophie en Devenir.* 2 vols. Paris: Vrin: 1970.

Tymms, Ralph. *German Romantic Literature.* London: Metheun, 1955.

Ueding, Gert. *Klassik und Romantik: Deutsche Literatur im Zeitalter der Französischen Revolution 1789–1815.* 2 vols. Munich: Hanser, 1987.

Uerling, H. *Friedrich von Hardenberg: Werk und Forschung.* Stuttgart: Metzler, 1991.

Vierhaus, Rudolf. *Deutschland im 18. Jahrhundert.* Göttingen: Vandenhoeck and Ruprecht, 1988.

Verschoor, A. D. *Die ältere deutsche Romantik und die Nationalidee.* Amsterdam: Paris, 1928.

Walzel, Oskar. *Deutsche Romantik.* Leipzig: B. G. Teubner, 1908. Translated by A. E. Lussky as *German Romanticism.* New York: Putnam, 1924.

––––––– "Wesenfragen deutscher Romantik," *Jahrbuch des Freien deutschen Hochstifts* 29 (1929), 253–376.

Wegengast, Margarathe. *Hölderlins Spinoza Rezeption.* Tübingen: Niemeyer, 1990.

Wiese, Benno von. "Zur Wesenbestimmung der frühromantischen Situation," *Zeitschrift für Deutschkunde* 42 (1928), 722–729.

Willoughby, L. A. *The Romantic Movement in Germany.* New York: Russell and Russell, 1966.

Weiland, Werner. *Der junge Friedrich Schlegel oder die Revolution in der Frühromantik.* Stuttgart: Kohlhammer, 1968.

Wellek, René. "The Concept of Romanticism," in *Concepts of Criticism,* pp. 128–198. New Haven: Yale University Press, 1963.

———— "Romanticism Reexamined," in *Concepts of Criticism*, pp. 199–221.

Wetzels, Walter. "Aspects of Natural Science in German Romanticism," in *Studies in Romanticism* 10 (1971), 44–59.

Wieland, Wolfgang. "Die Anfänge der Naturphilosophie Schellings und die Frage nach der Natur," in *Natur und Geschichte: Karl Löwith zum 70. Geburtstag*, pp. 71–90. Stuttgart: Kohlhammer, 1967.

Wild, Reiner. "Freidenker in Deutschland," *Zeitschrift für historische Forschung* 6 (1979), 253–285.

Wirz, Ludwig. *Friedrich Schlegels philosophische Entwicklung*. Bonn: Hanstein, 1939.

Wundt, Max. "Die Wiederentdeckung Platons im 18 Jahrhundert," *Blätter für deutsche Philosophie* 15 (1941), 149–158.

Ziolkowski, Theodore. *German Romanticism and its Institutions*. Princeton: Princeton University Press, 1990.

———— *Das Wunderjahr in Jena: Geist und Gesellschaft 1794–1795*. Stuttgart: Klett-Cotta, 1998.

INDEX